The Essential Book of Jewish Festival Cooking

The Essential Book of

Jewish Festival Cooking

200 Seasonal
Holiday Recipes
and Their Traditions

Phyllis Glazer with
Miriyam Glazer

HarperCollins*Publishers*

HarperCollins books may be purchased for educational, business, or sales promotional use. For information, please write: Special Markets Department, HarperCollins Publishers Inc., 10 East 53rd Street, New York, NY 10022.

FIRST EDITION

Designed by Ralph L. Fowler

Printed on acid-free paper

Library of Congress Cataloging-in-Publication Data
    Glazer, Phyllis.
        The esential book of Jewish festival cooking : 200 seasonal holiday recipes and their traditions / Phyllis Glazer and Miriyam Glazer.—1st ed.
            p.   cm.
        ISBN 0-06-001275-7
        1. Cookery, Jewish.   2. Fasts and feasts—Judaism.   I. Glazer, Miriyam.
    II. Title

    TX724.G595   2004
    641.5'676—dc21   2003056621

04 05 06 07 08   ❖/RRD   10 9 8 7 6 5 4 3 2 1

We dedicate this book

to our mother,
Ida Glazer,
whose passion for cooking filled our lives with joy,

to Nissan Balaban,
who lit a spark that turned into a flame,

to our cherished daughters,
Avigail, Yarden, and Zohar,

and in loving memory of both our father,
Harry Glazer,
who always insisted that garlic and onions purify the blood,

and our grandmother
Rose Soroka,
whose modest kitchen started it all.

Contents

The Festivals of Winter

Acknowledgments

Nearly more people than we can count have made invaluable contributions to this book, offering their expertise in Jewish culinary or religious tradition, contributing recipes, helping us in the testing—and tasting (!)—or, finally, in the preparation of the manuscript itself. But our very first debt of gratitude is to our editor, Susan Friedland, for proposing this project to Phyllis to begin with, out of her conviction that the time had come for a new approach to Jewish festival cuisine.

We are grateful to Rafi Aharonowitz, Tova Aran, Miri Ben Abu, Cherna Crome, David Eitam, Yonatan Frenkel, the Gamlieli family, Haim Gan, Galia Gavish, Rozanne Gold, Nadav Granot, the Gueta family, Noga HaReuveni, Ruth Keenan, Ephraim Lansky, Ya'acov Lishansky, Ran Oron, Yehiel Philosof, Elinoar Rabin, Rita Romano, Idele Ross, Adi and Leah Smaller, Ruthie Levi-Schuster, Riki Tankus, Laila Tukhi, and to the wonderful chefs who generously donated their time and recipes: Hanoch Bar Shalom, Moshe Basson, Tamar Blai, Jeki Dabah, Ezra Kedem, Erez Komorovsky, Yonatan Roshfeld, Mika Sharon, Ran Shmueli, and Daniel Zach. Thanks also to Shalom Kadosh and Avi Shteinitz.

Warm and abundant gratitude goes to Schelley Talalay Dardashti, for her generous contributions, and to Sara Nazarian and her family of Los Angeles, who introduced us to the delicacies of Persian cuisine.

We'd also like to thank Rabbi Meir Azari of Beit Daniel in Tel Aviv and Rabbi Prof. David Golinkin of Jerusalem's Schechter Institute of Jewish Studies, Rabbi Eliezer Shach, as well as Rabbi Ed Feinstein, Rabbi Prof. Pinchas Giller, and Rabbi Dan Shevitz of Los Angeles, for sharing their expertise with us.

We thank our agent, Jane Dystel, for her patience and support.

Special debts of gratitude, along with love, go to Nissan Balaban, Natasha Krantz, and Silvia Rosenberg.

To the many readers of Phyllis's newspaper columns over the years, who wrote in to share their favorite recipes and holiday memories, go special words of thanks.

To Califia Suntree, thank you!

Above all, we owe more gratitude than we can express to the indefatigable efforts, cherished recipes, and inspiration of our mother, Ida Glazer, whose own culinary expertise and vivid memories of her mother's kitchen left us all teary-eyed, and to the amazing patience and support of our beloved Zohar and Yarden Rose Oron.

Blessed be you in the city and you in the country,

Blessed be the issue of your womb, the produce of your soil,

    the offspring of your cattle, the calving

    of your herd and the lambing of your flock,

Blessed shall be your basket and your kneading bowl.

    —**Deut. 28:3–5**

Introduction

Long before timepieces and the Internet, our ancestors looked for agricultural signs to mark the passing of the seasons and the time for holiday rejoicing. Then as today, in the land of Israel, green garlic meant that Passover was near; the new barley and wheat harvests signaled the time for the Omer and then Shavuot; the vineyards with their ripened grapes was the setting for Tu b'Av; the firm little yellow Barhi date was a tangible sign of the approaching Days of Awe, and olive oil was plentiful at Hanukkah. With the exception of Hanukkah and Purim, which arose in later eras, the festivals—in biblical days—responded to the rhythms, seasons, and foodstuffs of the land.

But since ancient times Jews have lived mostly in exile. Uprooted from the earth of our ancestors in 70 C.E. after the Romans destroyed the Second Temple, our people could no longer see the blossoming of the almond tree in winter, summer's profusion of white squill flowers, or the ripening of the wheat in spring. They could no longer bring their *bikkurim*, their "first fruits," to offer to God in Jerusalem from late spring to early fall, from Shavuot to Sukkot, or sacrifice the Paschal Lamb at the Temple for Passover. The festival celebrations were forever changed.

But they scarcely disappeared. In the second century, the customs and laws of the holidays were collected in the Mishnah, and three centuries later, the detailed discussions about the Mishnah were in turn collected in the Babylonian and Jerusalem Talmuds (which we refer to as BT and JT in our book). Judaism survived—and flourished—in exile. With passion for protecting the legacy of the Jewish people, the rabbis of the Talmud evolved new meanings for each of the festivals to take the place of the Temple sacrifices, the tithing of the crops, and the agricultural symbolism that were part and parcel of our ancestors' daily lives. They drew their sources from the Bible, from the teachings of their own forebears, the earliest rabbis in Palestine, and from the nations around them. The Judaism they developed has succeeded in surviving to this day—through crusades, pogroms, and the Holocaust.

In an era like ours, which is actively reclaiming a true appreciation of nature and natural foods, understanding how the festivals began can awaken a fascination with the very same foods that nourished and inspired our ancestors, each in its own season—and each with its own special significance. At the same time, Jews have a rich culinary heritage from our centuries in the vast Diaspora, from Morocco to Poland, from the Black Sea land of Georgia to Persia. As you turn the pages of *The Essential Book of Jewish Festival Cooking*, you'll therefore discover recipes for the seasonal foods of the land that gave birth to the festivals to begin with, along with those developed by Jewish communities around the world.

You'll also find, possibly to your surprise, that unlike every other Jewish holiday cookbook, ours begins with the full-moon festival of Passover in the month of Nisan (March/April). That's because Nisan, in the spring, was the "first month" in the Bible, the original beginning of the Hebrew calendar year. Autumn's Rosh Hashanah emerged as the new year only during the Babylonian exile.

Join us as we wind our way through the seasons of the land of Israel, and the lands of the Diaspora, in what has been for us a spiritual, soulful, and, most of all, an exciting culinary journey into our roots.

—*Phyllis Glazer, Tel Aviv, Israel*
 Miriyam Glazer, Santa Monica, California

A Note on Ingredients

a land of streams
of springs and underground waters flowing
out in valley and hills,
a land of wheat and barley, of vine
and fig trees and pomegranates,
a land of olive trees and honey.

—Deut. 8:7–8

As you glance through this book, you'll notice that many of the tempting recipes reflect the foods and flavors of the seasons in the ancient land of Israel. Many of them are also inspired by the Seven Species—the foods, says the Bible, that most characterized the land and its traditions, and are part and parcel of Jewish festival life.

Today, all of these foods—wheat, barley, grapes and wine, figs, pomegranates, olive oil, and the dates that served as our biblical honey—are available almost all year round in America, shipped in from the far corners of the world. They are, of course, suitable for the recipes in this book. But if you wish to enrich and add more meaning to festival dishes, we suggest using, when possible, ingredients derived from the same soil that sustained and nourished our ancestors. These might include Israeli cold-pressed extra-virgin olive oil, olives, goat cheeses, and wines.

Most of the ingredients called for in the recipes are available at every supermarket. Some—such as carob powder, turbinado sugar, and fruit leathers—you'll find in health-food stores. The more exotic ingredients—such as zahtar, Persian lemon, and sumac—are easy to find at Middle Eastern and Persian food shops. You may also note that I try to avoid using commercial stocks, artificial ingredients, and those that involve cruelty to animals—such as fois gras and milk-fed veal—and prefer instead to enhance the dishes in this book with fresh herbs and spices and other natural ingredients. For those like myself who use natural and unprocessed alternatives, such as whole-wheat flour and unrefined sugars, I've included them in suitable recipes as well. All flour is unbleached and all eggs are large unless otherwise indicated. Recipes are marked with an **(M)** for meat, **(D)** for dairy, and **(P)** for pareve. Some recipes may have two versions.

And finally, to make re-creating these biblical, Diaspora, and contemporary recipes easier, I've given produce in units, volume, and/or weight where appropriate, since, while a "large onion" or a "medium carrot" may vary from place to place, some people prefer to shop and cook by size of their produce rather than check the weight (the difference is not crucial in some recipes).

I hope that *The Essential Book of Jewish Festival Cooking* will add new dimension to the way you look at food, and give you new understanding of what foods, and not just the Seven Species, can mean not only to the stomach, but also to the human spirit, soul, and psyche.

—*P. G.*

The Festivals
of Spring

For now, the winter is past,
The rains are over and gone,
The blossoms have appeared in the land . . .
The time of pruning has come . . .
The green figs form on the fig tree,
The blossoming vines give off fragrance.
  —Song of Songs 2:11–13a

Passover

Z'man Heiruteynu:
The Season of Our Liberation

From the mountains of Nepal, where they may be trekking, to the 2,000-year-old Jewish community on the Tunisian isle of Djerba; from Buenos Aires to Southern California, a kind of homing instinct makes Jews all over the world seek out other Jews on the night of the fourteenth of the Hebrew month of Nisan (late March or April).

For that's the night of the Passover Seder, the first festival of the first month of the Jewish lunar year.

Maybe the "homing instinct" is a modern expression of the Passover pilgrimage of two millennia ago, when thousands of Jews from all over Israel flocked to the Temple in Jerusalem to celebrate the festival. In recent years, our own widespread family has joined together to hold the Seder at the shores of the Red Sea; in Tel Aviv, where our guests hailed from Colombia, Congo, Russia, and all over America; at our old family home on Rockaway Beach in New York; and even in Barcelona.

The way the Seder is conducted varies almost as much as its settings. Some of our friends chant the Haggadah, the ancient story of the liberation of the Israelites from slavery in Egypt, in the original Aramaic; others, alongside guests from across the racial and ethnic spectrum, relate it to contemporary issues of individual freedom or social justice. A family we know hangs sheets from the ceiling in their living room to make a tent, and the Seder participants lounge on pillows on the floor within it. Our own Ashkenazic family has adopted traditional Sephardic customs: The children dress as wayfaring Israelites at the outset of the Seder, and as we recite the Haggadah's description of slavery, we mimic the taskmasters of Egypt, gleefully "beating" each other with fresh green onions.

However and wherever the Seder is held, though, its symbolic foods, displayed on the Seder plate, include those laid down in the Talmud two thousand years ago: bitter herbs—originally wild romaine lettuce—to recall the harsh conditions the Israelites endured; haroset, to remind us of the mortar they had to form; and above all matzah, called *lechem oni*, the unleavened bread of poverty, but also the bread of freedom, for on the night the Israelites left Egypt, their sourdough starter, the yeast of biblical times, had had no time to rise.

Still, how startlingly different our celebrations are today from the first Passover described in the Bible or, generations later, held at the Temple. Ours comes from the Talmud, which evolved the rituals of the Seder based on the customs of Greek and Roman symposia in the centuries after the destruction of the Second Temple in 70 C.E.

But the Passover held on the night before the Hebrew slaves left Egypt, and, generations later, at the Temple in Jerusalem, was a true carnivore's delight. Each clan was to slaughter a lamb, roast it, and then eat it entirely that night, along with bitter herbs and unleavened bread. On the verge of their liberation, the Hebrews in Egypt also took a bunch of hyssop, dipped it into the animal's blood, and marked the doorposts and the lintels of their homes.

Unlike traditional meals, which our ancestors ate sitting cross-legged and barefoot on a straw mat, the Passover lamb had to be devoured as quickly as possible—in fact, says the Bible, with "hips girded . . . sandals on your feet," and a walking stick in your hand (Exod. 12:11), as if ready at a moment's notice to march to freedom.

After the Temple was destroyed, the rabbis living in exile in Babylonia did away with the biblical tradition of rushing. Instead, intent on honoring the biblical commandment to "keep this service" (Exod. 12:25), they created the Seder, transforming the Roman custom of ongoing discussion, reclining at the table as a sign of one's social status, eating and dipping hors d'oeuvres (bitter lettuce dipped in salt water), and drinking wine into a religious occasion. Eager to keep the children awake, they encouraged their questions and ritualized the recitation of the wonders and miracles accompanying the exodus from Egypt. Thanks to them, the once-famous centerpiece of the Passover celebration, the Paschal Lamb, was reduced to a shadow of its former self, becoming the little roasted shank bone on our Seder plate.

Even the original Passover, with its emphasis on eating the sacrificial lamb and unleavened bread, may have originated in two seasonal rites predating the Bible. Since the month of Nisan, the lunar new year heralding the arrival of spring, is also a time of lambing, "the Feast of Passover" may have been a joyous time once celebrated by shepherds with rituals that included offering a firstborn lamb as a thanksgiving sacrifice. "The Festival of Matzah," on the other hand, may have been the time that farmers rid their larders of the sourdough starter they had used for leaven in the previous year, relying on plain unleavened bread—matzah—until the new grain was winnowed, ground, and turned into new starter.

Whatever its origins, the fourteenth of Nisan has been a special night "for all the Children of Israel, throughout the ages" (Exod. 12:42), and the most often-repeated line in the Bible, "Remember you were slaves unto Pharoah in Egypt" (Exod. 13:3), became the basis of the Jewish pursuit of justice, generosity toward the poor, and concern for minorities. The journey from slavery to political freedom is the very pulse of the Jewish story.

There's always a flurry of activity preparing for Passover: ridding our homes of *hametz* (leaven), bringing out the special dishes and pots, preparing the Seder meal. In fact, for our great-grandparents and those before them, Passover took months of preparation.

In Eastern Europe, the fat of the goose served on the previous Hanukkah was rendered and put aside for Passover.

Purim, falling a month before Passover, was the time to begin making *russel,* a beet-based substitute for vinegar. A Yiddish word derived from the fifteenth-century Polish term for the salt solution used to preserve food, *russel* was also used to make *russel borscht,* beet soup. Even matzah was made just after Purim, with individual households or whole communities purchasing wheat flour and baking the matzot together in hovels-cum-bakeries especially set up for this purpose. The more well-to-do customers enjoyed thin, round matzah, and the men of the household crushed some to make matzah meal and farfel, larger crumbs.

It was even customary to make your own yellow-brown Passover wine from raisins, possibly deriving from a rabbinic prohibition against using red wine during the eras when the blood-libel accusations against Jews were rife. Many people also made mead, an ancient drink based on hops, sugar, and honey, fermented by dipping a coarse string in an egg white and inserting it into a pot.

In recent years, it's become increasingly hard to remember the flavors, sights, scents, and smells that were once integral parts of the entire week of

Passover. One doubts that our ancestors would have approved of the New Age Passover Pasta, Passover self-rising flour, Passover wafers, cake mixes, breakfast cereals, and other Passover clones, all made of matzah. They're so perfected, you almost can't tell the difference. And that's the problem. Today, even Fido can eat kosher for Passover.

As the older generation moves on, the art of making classic dishes such as gefilte fish or Iraqi chicken-stuffed fritters is being lost irretrievably, as is the time-honored process of intergenerational teaching in the kitchen. And growing up with Passovers that rely on "virtual" products such as pasta and Cheerios-type breakfast cereals will ultimately mean that the "difference" intended by Passover will scarcely be felt, unless we make the effort to make it so.

Whether you're planning a Passover Seder menu or looking for delicious foods to serve throughout the Passover week, you'll find a variety of recipes in this and other chapters. For ideas on how to combine them all, check the menu suggestions in Appendix I (page 301).

Passover Recipes

Appetizers

Roasted Vegetables in Olive Oil and Spring Herbs **P**
Nanuchka's Fabulous Walnut-and-Herb-Stuffed Eggplant Rolls **P**
Parsley-and-Garlic-Stuffed Portobello Mushrooms **P**
Mom's Russian-Style Gefilte Fish **P**
Leah Gueta's *Harime* **P**

Soups

Golden Thyme-Scented Vegetable Broth **P**
The Perfect Knaidlach **P**
Cream of Root Vegetable Soup **D**

For the Seder Plate

Glazer Family Haroset **P**
Yemenite Haroset **P**

Main Dishes for Seder

Roasted Chicken with Two Potatoes, Garlic, and Rosemary **M**
Roasted Salmon with Marinated Fennel and Thyme **P**
Stuffed Shoulder of Veal **M**

Side Dishes

Spring Vegetable Kugel (P)

Braised "Bitter Herbs" with Pistachios (P)

Baby Spinach Salad with Arugula, Basil, and Pine Nuts (P)

Ideas for Passover Week

Tarragon-Scented Savory Goat Cheese Cheesecake (D)

Moroccan Egg-Stuffed Potato *Pastelim* (P)

Iraqi Chicken-Stuffed Patties (M)

Fresh Mushroom and Vidalia Onion Frittata (P) (D)

Glazer Family Matzah Brei (D)

Fresh Beet Salad in Honey Dressing (P)

Marinated Fennel in Olive Oil and Herbs (P)

Passover Thumbprint Seeded Rolls (P) (D)

Desserts

Melon with Crystallized Ginger (P)

Pecan Meringue Cookies (P)

Lemony Nut Cake with Lemon Topping and Berries (P)

Fudgy Passover Brownies (D)

Moshe b'Tayva (Moses in the Basket) (P)

Eingemacht (P)

Cherna's Favorite Lemon Curd (D)

Roasted Vegetables in Olive Oil and Spring Herbs

Serves 6 to 8

We sometimes begin the Seder sitting comfortably in the living room, and serve these fragrant herb-infused roasted vegetables there after the *Karpas* ritual, when a vegetable is dipped in salt water. Colorful and delicious, the roasted vegetables take the edge off everyone's appetite, so that the *Maggid*, the heart of the Seder, as well as all the subsequent rituals, can be recited—and discussed—in a more leisurely way. We move to the dining table only when we reach *Shulchan Orekh*, the festive meal.

Although some of the vegetables need to be steamed before roasting, it's possible to prepare and marinate all the vegetables together even 24 hours beforehand. In just a few weeks, you can vary the recipe for a Lag b'Omer barbecue by cutting the vegetables into chunks for kabobs, and grilling them for 10 to 15 minutes on low-glowing coals, turning and basting occasionally.

Marinade

2 teaspoons mustard seeds (optional)
1 cup extra-virgin olive oil
⅓ cup white or red wine Passover vinegar
3 tablespoons minced garlic
¼ cup thinly sliced fresh basil leaves
1 tablespoon chopped fresh thyme leaves, or 1 teaspoon dried
1 tablespoon chopped fresh oregano, or 1 teaspoon dried
1½ teaspoons chopped fresh rosemary leaves, or ½ teaspoon dried
¼ to ½ teaspoon freshly ground black pepper

Vegetables

1¼ pounds (about 18) very small thin-skinned potatoes
3 large carrots, sliced into ½-inch pieces on the diagonal
1¾ pounds eggplant (about 1 medium), sliced widthwise into ½-inch slices
1 pound zucchini (about 3 medium), sliced into ½-inch pieces on the diagonal
1¼ pounds (about 4 medium) assorted-color bell peppers (red, yellow, orange, green), seeded and cut into 1½-inch squares
16 medium fresh mushrooms
Coarse sea salt or kosher salt to taste

1. Prepare the marinade first: Toast the mustard seeds, if using, in a dry skillet over low heat, stirring occasionally, until they pop. Set aside.

2. Put the olive oil, vinegar, garlic, basil, thyme, oregano, rosemary, and black pepper in a blender and whirl until well blended. (Or whisk together the vinegar, garlic, herbs, and pepper and add the olive oil in a slow, steady stream, whisking constantly.) Stir in the toasted mustard seeds.

3. Prepare the vegetables: Heat 1 inch lightly salted water in a large saucepan to boiling, add the potatoes, cover, and lower heat (you may use a steamer basket). Simmer about 20 minutes, or until just tender. Do not overcook. Remove with a slotted spoon and place in a large bowl. Check the water level, adding more water if necessary. Add the carrot slices and cook for 3 minutes, then add the eggplant and continue to cook an additional 3 to 4 minutes, until carrots are crisp-tender and eggplant is just slightly tender. Drain and add to the bowl along with the zucchini, sliced bell peppers, and mushrooms.

4. Stir the prepared marinade and pour over the vegetables in the bowl. Mix gently, cover with plastic wrap, and refrigerate for at least 3 hours or overnight, stirring occasionally.

5. Heat the oven to high. Drain the vegetables, but reserve the marinade. Line a large baking pan with parchment paper, and lay the vegetables out as evenly as possible. Brush with the marinade and place on the middle rack of the oven. Roast the vegetables for 15 to 20 minutes, or until golden brown, turning occasionally and basting with the reserved marinade. Transfer to a serving platter, pour over the marinade left in the pan, and serve hot or warm. Sprinkle with salt just before serving.

Nanuchka's Fabulous Walnut-and-Herb-Stuffed Eggplant Rolls

**Makes about
20 to 30 pieces**

T his traditional Passover dish comes from Georgia (not the Deep South, but rather the Caucasus country on the Black Sea), and was given to us by Nana Shrier and her head cook, Marina Tofuria, at Nanuchka, the only Georgian restaurant in Tel Aviv.

Our dear friend Natasha Krantz, also Georgian, re-created the stuffing for us and turned it into a scrumptious base for salads, a great filling for fresh vegetables, or a spread for matzah. You might want to experiment with different nuts such as macadamias and hazelnuts or different herbs such as basil, sage, and cilantro throughout Passover week.

Use either elongated or round, fat eggplant for this recipe. The longer eggplant results in smaller, more delicate rolls with less filling, suitable for a first course, while the fatter eggplant is better for larger rolls, suitable as a main course.

While at Nanuchka they salt the eggplant first and let it drain for fifteen minutes, Natasha goes right ahead and fries it, the latter method recommended only for the freshest eggplant. If you prefer to avoid frying, just brush the thinly cut slices with olive oil and bake on both sides on a parchment-lined baking sheet in the oven until tender and golden brown. For even browning, turn occasionally and shift positions of the slices on the sheet if necessary. Serve 2 pieces per person as a first course, 3 or more as a main course.

3¾ pounds eggplant (2 to 3
   medium)
Coarse sea salt or kosher salt
Freshly ground black pepper
About 1 cup vegetable oil
1½ cups walnut halves (about
   1 pound)
2 medium garlic cloves, pressed
   (1 tablespoon)
½ teaspoon white or red wine
   vinegar

⅓ cup chopped onion
Scant ¼ teaspoon ground
   coriander
1 teaspoon salt, or more to taste
1 small dried hot pepper or
   cayenne to taste
½ cup packed chopped cilantro
⅓ cup packed chopped fresh
   Italian parsley

1. Cut the stem end off the eggplant and slice the eggplant lengthwise into ⅜-inch slices. Sprinkle both sides with a little coarse salt and pepper and rub in. Let stand for 10 minutes, rinse off, and pat dry.

2. Heat half the oil in a skillet and sauté half the eggplant slices on both sides until golden brown. Remove and place between two sheets of paper towel to absorb excess oil. Repeat with the rest of the oil and eggplant.

3. In a food processor, grind the walnuts to a powder. Add the remaining ingredients, blending until the paste forms a ball. Lay the eggplant slices on a work surface and place 2 or more tablespoons of filling (depending on type of eggplant) at the base. Carefully roll from the bottom into a compact roll. Serve on a serving platter decorated with fresh greens, if desired.

Variations

Cabbage Walnut Salad: Cook ½ medium cabbage in boiling water until very tender, and squeeze out excess moisture by hand. Chop coarsely by hand together with a few tablespoons of the walnut mixture. Season to taste with salt and pepper.

Roasted Eggplant Walnut Salad: Roast 1 to 2 small eggplants (see Roasted Eggplant and Pomegranate Seed Salad, page 142, for instructions on how to roast eggplant). Chop by hand, blending in a few tablespoons of the walnut mixture.

Use the filling to stuff fresh mushrooms, celery ribs, and cherry tomatoes.

Parsley-and-Garlic-Stuffed Portobello Mushrooms

Serves 6 to 12

Garlic, or *shum* in Hebrew, was used extensively in biblical times, and freshly picked purple-tinted garlic was always a sign that heralded the coming of spring and Passover. Not only did it help sustain our foreparents in the Holy Land, it may have been an integral part of their Egyptian diet as well: The Greek historian Herodotus describes an inscription on the Great Pyramid recording the sums of money spent during construction on onions, garlic, and radishes for the workers.

Inspired by this flavor of spring, these fragrant and satisfying stuffed mushrooms make a lovely starter (serve 1 per person), or the basis for a light Passover lunch (serve 2 per person) with a salad of baby greens.

Note: If no portobellos are available, use large button mushrooms. Serve 2 to 3 as a starter, and 4 to 5 for a light lunch.

12 large portobello mushrooms
  (four 16-ounce packages)

Stuffing
½ tablespoon minced garlic
  (about 1 large clove)
1 cup matzah meal
¼ cup finely chopped Italian
  parsley
1 cup chopped onion (about
  2 medium onions)
¼ cup dry white wine
Salt to taste
Freshly ground black pepper
  to taste
6 tablespoons extra-virgin olive
  oil plus oil or nonstick
  cooking spray for the pan

1. Preheat the oven to 350°F. Line a large baking pan with parchment paper, and lightly grease the paper with additional oil or nonstick cooking spray.

2. Clean the portobello mushrooms with a damp paper towel and set aside.

3. In a medium bowl, combine all the stuffing ingredients, finally adding 3 tablespoons of olive oil.

4. With a spoon, fill the mushrooms with equal amounts of stuffing, and flatten down with the back of the spoon. Place the mushrooms in the prepared baking pan. Pour the remaining olive oil evenly over mushrooms. Bake for 20 minutes, or until golden brown. Serve warm.

Variations

Add 3 to 4 tablespoons lightly toasted pine nuts or shelled pistachios to the stuffing. To toast pine nuts, place in a dry skillet over medium-low heat, stirring often, until they are light tan in color. Pistachio nuts are best if you toast them in a 375°F oven for 8 to 10 minutes, shaking the pan occasionally.

Add 2 tablespoons chopped fresh oregano, basil, or sage, or 1 tablespoon thyme or marjoram, to the stuffing, or 2 tablespoons of a combination of fresh herbs. Add both herbs and nuts, if desired.

The Haggadah: A Telling Story

The story of Passover was not always passed down from generation to generation with a paperback Haggadah (a word that means "the telling"). In fact, for thousands of years the story of Passover was transmitted only by word of mouth.

Our modern Haggadah originated in Mishnah tractate Pesachim, but it was only in thirteenth-century Spain that the earliest handwritten Haggadot were produced. Just three hundred years later there were 25 printed versions; by the seventeenth century, there were 37; by the eighteenth, 230; the nineteenth, about 1,500 . . . and by the twentieth, over 3,000!

Today the Haggadah is a collection of narrative sources interspersed with ritual, legend, prayers, blessings, and songs of thanksgiving developed over the ages. There are ecological, vegetarian, feminist, socialist, kibbutz, Reform, Conservative, Reconstructionist, Hasidic (Bratislaver, Lubavitch), Modern Orthodox, gay-and-lesbian, and "multicultural" versions, all with their own interpretations of the Season of Our Liberation.

In 1937, even the General Foods Corporation produced its version of one of the most popular Jewish books of all time (". . . Maxwell House Coffee, whose relations with the Jewish people have always been the most friendly, takes pleasure in presenting this new, up-to-date edition of the Haggadah!," undoubtedly attempting to make the fourth glass of wine "good to the last drop"). Of course, the bare-bones mass-marketing format of the once nearly ubiquitous *Maxwell House Coffee Haggadah* had little in common with the elaborately illustrated Haggadot that had been produced ever since the Middle Ages, except for one very important thing: Its written content was nearly exactly the same as that of the Haggadot whose development began nearly two thousand years before!

Mom's Russian-Style Gefilte Fish

Makes approximately 20 pieces

One of the great classics of the European Jewish menu, gefilte fish is a centuries-old dish dating back to medieval times, served on both Sabbath and the holidays. The tradition probably arose from Jewish mystical teachings linked to an old legend that the Messiah will appear to the Jewish people in the form of the Leviathan, a giant fish from the sea, from which only the righteous may eat.

Practically speaking, however, the original gefilte fish was born out of poverty. Since fresh fish was always very expensive, ground fish was "stretched" with fillers such as matzah meal, eggs, and onions, to serve more people with less fish.

Our mother, who was born in Philadelphia, remembers that her mother and many other Eastern European Jews bought the fish live and let it have its cleansing swim in the bathtub for several days before whacking it over the head and cleaning, gutting, and scaling it. You can (and should) ask the fishmonger to fillet the fish, remove all scales, and place the skin, bones, fins, tail, and head (with eyes removed) in a separate bag. Although many people ask the fishmonger to grind the fish fillets for them, our mother insists that for best flavor you should grind them at home using the fine disk of an electric grinder.

During all the years she lived in America, Mom used to make her renowned gefilte fish with carp, whitefish, and pike, but in Israel, where the types of fresh fish differ according to the seasons, she learned to make it as most Israelis do—with carp only.

Although making good gefilte fish may seem like an awesome task, it can be relatively painless if you follow the instructions on pages 15 and 16. The best pot to use is one with a wide bottom, so that the fish will not be too tightly packed. Mom used the same trusty enormous yellow enamel pot in our home in Rockaway Beach, New York, for decades. That pot now resides in my kitchen in Tel Aviv.

Broth

Skin, bones, fins, tail, and head
  of the fish, eyes removed
6 large carrots, scraped clean
1 pound onion (about 2 large),
  thickly sliced
3 ribs celery with leaves, thickly
  sliced
2 teaspoons salt
1 teaspoon white pepper

Fish Balls

1 large carp (about 5½ pounds
  filleted fish) or 1½ pounds
  whitefish, 2 pounds pike, and
  the rest carp fillets
1 extra-large onion, cut into
  chunks
½ cup matzah meal*
3 large eggs, lightly beaten
  with a fork
1 tablespoon salt
1 teaspoon white pepper, or
  more to taste

Make the Broth

1. The secret of our mother's incredibly rich, clear fish broth, she always told us, begins with how you prepare the ingredients for the broth. This requires, first and foremost, scrupulous cleaning of the skin, bones, fins, tail, and head, to remove any imperfections. Wash them under cold running water, using a small, sharp knife to remove any scales remaining on the skin and blood spots remaining on the bones. Place washed items in the bottom of a large wide-bottomed pot.

2. Cut 3 of the carrots into coarse chunks, and layer on top of the fish parts in the pot with the sliced onions and thickly sliced celery stalks with leaves. Add water to cover the ingredients in the pot, plus 2 inches. Season with the salt and white pepper. Partially cover, bring to a boil, and lower heat to simmer for 60 minutes.

3. Using a slotted spoon, remove large bones and fish head, leaving the vegetables and rest of the bones at the bottom as a bed for the fish balls. Taste and adjust seasoning, and simmer while preparing the fish balls.

Make the Fish Balls

4. Quickly rinse fish fillets under cold running water, pat dry, and cut into chunks. Grind the fish and onion chunks together with a food grinder, or the food grinder attachment on a standing mixer. A food processor is not a good option, because it turns the fish into a paste. If no grinder is available, ask the fishmonger to grind the fish. If you have a friendly fishmonger, bring the onion to the store and ask him to grind it with the fish.

*On other holidays, Mom replaces the matzah meal in the mixture with a thick slice of soaked and squeezed (home-baked) challah.

5. Transfer the ground mixture to a wooden chopping bowl and chop in the matzah meal until it disappears into the mixture. Chop in one beaten egg at a time, then chop a little more until smooth. Add ¼ cup cold water and continue chopping lightly about 2 minutes, until smooth and fluffy. Let stand 10 minutes.

6. Make a ball of the mixture to see if it holds together well, and chop 2 to 4 tablespoons additional matzah meal into the bowl only if the mixture is too wet. Season with the salt and white pepper.

7. Place a bowl of cold water within reach of the simmering broth. Moisten your hands. In the palm of your hand, form an oval-shaped fat little ball of the mixture about 3 inches long. Slide the balls as you make them gently into the simmering broth in even layers, and repeat until all fish is used.

8. Slice remaining 3 carrots into ¼-inch rounds or on the diagonal into ovals (for garnish) and add to the pot. All fish should be submerged in the broth. If not, add just enough water to immerse the fish. Partially cover pot, gently bring to a boil, and simmer for 1½ hours. (Do not add any more water to the pot, even if the fish is no longer submerged.) Taste the broth and add salt and pepper if necessary.

9. Partially cover again and cook for an additional 15 minutes. Remove from heat, and let fish cool in the broth. Remove from heat with a slotted spoon and decorate each piece with a slice of carrot. Cover the pieces with clear broth, thoroughly cool, and refrigerate. (Keeps at least 3 to 4 days covered with broth in a closed container in the refrigerator. Gefilte fish can be frozen, but will lose some flavor.)

Like gefilte fish, hot and spicy *harime* (pronounced ha-RI-meh) was originally a holiday fish dish for poor people, since it was eaten with a lot of matzah—or bread on other holidays—to sop up the sauce and fill many hungry mouths with just one little potful. Every self-respecting Libyan or Tunisian Jewish family has its own special recipe for *harime*, served as a first course on Passover and other special occasions. This version comes from Leah Gueta, who, together with two of her many sons, is the owner and proprietor of Gueta in Jaffa, the best Tripolitan (Jewish) restaurant we have ever known.

Note: To make this recipe, you can either follow the instructions below, which will result in a very spicy dish, or do as the Tripolitans do, and prepare a combination of hot paprika and garlic called *Filfil v'Chuma*, which you add according to taste: Mince or press 3 to 6 large garlic cloves (1½ to 3 tablespoons minced) and pound together with a mortar and pestle a tablespoon of hot paprika or chili pepper. Add enough olive oil to make a paste. Store in a covered jar in the refrigerator with a thin layer of oil on top to prevent mold.

To use: Substitute 3 to 4 tablespoons *Filfil v'Chuma* for the garlic and hot paprika in the recipe, and mix in sweet paprika and salt as below.

6 pieces firm white fish, cut into chunks 1½ inches thick (about 2 pounds)	1 tablespoon sweet paprika
	¼ cup oil
	1¼ cups water
1 teaspoon salt	2 heaping tablespoons tomato paste
3 to 5 tablespoons freshly squeezed lemon juice	
	¼ teaspoon sugar
1 head garlic, cloves peeled and crushed	1 level teaspoon ground cumin
	1 level teaspoon ground caraway
1 to 2 tablespoons hot paprika	

1. Wash the fish and season with a little salt. (If using frozen fish, sprinkle with a little lemon juice as well.) Let stand 5 minutes. Pat dry and place on a plate. Using a mortar and pestle, pound together crushed garlic and salt. Add the hot and sweet paprika and mix well.

2. Heat ¼ cup oil in a large skillet and cook the garlic-paprika mixture over low heat. Lightly sauté for 2 or 3 minutes, stirring constantly to prevent burning, until it turns a burgundy color.

3. Stir in ¼ cup water and the tomato paste (the "secret," according to Leah, is to add the same amount of tomato paste as the garlic-paprika-

water mixture). Cook 5 minutes over high heat, stirring constantly, until the sauce is fragrant and bubbly.

4. Add the remaining 1 cup water and the sugar. Lower heat and cover, scraping the bottom of the pan occasionally (the paprika has a tendency to stick to the bottom), for 10 minutes. The oil will separate from the paprika. The consistency of the sauce should be "thinner than ketchup," Leah adds.

5. Place the fish in the pan in one layer, and add warm water to almost cover. Sprinkle the cumin and caraway, and a little more salt if necessary, over the fish. Bring to a boil, cover, and cook on high heat for 5 minutes. Lower heat and squeeze the lemon juice to taste on top. Cover and simmer 7 to 10 minutes, until done.

The Night of Lettuce and Flowers

For the Jewish communities of Tripoli, the last night of Passover was a time of romance known as "the Night of Lettuce and Flowers." In the early afternoon in the old quarters of the city, neighborhood bachelors would meander through the streets while young single women stood at the doors of their houses, dressed in traditional finery: velvet blouses embroidered in silver, silk waistcoats with golden threads, gold and silver bracelets and necklaces.

If a bachelor saw a young woman he wanted to meet, he'd give her a flower. Her acceptance was a sign that he interested her and was welcome to her home to meet her parents. If they became engaged that very evening, the young man would send a youngster in his family to her home with a basket of lettuce and flowers—a *kertella*—along with perfumes, fruits, and presents meant to bring her whole family delight.

Though homemade chicken soup is the traditional choice for Jewish festivals and occasions, some people find the process of making it too time-consuming, and an increasing number of people would prefer a vegetarian choice, providing it is rich and flavorful. This delightfully rich consommé makes a great alternative, and is a wonderful medium for either The Perfect Knaidlach (recipe follows) or Any-Way Kreplach (page 130), and a handy answer to recipes that call for chicken or vegetable stock. It may also be served as a delicious vegetable soup.

If you wish to use this recipe as a broth, coarsely chop the vegetables and add the celery leaves. It is unnecessary to peel the squash or skin the tomatoes because the soup will be strained. For a vegetable soup, dice the vegetables, peel the squash, and skin the tomatoes by dipping in boiling water for a minute to blister skin. Remove the tomatoes with a fork, skin, de-seed, and chop.

For The Ultimate Chicken Soup (*Goldene Yoich*), see page 128.

Golden Thyme-Scented Vegetable Broth

Makes about 10 cups clear broth (serves 6 to 8) or 15 cups vegetable soup (serves 8 to 10)

¼ cup extra-virgin olive oil

½ pound chopped onions (about 2 large)

1 pound chopped carrots (about 6 medium)

2 cups chopped celery (about 4 ribs), leaves reserved for broth

2 cups coarsely chopped fresh mushrooms

12 cups water

2 large ripe tomatoes, quartered

1½ cups halved and sliced zucchini (about 1 medium)

1½ cups cubed butternut squash (optional)

2 bay leaves

¾ cup coarsely chopped Italian parsley

1 sprig fresh thyme, or ½ teaspoon dried

1 tablespoon coarse salt (sea salt if possible)

1 teaspoon fresh chopped Italian parsley, cilantro, or dill per person, for garnish

1. Heat the oil in a large soup pot, and cook the chopped onion, carrots, and celery ribs over medium-low heat, stirring often, until they are tender but not browned. Raise heat slightly, add the mushrooms, and cook an additional 3 minutes, stirring often to prevent browning.

2. Add water, celery leaves, tomatoes, zucchini, and squash if using, bay leaves, parsley, thyme, and salt. Bring to a boil and simmer, partially covered, over low heat for 60 to 90 minutes, adding additional boiling water if necessary, until the broth is a rich golden color. Stir occasionally.

3. Remove from heat and serve or strain for broth: Set a wire-mesh strainer over a large bowl placed on a kitchen towel to avoid spilling. Strain the soup, then use the back of a ladle to press the vegetables remaining in the strainer, extracting as much broth as possible. Discard the vegetables, bay leaf, and parsley. To serve, reheat the broth gently and garnish with fresh chopped parsley, cilantro, or dill. Serve with The Perfect Knaidlach (recipe follows), if desired.

Once asked on a radio show about the derivation of knaidlach, I explained that the original knaidlach were actually rock hard, and were created by Ashkenazic housewives as a weapon of self-defense. If dinner went smoothly, they were eagerly consumed, but should a pogrom suddenly come to pass, they could be thrown at their adversaries. Though of course I meant it in jest, the show's announcer liked it so much that he has asked me to repeat it every year since.

The real origin of the knaidel, according to author John Cooper, is the south German *Knödel,* or dumpling—popular in German cuisine since the Middle Ages.

The Perfect Knaidlach

Makes 16 or more

4 eggs	1 teaspoon salt
½ cup water, seltzer, or cold chicken soup	⅛ teaspoon pepper
	1 cup matzah meal

1. Using a fork or wire whisk, beat eggs until frothy. Beat in water, salt, and pepper. Gradually stir in the matzah meal with a fork. Cover and refrigerate for at least one hour. (The batter can also be prepared ahead, covered tightly with plastic wrap, and stored in the refrigerator for several hours or overnight.)

2. Remove the knaidlach mixture from the refrigerator and stir with a fork until smooth. Bring a large pot of lightly salted water to a boil. Lower heat to a simmer.

3. Rub a little oil in the palms of your hands and place a heaping teaspoon of the mixture in one palm. Gently roll the mixture between the palms to form a neat matzah ball. Drop immediately into the simmering water. Repeat with the rest of the batter. Gently submerge the balls in water as you add the additional knaidlach to the pot.

4. Partially cover the pot and let cook for 30 minutes, lifting lid occasionally to turn the balls over. Remove with a slotted spoon and place in a bowl or a container large enough to hold them. (Knaidlach may be prepared up to 2 days in advance. Reheat in soup.)

Variation

Add ¼ teaspoon nutmeg or freshly grated, peeled gingerroot, and/or 3 tablespoons minced fresh Italian parsley to the egg mixture before stirring in the matzah meal.

Cream of Root Vegetable Soup

Serves 8 to 10

Light but satisfying, this soup is delicious served with Roasted Salmon with Marinated Fennel and Thyme (page 27) at a dairy Seder dinner, or in mugs alongside a Spring Vegetable Kugel (page 29) or Fresh Mushroom and Vidalia Onion Frittata (page 35) at a Passover week lunch.

8 cups water
1 pound parsnip
1 large potato (about 1 pound), peeled
1 large carrot
1 leek, white part only, sliced, or 2 large shallots
1 large onion, coarsely chopped (about 1 cup)

1 bay leaf
5 whole allspice berries
4 tablespoons (½ stick) butter
Pinch of nutmeg
Salt
White pepper
1 cup half-and-half or heavy cream
½ cup chopped cilantro

1. Put 8 cups of cold water in a large bowl. Peel the parsnip and slice down the center lengthwise, into two halves. Cut into quarters lengthwise, coarsely chop, and place in the bowl with the water. Cut potato into coarse chunks. Scrape the carrot and cut into 6 pieces. Add potato chunks and carrot pieces to the parsnips. (Vegetables can be prepared in advance and kept soaking in the refrigerator for up to 2 hours. For longer storage, up to 4 hours, add a teaspoon of lemon juice to the soaking water.)

2. Trim, rinse, and chop the leek or shallots, and mix with the onion. Set aside.

3. Put the bay leaf and allspice berries in a small piece of cheesecloth, and tie the tops into a bouquet garni. Drain the vegetables but reserve soaking water.

4. Melt butter in a wide-bottomed soup pot. Add the drained vegetables, leeks, and onions, and cook on medium-low heat for 5 minutes, stirring often to coat the vegetables with butter.

5. Pour the soaking water into the pot and add the bouquet garni and nutmeg. Season with salt and white pepper and bring to a boil. Lower heat to a simmer and cook, covered, for 40 minutes, or until the vegetables are tender.

6. Cool slightly, remove carrots and the bouquet garni, and puree the vegetables in a food processor or blender in batches, along with broth as

needed. Mix the pureed vegetables with any broth remaining in the pot. (At this point the soup may be brought to room temperature, transferred to a closed container, and refrigerated. Best used within 6 to 8 hours.)

7. Before serving, return the soup to the pot. Puree the half-and-half or cream together with the cilantro, stir into the soup, and heat but do not boil. Taste, adjust seasonings, and serve. Any remaining soup can be stored in a closed container in the refrigerator. Reheat in a pot or the micro-wave, but do not boil. Best used within 2 days.

The Origins of the Seder Plate

Today you can choose a Seder plate made of glass, ceramic, bronze, burnished pewter, or the finest silver. But originally the "Seder plate" was actually just a small low table set in front of the leader of the Seder—removed when the Four Questions were recited, and returned afterward.

Though the rabbis of the Talmud decided what special foods were to be displayed, in typical Jewish fashion there are several interpretations for the meaning of each food and even for their arrangement on the plate. Sephardim, for example, display three *matzot shmurot,* specially made matzot, on the Seder plate, whereas Ashkenazim place the matzot on a separate plate entirely.

All Seder plates feature a roasted egg, but what does it mean? Most authorities agree that the egg symbolizes the festival's Temple Sacrifice. But others suggest that it symbolizes the birth of Judaism, and still others that it is a symbol of mourning for the loss of the Temple. On the other hand, all regard the roasted bone, usually a shank bone, as a symbolic substitute for the Paschal Lamb—but vegetarians may substitute a roasted or boiled beet (BT Pesachim 114b). Most of us have come to believe that the haroset, originally meant to be eaten with the bitter herbs to make them more palatable, symbolizes the mortar that held the building stones of Egypt in place. But one rabbi in the Talmud claims the haroset is rather an allusion to the apple of the Song of Songs and signifies our freedom. Of course, the actual ingredients for haroset vary all over the Jewish world.

And then there's the question of the *maror.* Most Seder plates have two kinds of the bitter herb—called *maror* and *hazeret.* They may both be horseradish—but one is used to remind us of the bitterness of slavery in Egypt, and the other

to make the *korech,* or Hillel sandwich, consisting of the bitter herb and two small pieces of matzah. Instead of fresh horseradish, one can use the more traditional escarole or romaine lettuce for the *maror,* reminiscent of the bitter lettuces that grew in biblical times. Also on the Seder plate is the *karpas,* a green vegetable, usually celery but possibly parsley. Because the fresh vegetable is fragile, and salt traditionally a preservative, when the *karpas* is dipped in salt water as part of the Seder ritual, it is as if we are dipping the fragility of life itself into the eternal.

Alongside all of these interpretations, there are fascinating kabbalistic ones: For mystics, the Seder plate becomes a spiritual Tree of Life, with each of the foods symbolizing one of its branches.

And, inevitably, there are new customs emerging in our generation. Some people have added a potato, to symbolize the hungry of the world for whom a simple potato would constitute a major meal. And there are others who add an orange, which has come to symbolize all those whose full participation in Judaism has yet to be fully acknowledged, including, indeed, both women and homosexual men *and* women.

Haroset East and West

Of all the ritual foods that grace the Passover table, there is probably none that has so many variations as haroset. We even have some ancient "recipes": Rabbi Elijah of London, a medieval sage, suggested that all the fruits mentioned in the biblical Song of Songs should be used as ingredients, including apples, dates, figs, pomegranates, and nuts, crushed together with almonds and moistened with vinegar. Another recipe, dating back to 1726, found in the seventeenth-century Bevis Marks synagogue in London, included raisins, almonds, cinnamon, pistachios, dates, ginger, hazelnuts, walnuts, apples, pears, and figs.

Iraqi Jews make haroset out of date syrup (*silan*) and ground almonds. Yemenites prepare a variety of haroset called *duka* combining pomegranate seeds, apples, raisins, nuts, and toasted sesame seeds, seasoned with cinnamon, ginger, and sweet wine.

In the old days, the consumption of haroset wasn't limited to Seder night, but was served as a spread, stuffing, and treat all through Passover week. Of all the recipes we tried, we like the next two best.

Glazer Family Haroset

Makes 2 cups

Although our family haroset was typically Ashkenazic, to us it always had a special flavor. Perhaps it was the magic of the forty to sixty family and friends who packed our family basement on both Seder nights. Since our mother always insisted on cooking everything herself, with our Bubby second in command as pot watcher and knaidel shaper, only the haroset making was left to us, the four sisters.

1½ pounds (about 4) large Gala, Fuji, or Granny Smith apples, seeded and finely chopped
1 cup walnuts, finely chopped
1½ teaspoons cinnamon
½ teaspoon nutmeg
Sweet red wine to moisten
1 to 2 teaspoons sugar

Combine all the ingredients in a wooden bowl, and chop with a mezzaluna. Make sure the haroset looks like the mortar Pharaoh would have needed for his pyramids. Cover tightly and store in the refrigerator. Best used within 4 days.

Yemenite Haroset

Makes about 3 cups

Redolent with the spices brought to King Solomon by the Queen of Sheba, and chili peppers, introduced by the New World, this mildly hot haroset recipe was given to us by Schelley Talalay Dardashti.

15 dried figs, chopped
15 medium dates, chopped
2 to 3 tablespoons sesame seeds, lightly toasted
1 teaspoon ground cinnamon
1 tablespoon freshly grated, peeled gingerroot
Dash ground cardamom
⅛ teaspoon cayenne pepper, or more to taste
Dry red wine

Finely chop figs and dates, and add sesame seeds and spices. Stir in enough wine to make a paste. Store in refrigerator. Serve at room temperature.

Roasted Chicken with Two Potatoes, Garlic, and Rosemary

Serves 6

The scent of fresh garlic heads still on their stalks fills the air of the Carmel Market in Tel Aviv in the days before Passover, just as it filled the markets in ancient times. I choose the garlic and the vendor plaits it on the spot into a splendid garlic braid, which will hang in my kitchen for use in the months to come. Its heady aroma fills the house, and outside the sweet scent of fresh rosemary fills the air. Both were the inspirations for this dish.

If you're lucky enough to find fresh garlic heads with their stalks in farmers' markets, use 4 for this recipe, and cut the heads and tender parts of their stalks in halves or quarters. Lay them in the baking dish, interspersed between the chicken. A real treat.

Easy to prepare, this casserole combines main dish and side dish. Don't be afraid it will be too garlicky—the garlic flavor mellows during baking.

1 3- to 4-pound roasting chicken, cut into 6 to 8 pieces
1 pound sweet potatoes or yams
1½ pounds small unpeeled potatoes, halved
1 medium onion, cut crosswise in rings
20 unpeeled garlic cloves (about 2 heads)
2 sprigs fresh rosemary, each broken into 3 to 4 pieces
Salt
Pepper
¾ cup extra-virgin olive oil

1. Preheat the oven to 425°F.
2. Wash the chicken, pat dry, and place in a roasting pan. (Our mother also uses the boiling water bath method described in the chicken soup recipe [page 128] to prepare the chicken for baking or roasting.)
3. Wash, dry, and peel the sweet potatoes and cut into large chunks. Scatter the sweet potatoes, potatoes, onion, garlic cloves, and rosemary around the chicken. Season with salt and pepper. Pour the olive oil over all.
4. Roast for 20 minutes. Turn the heat down to 350°–375°F and continue to bake for 45 to 60 minutes, until the chicken and potatoes are golden and the garlic is crisp. Turn the chicken and potatoes over occasionally during baking. (If the vegetables are browning too fast but the chicken is still not done, cover the pan with aluminum foil during baking.)

This gorgeous main course can be put together in minutes, once you prepare Marinated Fennel in Olive Oil and Herbs (page 38). It goes well with Spring Green Salad with Tangerine and Fennel Seed Vinaigrette (page 92), and, after Passover, Baked Potato and Sprout Salad with Fresh Parsley Dressing (page 57).

2 large bunches fresh thyme	⅓ cup oil from Marinated
One 2-pound center-cut salmon	Fennel
fillet with skin	Coarse salt
2 to 4 cups Marinated Fennel in	White pepper
Olive Oil and Herbs	

1. Preheat oven to 500°F.

2. Arrange the thyme sprigs in single layer in center of heavy baking sheet. Place salmon skin side down atop the thyme.

3. Use a slotted spoon to remove 2 cups of the marinated fennel mixture, including lemon slices and thyme sprigs, from the jar (or use enough to cover the entire piece of salmon). Spread over the fish. Drizzle olive oil from the marinade onto the salmon and season with coarse salt and white pepper. (Can be prepared up to 6 hours ahead. Cover and refrigerate.)

4. Roast salmon about 20 minutes, until just cooked through. Lower heat to 200°F and continue to roast about 10 minutes more, or until opaque throughout. Slice and serve with a spoonful of the marinated fennel and pan juices on top.

We remember the fish, which we ate in Egypt . . .
the cucumbers and the leeks, the onions
and the garlic.

—Num. 11:5

Roasted
Salmon
with
Marinated
Fennel and
Thyme

Serves 8

Stuffed Shoulder of Veal

Serves 6

For this elegant and satisfying main course for a Passover meal, we prefer to use veal rather than milk-fed veal for humane reasons.

4 to 5 pounds shoulder of veal
(about ½ pound per person)
(Ask the butcher to cut a
deep pocket in the center of
the veal.)

For the Stuffing
¼ cup olive oil
1¼ cups chopped onion
⅔ cup coarsely shredded carrots
½ cup finely diced celery
1 medium Granny Smith apple,
   peeled and cut into thin slices
2 cups thinly sliced mushrooms
   (use a mixture of button,
   porcini, or other wild
   mushrooms)
½ cup matzah meal

1 teaspoon salt
1 teaspoon white pepper
2 teaspoons chopped fresh sage,
   or ½ teaspoon rubbed sage
1½ teaspoons fresh thyme leaves,
   or ½ teaspoon dried
2 eggs, lightly beaten

For the Meat and Roasting Pan
¼ cup olive oil
½ teaspoon paprika
1 teaspoon salt
¼ teaspoon freshly ground black
   pepper
2 cups dry or semidry white
   wine (or use 1 cup water and
   1 cup wine)

1. Preheat the oven to 325°F.

2. Heat the olive oil in a large skillet. Sauté the onion until golden (don't brown). Stir in the shredded carrots, celery, and apple slices, and cook until softened. Add the mushrooms. Cook, stirring for 3 to 4 minutes over a medium flame, until mushrooms are tender.

3. Off heat, add the matzah meal and seasonings and mix thoroughly. Let cool and mix in the eggs.

4. Stuff the veal pocket with a spoon or use your hands, gently packing the stuffing in. Any remaining stuffing can be baked in the pan with the roast.

5. Put the stuffed veal in a roasting pan, and rub it with the oil, paprika, salt, and black pepper. Pour the wine into the pan. Lightly cover with aluminum foil and bake in the preheated oven about 2 hours, basting with the juices in the pan every 15 to 20 minutes. The roast should look lightly browned.

6. Lower heat to 300°F. Continue roasting, uncovered, for another 30 minutes, until the meat is tender (cut off a little piece to taste for tenderness and seasoning). Slice to serve.

Serves 8 to 10

ather than serve a rib-sticking potato kugel at our Seders, we were inspired by our mother to make this colorful, tasty, and healthy kugel, fragrant with vegetables. You can use yellow summer squash instead of, or along with, the zucchini, and use any combination of button or wild mushrooms (sold in bulk in many gourmet supermarkets).

4 matzot (we have a special
   fondness for egg matzah)
⅔ cup canola or olive oil
½ cup chopped onion
1 cup celery, cut into ¼-inch
   slices (2 medium ribs)
2 cups sliced mushrooms
   (button, portobello, oyster,
   porcini—use any combination
   you wish)

2 cups grated carrots
2 cups grated zucchini
6 eggs
¾ cup finely chopped Italian
   parsley
2 teaspoons salt
1½ teaspoons freshly ground
   pepper

1. Preheat the oven to 350°F. Lightly grease a 2-quart baking pan. Set aside.

2. Break the matzot into small pieces (about the size of a quarter). Place in a strainer, and let a stream of cold water run over them until softened. Squeeze out and place in a large bowl.

3. Heat ⅓ cup of oil in a large skillet. Add the onion and celery. Sauté over medium-low heat, stirring occasionally, until the onion is translucent. Add the mushrooms, and continue sautéing and stirring, until the mushrooms are just softened. Transfer to the bowl with the squeezed-out matzot.

4. Heat the remaining oil in a separate skillet, and sauté the carrots about 4 minutes, until nearly soft. Add the zucchini and sauté an additional 3 to 4 minutes, until both the vegetables are soft. Add to the bowl with the matzot, and mix gently to cool.

5. Stir in the eggs, parsley, salt, and pepper, mixing thoroughly. Place in the prepared pan and bake for 30 minutes, or until golden brown on top. Fabulous!

Braised "Bitter Herbs" with Pistachios

Serves 4

This unusual biblically based vegetable side dish is inspired by the little plants that look remarkably like miniature romaine lettuces dotting the roadsides of Israel in spring. These distant ancestors of the romaine, which served the ancients as "bitter herbs," were cultured into their sweet dispositions only in later eras.

½ cup finely chopped cilantro
½ cup finely chopped parsley
1½ pounds romaine lettuce
   (1 large head)
½ pound curly chicory lettuce
2 tablespoons extra-virgin olive
   oil or cold-pressed sesame oil

2 garlic cloves, minced or
   diagonally sliced
Salt
Coarsely ground black pepper to
   taste
1 to 2 tablespoons toasted whole
   pistachios, shelled

1. Rinse the lettuces well, especially at the base of the leaves. Remove the tough outer leaves, and break into bite-size pieces. Drain and pat dry with a paper towel.

2. In a wok or medium skillet, heat the oil and sauté the cilantro, parsley, and garlic over low heat until the herbs wilt. Add the chicory and sauté for 2 minutes, stirring frequently. Add the romaine and cook quickly over medium heat, until the lettuces are just tender but still bright green and crisp, and not completely wilted. Add more oil or a tablespoon or two of water if necessary to prevent burning.

3. Season with salt and pepper, and transfer to a shallow bowl. Garnish with pistachios and serve immediately. (To prepare ahead of time, sauté garlic and herb mixture and let stand in the wok or skillet. Rinse, dry, and chill lettuces. At serving time, heat the garlic-herb mixture and sauté the lettuces as indicated in the recipe.)

Variation

Substitute raisins for the pistachios.

The winter rains have made the earth fertile once again, and like the little lettucelike plants that dot the roadsides, so the hills in spring are filled with young and tender leaves and flowers, echoed in the reds and greens of this salad.

Serve as a light side dish with any of the main courses, or Tarragon-Scented Savory Goat Cheese Cheesecake, Moroccan Egg-Stuffed Potato *Pastelim*, Iraqi Chicken-Stuffed Patties, or Fresh Mushroom and Vidalia Onion Frittata—all found in this chapter.

Baby Spinach Salad with Arugula, Basil, and Pine Nuts

Serves 6 to 8

6 cups baby spinach leaves, stems trimmed before measuring

3 cups arugula leaves, stems trimmed before measuring

1½ cups fresh basil leaves

1 medium head radicchio

½ cup thinly sliced red onion

¼ cup pine nuts, toasted in a dry skillet

½ cup extra-virgin olive oil

¼ cup freshly squeezed lemon juice

2 large garlic cloves, minced or pressed

Salt

Freshly ground black pepper to taste

1. Rinse the trimmed spinach, arugula, and basil leaves. Pat dry, then let dry thoroughly. Wrap in a kitchen towel, place in a plastic bag, and chill until just before serving. Cut the radicchio in half, remove the core, and shred thinly with a sharp knife. (May be prepared several hours in advance. Place in a bowl, cover tightly or seal with plastic wrap, and chill.)

2. Combine the chilled greens, radicchio, red onion, and toasted pine nuts in a salad bowl.

3. Just before serving, whisk the olive oil, lemon juice, and garlic in a small bowl, season with salt and pepper, and pour over the salad. Gently toss and serve.

Variations

Add 1 cup sliced fresh mushrooms.

Omit the basil leaves, pine nuts, lemon juice, and garlic. Reduce olive oil to ¼ cup. To dress the salad, mix the remaining ¼ cup olive oil with ¼ cup or more Honey-Basil Pesto (page 171).

Tarragon-Scented Savory Goat Cheese Cheesecake

Serves 10 to 12 as a main course, 15 to 20 as hors d'oeuvres

While we're accustomed to thinking of cheesecake as sweet, this savory one is more like a quiche, delicious served warm or at room temperature for a quick lunch or dinner, and for entertaining during both Passover and Shavuot. It goes well with Marinated Fennel in Olive Oil and Herbs (page 38).

Crust
2 cups matzah meal
¾ cup unsalted butter, melted
¼ cup ground or finely chopped walnuts

Filling
12 ounces soft uncoated goat cheese (preferably Israeli), at room temperature
3 8-ounce packages cream cheese, at room temperature
4 eggs, beaten
1⅓ cups dairy sour cream
½ teaspoon salt
3 to 4 tablespoons coarsely chopped fresh tarragon leaves
Generous grind of freshly ground black pepper to taste

1. Preheat oven to 325°F. Cut a circle and a 3-inch-wide strip of parchment paper to fit the bottom and sides of a 10-inch springform pan. Affix with butter.

2. In a bowl, blend the matzah meal, melted butter, and walnuts together with a wooden spoon. Press the mixture into the bottom and slightly up the sides of the pan. Chill while preparing the filling.

3. In the bowl of a food processor or using an electric mixer, blend the goat and cream cheeses together. Mix in the eggs, followed by the sour cream, salt, tarragon, and pepper, beating well.

4. Pour the mixture into the chilled crust and place the pan on a baking sheet to avoid dripping onto the bottom of the oven. Bake for 1 hour. Turn off the oven and let the cake remain in the oven for 30 minutes.

5. Remove from oven. Cool down to just warm. Carefully remove the outer ring and remove the bottom disk by placing the cheesecake on the serving platter, inserting a flat spatula between the disk and cheesecake and circling around gently to detach it (do not attempt to remove the paper if it sticks). Place the cheesecake on a serving plate.

6. (Cheesecake may be prepared in advance and chilled in the pan. Just before serving, remove the outer ring and bottom disk. Serve at room temperature or rewarm in a preheated 250°F oven for 8 minutes. Remove and carefully transfer to a serving plate. Individual slices may also be reheated in the microwave.)

7. Slice the cheesecake with a knife dipped in ice water and serve. Best consumed within 3 to 4 days.

These crowd-pleasing potato patties that both adults and children tend to nosh on warm or cold throughout the day come from the large family of dishes known as *pastelim*, which also include stuffed pies. They are found in every Moroccan Jewish home on Passover, when they are made with matzah meal, and during the year, when they are made with bread crumbs.

My Moroccan neighbor Miri, who shared this recipe with me, likes to stuff them with hard-boiled eggs, which she cuts with an egg slicer into thin slices. "It's very pretty when you take a bite and see the little slice inside," she says, "but they can also be stuffed with cooked ground beef or chicken if you like. On Passover they go like hotcakes." My daughters are no doubt responsible for the disappearance of a goodly few.

While these Moroccan patties are traditionally made with parsley, you may want to experiment with cilantro, dill, or a combination of fresh herbs.

Note: The best way to mash the potatoes is to put them through a ricer. Once you try a ricer, you'll wonder how you ever lived without one.

1½ pounds boiling potatoes (about 4 to 5 medium), cooked, peeled, mashed, and chilled	¼ cup matzah meal
	Salt
	Freshly ground black pepper
4 eggs	3 hard-boiled eggs, sliced thinly
½ teaspoon ground turmeric	with an egg slicer
½ cup chopped Italian parsley	Vegetable oil for frying

1. In a bowl, beat 3 eggs and turmeric. Combine with chilled mashed potatoes, parsley, and matzah meal. Season with salt and pepper. Cover and let stand 10 minutes. Beat the remaining egg and reserve in a dish for dipping.

2. Heat ¼ inch oil in a large skillet over medium-low heat. Grease your hands with a little oil. Take about 2 tablespoons of the mixture and flatten it out in the palm of your hand. Make an indentation in the center with your fingers, and place a hard-boiled egg slice inside. Take a heaping tablespoon more of the potato mixture and place it on top of the egg. Gently flatten with the fingers into a closed patty.

3. Dip the patty lightly on both sides in the beaten egg and fry in hot oil until golden. Carefully turn and fry the other side. Transfer to a paper towel-lined plate to absorb excess oil. Serve hot or at room temperature.

Iraqi Chicken-Stuffed Patties

Makes about 25

Like the Moroccans, Iraqi Jews also enjoy making stuffed potato *pastelim* on Passover, when potato dishes are especially popular in lieu of grains. While these use a potato mixture similar to the Moroccan for the outside, they're stuffed with a terrific Iraqi chicken mixture given to us by Jerusalem chef Moshe Basson. The recipe has been passed down in his family for generations.

1½ pounds boiling potatoes
    (about 4 to 5 medium), cooked,
    peeled, mashed, and chilled
¼ cup matzah meal plus extra
    meal for dipping
3 eggs, beaten
Salt
Freshly ground black pepper
Olive or vegetable oil, for
    frying

Stuffing

3 tablespoons vegetable oil
1 cup finely chopped red onion
2 butterflied chicken breasts,
    deboned, chopped into
    ¼-inch pieces
½ cup raisins
½ cup toasted pine nuts
    (optional)
⅓ teaspoon *each* black pepper,
    allspice, cinnamon, nutmeg,
    and cardamom

1. Combine the mashed potatoes, matzah meal, and eggs in a bowl. Season with salt and pepper. Cover and let stand 10 minutes.

2. For the stuffing: Heat 3 tablespoons oil in a skillet and cook the onion until golden. Add the chicken, raisins, and pine nuts, if using, and stir in the spices. When the chicken turns opaque, remove from the heat. Let cool slightly, then cover and chill.

3. Oil hands and make a ball of potato mixture the size of a large egg. Flatten it out between your palms and make an indentation for the filling. Put a heaping tablespoon of filling in the center, and fold the edges over it. Close and flatten out to make sure that there are no holes with stuffing peeking through.

4. Dip on both sides in matzah meal and deep-fry as the Iraqis do, or fry in a generous amount of hot oil until golden. Turn carefully, and fry the other side. Place on a paper towel to absorb excess oil. Serve hot.

Inspired by the Sephardic tradition of frittatas (or *fritadas*) on Passover, this tender and delicious one makes a quick lunch, appetizer, or main dish for brunch.

4 regular or egg matzot	Freshly ground black pepper
8 large eggs	2 tablespoons extra-virgin olive
¼ cup water, milk, or half-and-half	oil
	1 tablespoon canola oil
¼ cup coarsely chopped fresh tarragon or chives	1 large Vidalia onion (8 ounces), halved and thinly sliced
Salt	2 cups fresh mushrooms, sliced

1. Place the matzot in a colander and moisten under running water. Let stand until fully drained and break into small pieces.

2. In a separate bowl, beat the eggs, water or milk, tarragon or chives, salt, and pepper. Add the matzah pieces. Set aside.

3. Heat the oils in a large skillet and sauté the onion until translucent. Add the mushrooms and sauté for 2 to 3 minutes, stirring frequently, until wilted.

4. Pour the matzah mixture over the vegetables in the skillet, and smooth out to an even layer with a fork. Cover and let cook on low heat undisturbed for 5 minutes, or until bottom is golden brown.

5. Remove the cover, turn over on a large plate, and slip back into the pan. Cook the underside for 3 minutes, cover, and let cook an additional 3 to 5 minutes until set. Slip out onto a serving platter and cut into wedges. Serve hot.

Note: This recipe can also be made like matzah brei: Pour the egg-matzah mixture over the onions and mushrooms, and let set at the edges before cooking as in the following recipe.

Fresh Mushroom and Vidalia Onion Frittata

Serves 6

Glazer Family's Matzah Brei

Serves 2 if greedy, 3 if reasonable

Simple and irresistible, matzah brei is a family favorite. Some of us like it sweet and drowned in maple syrup; others just add more salt.

Serve with cinnamon and sugar, real maple syrup, salt, honey, or Raw Applesauce (page 245). Makes a great breakfast with Warm Casserole of Seven Dried Fruits (page 269) laced with yogurt, cream, or crème fraîche if desired.

3 plain or egg matzot	¼ teaspoon salt
3 eggs	3 tablespoons butter

1. Break up matzot in small pieces. Put pieces in a colander and let cold water run through. Let stand about 5 minutes, until thoroughly drained.

2. Beat eggs with salt. Add matzah and mix thoroughly. Let stand 5 minutes, until the eggs are absorbed.

3. Melt butter in a large skillet over medium heat. If you prefer your matzah brei pancake style, let it cook until lightly brown on bottom and turn over with two spatulas. It can also be scrambled like scrambled eggs.

The Origin of Matzah

In ancient times matzot were an inch thick or more, and were frequently decorated with figures of doves, fish, and animals, or—in one Italian manuscript from the fourteenth century—a flowered border with a four-legged animal sporting an Egyptian-featured face. The famous "matzah holes" were made with a special sharp-toothed comb called a *redel*. Matzot were also always round; square matzot, or what came to be known as American-style matzot, were first manufactured by machine in Austria around 1857.

Before World War I, matzah production in the United States was designed for an exclusively Jewish market and solely for Passover. It was only in 1918 that an enterprising firm called Horowitz Brothers began producing matzah all year round. In 1925 the brothers began manufacturing the first "kosher for Passover" products under religious supervision.

Today, there are all kinds of matzot—whole wheat, garlic flavored, or those made with eggs or bran. And for those who are very particular, there's *shmura matzah*—round matzot created from wheat that is under religious supervision from the moment it's harvested to the moment it's baked and boxed, to ensure that it becomes neither damp nor fermented during the manufacturing process.

Beets—*selek*—were a popular vegetable in ancient times, particularly during the Second Temple period (537 B.C.E.–70 C.E.). Both green leaves and bulbous red root held culinary value. The leaves could be eaten fresh or added to various stews, and the flamboyantly red root was perfect for colorful croquettes, salads, and pickles. Long before rouge was invented, slices of *selek* brushed over the cheeks gave a rosy glow to those women clever enough to use them. Mix together in a bowl, or serve ingredients in separate bunches on a serving platter and let guests mix their own.

Serves 4

½ small head cabbage
1½ cups grated carrots
1 cup peeled and grated fresh
   beets
½ cup radish sprouts
½ cup raisins
⅓ cup sliced scallions (white and
   tender part of green)
1 Granny Smith apple, cored,
   seeded, and diced

Dressing
¼ cup freshly squeezed lemon
   juice
½ cup olive or other oil
1 tablespoon honey
Coarse sea salt or kosher salt
Freshly ground black pepper

1. Wash and dry vegetables. Remove the tough core of the cabbage and lay the cabbage cut side down. Using a very sharp large knife, shred the cabbage finely (all shredding and grating may also be done in a food processor). Remove and transfer to a serving bowl or platter.

2. Grate carrots and beets on the medium side of a grater. Arrange the carrots, beets, sprouts, raisins, scallions, and apple on top of or alongside the cabbage. (All salad ingredients may be prepared several hours in advance, and kept in separate plastic bags or containers covered tightly with plastic wrap in the refrigerator. Sprinkle a little lemon juice over the apple and diced avocado (see Variation below) to prevent darkening.)

3. Before serving, whisk the lemon juice, oil, and honey in a small bowl. Season with salt and pepper and pour over the salad, or pass the dressing separately, if desired.

Variation

Add 1½ cups peeled and diced avocado.

Marinated Fennel in Olive Oil and Herbs

Fills a 2-quart Mason jar

These fennel "pickles" make a deliciously different condiment on the Seder table, as well as an accompaniment to both hot and cold dishes and salads throughout Passover week. They're a fiber-rich snack to munch on, and perfect on pasta throughout the year.

Thyme, which adds a subtle flavor and fragrance to this pickle, once grew wild in the hills of ancient Israel. The Mishnah mentions it both as a flavoring herb and as a plant suitable as tinder for fuel. It was traditionally eaten with fatty or heavy dishes made with lamb or beans, probably because it was discovered to help improve digestion.

3 pounds fennel (3 bulbs with 1-inch stalks)
2 medium onions, sliced
4 garlic cloves, peeled and sliced
2 lemons, scrubbed and sliced thinly lengthwise (unpeeled)
4 sprigs fresh thyme
⅔ cup Passover white wine vinegar (optional)
Pinch of sugar dissolved in 1 teaspoon water
Coarse sea salt or kosher salt
Coarsely ground black pepper
Extra-virgin olive oil, to cover

1. Wash, dry, and trim the fennel stalks where they meet the top and sides of the bulb. Remove dry or pulpy outer leaves, stalks, and edible leaves. Save the outer leaves and stalks for soup, and the leaves for garnishing.

2. Slice the bulbs thinly crosswise. Place the slices in a large bowl with the onion, garlic, lemon, and thyme. Mix in vinegar, if using, and sugar water. Season with salt and pepper and cover with extra-virgin olive oil (or half olive oil, half vegetable oil), making sure that the olive oil covers the fennel.

3. Use a dish smaller than the circumference of the bowl and a kettle half-filled with water on top as a weight to help submerge the vegetables. Let sit several hours at room temperature before serving.

4. Remove thyme sprigs and transfer to a 2-quart Mason jar. Store tightly closed in the refrigerator. More fennel may be added to the same marinade throughout the week. Top up with olive oil so fennel is submerged.

For those who tire of matzah on Passover, these seeded rolls will help pass the week with style. Serve them as is, with butter and jam, or slit and filled with chopped liver, tuna salad, or other favorite filling.

Passover Thumbprint Seeded Rolls

2 cups matzah meal
½ teaspoon salt
½ cup butter or pareve
   margarine, cut into cubes
1 cup boiling water

3 large eggs, beaten
Approximately 1 tablespoon *each*
   sesame seeds, caraway seeds,
   pumpkin seeds, sunflower
   seeds, and dried rosemary

Makes 20

1. Preheat the oven to 400°F. Lightly grease a baking sheet with oil or nonstick cooking spray, or line with parchment paper.
2. Place the matzah meal and salt in a bowl of a mixer (or beat by hand) and add the butter or margarine. Pour the boiling water over and stir or beat with a wooden spoon until butter or margerine is dissolved.
3. Cool slightly and beat in the eggs one at a time.
4. Grease hands with oil and form 20 balls. Flatten them slightly and make a thumbprint in the middle of each. Sprinkle each with a different spice or seed and bake for 15 to 20 minutes, or until golden.

Kicking the *Kitniot* Habit

Ashkenazim probably never give as much thought to *kitniot*—legumes—as they do on Passover. To eat or not to eat? Many of us spent many a Passover believing that beans, corn, lentils, millet, peanuts, peas, and sesame and sunflower seeds are *hametz* and thus forbidden (like leavened wheat, and barley, spelt, rye, and oats). Also, most Sephardim eat rice; according to custom, Ashkenazim don't. But . . .

Rabbis in both the United States and Israel have pointed out that early authorities such as Samuel of Falais and Rabbi Yeruham called avoiding *kitniot* a "mistaken" and "foolish" custom, and that all Jews are permitted to eat both legumes and rice on Passover "without fear of transgressing any prohibition."

Ashkenazim who nevertheless want to stick to "the custom of their ancestors," says Rabbi David Golinkin, should observe the original custom of no rice or legumes but "use oil from legumes and all the other foods 'forbidden' over the years, such as peas, beans [like soy], garlic, mustard, sesame, sunflower seeds, peanuts, etc. This will make their lives easier and will add joy and pleasure to their observance of Pesach."

Melon with Crystallized Ginger

Serves 8 to 10

A straightforward light dessert or snack, the melon is enhanced many-fold by the simple addition of crystallized ginger. In season, I also add sliced carambola (Chinese star fruit) for a decorative touch.

1 honeydew melon (about 2 to 3 pounds), peeled and sliced 1 inch thick
1 ripe cantaloupe (about 2 to 3 pounds), peeled and sliced 1 inch thick

⅓ cup chopped crystallized ginger
A little bowl of *Eingemacht* (page 46), optional

1. On a serving platter, lay the honeydew slices on their sides, alternating with slices of cantaloupe. Cover with plastic wrap and chill until serving time.

2. Before serving, sprinkle over the crystallized ginger, and let stand a few minutes before serving. Pass a little bowl of *Eingemacht,* and let guests take a spoonful, if they like.

Pecan Meringue Cookies

Scented with nutmeg, these distinctive light little cookies have been a family favorite for many years. They are easy to make, melt in your mouth, and are far better than store-bought meringue cookies.

1 large egg white
1 cup light brown granulated
    sugar, regular light brown
    sugar, or turbinado sugar

Pinch of salt
¼ teaspoon ground allspice or
    nutmeg
1½ cups finely chopped pecans

Makes 24 to 30

1. Preheat oven to 250°F. Line a baking sheet with parchment paper and set aside.

2. Using an electric mixer, beat the egg white until stiff and gradually add the sugar, salt, and desired spice. Beat until the mixture looks shiny. Stir in the nuts.

3. Using two spoons, place full teaspoons of the mixture on the sheet, leaving 1½ inches between each cookie. Flatten out the tops.

4. Bake in the preheated oven for 25 to 30 minutes, or until the cookies appear dry on top. Use a spatula to gently remove the warm cookies from the oven and cool on a wire rack. Store in a sealed jar.

Lemony Nut Cake with Lemon Topping and Berries

Serves 6 to 8

When I first made this cake at home, I topped it with the luscious mulberries growing outside on the 70-year-old tree in my yard, but it is also lovely with fresh raspberries, little strawberries, or a mixture of seasonal berries. You can vary the nuts you use, as long as the total is 1⅔ cups, and use lime juice instead of lemon juice in the topping, if preferred.

½ cup hazelnuts (filberts)
½ cup walnuts
⅔ cup unblanched almonds
¼ cup matzah meal
1 cup sugar
4 large eggs, separated
Pinch of salt
1½ teaspoons grated lemon zest

Topping
2 tablespoons freshly squeezed lemon or lime juice
1 cup confectioners' sugar
1 cup assorted fresh berries (sliced or chopped if large)

1. Preheat the oven to 350°F. Line the bottom and sides of a 9-inch springform pan with parchment paper, affixing with a little oil to help it stay in place. Alternately, line the bottom of the pan with parchment paper, grease the sides, and sprinkle with dried coconut, knocking out excess.

2. If using unpeeled hazelnuts, put in a baking dish and toast in the oven about 8 minutes, until lightly browned. Rub between paper towels while hot to remove brown skin and set aside to cool.

3. In the bowl of a food processor, using the metal blade, process the nuts, matzah meal, and ¼ cup of the sugar together until powdered.

4. In the bowl of a standing electric mixer, beat egg whites with ¼ cup sugar and a pinch of salt until stiff peaks form. Remove from the bowl and set aside.

5. Place the egg yolks and remaining ½ cup sugar in the bowl of the mixer and beat until thick and fluffy. Beat in lemon zest. Fold ⅓ of the egg whites and ⅓ of the ground nuts alternately into egg yolk mixture, then repeat using ⅓ of each mixture each time until all the ingredients are incorporated.

6. Pour into the prepared baking pan and bake for 35 minutes. Let cool 10 minutes, then run a knife around the edges to help release the cake. Remove the outer ring of the springform pan, run a knife between the bottom of the cake and the bottom of the pan, and turn it out onto a wire rack.

7. In a small bowl, blend lemon or lime juice with confectioners' sugar and smooth over the top of the cake. Top with the berries and serve, or chill until serving time.

R ich and fudgy, these brownies will be devoured within minutes.
Note: This recipe makes twenty-four ½-inch-high brownies. The same recipe can be baked in an 8-inch round pan as a cake. Save the nuts and sprinkle them on top, or use them in the cake and sprinkle confectioners' sugar over the top.

4 ounces bittersweet chocolate
¼ cup (½ stick) butter, at room temperature
⅓ cup cream cheese, at room temperature
1 cup turbinado sugar or granulated sugar

2 eggs, beaten
1 teaspoon "kosher for Passover" vanilla extract
½ cup matzah cake flour
2 tablespoons potato starch
1 cup finely chopped pecans

1. Preheat the oven to 325°F. Butter an 8-by-12-inch cake pan, or line it with parchment paper and butter the sides.

2. Break the chocolate into pieces and melt in top of a double boiler, stirring occasionally. Remove from heat and let cool slightly. (Chocolate may also be softened in the microwave.)

3. In the bowl of a standing electric mixer, or using a wooden spoon or a whisk, cream the butter and cream cheese. Beat in the sugar, eggs, and vanilla, mixing well. Add the cake flour, potato starch, cooled chocolate, and nuts, and mix on low speed, stopping to scrape down the sides of the bowl occasionally with a rubber spatula.

4. Pour into the prepared pan and bake for 25 to 30 minutes (an 8-inch round cake will take slightly more time), or until a toothpick inserted in the center comes out clean. Cut with a sharp knife while still warm.

Moshe b'Tayva (Moses in the Basket)

Dates Stuffed with Homemade Marzipan

Makes 14 to 16

Part of the Passover story begins with baby Moses bundled into a little date frond basket to float on the Nile under the watchful eye of his sister Miriyam until Pharaoh's daughter found him. Making these adorable and delicious little sweets with friends and family could start a memorable, meaningful, and creative Passover tradition.

Medjool dates are very large, are usually found in Middle Eastern stores, and should be tender to the touch and slightly moist inside. Although they are the perfect size, do not buy them if they appear very dry. Substitute another type of date if necessary. Your *Moshe* will be smaller, but just as sweet.

Caution: Before you start, ask everyone to refrain from eating more than one *Moshe* until they are all made, so that you can compare styles and techniques. Otherwise, before you know it, they'll just be a memory.

Note: This same delicious marzipan can be used to stuff apricots, or it can be placed between walnut or pecan halves.

14 to 16 large Medjool dates

Marzipan
3½ ounces (a slightly rounded cup) slivered or whole blanched almonds, ground
3½ ounces (⅔ cup) confectioners' sugar
¼ teaspoon "kosher for Passover" vanilla extract
A few drops rose water or almond extract
1 to 2 teaspoons hot water

Garnish
¼ cup crushed, toasted, unsalted pistachio nuts
Whole cloves as needed
Coriander seeds or mustard seeds (for the eyes)

1. Use a sharp, pointed knife to slit the dates lengthwise, and remove the pits. Set aside.

2. Grind the almonds in a food processor to a powder consistency. Add the sugar, and with the machine running, add the vanilla, rose water or lamond extract, and 1 teaspoon hot water. The mixture should come together like a ball. If not, add another 1 to 2 teaspoons water, but be careful not to add too much or the marzipan will be too soft.

3. For each little *Moshe*, make a small ball of marzipan for the head, and an elongated oval-shaped piece for the body. (The total length of both together should be slightly smaller than the length of a date.)

4. Roll the "body" in the crushed pistachio nuts (to add color and to represent the "bunting"). Attach the head to the body and stick the whole in one of the dates, gently pressing the sides of the date around him to make him snug. Round the top and the bottom with a gentle pinch, to make a little boat.

5. To make the eyes, use the tip of a whole clove to pierce 2 holes in the "head." (We considered using cloves for the eyes themselves, but were afraid of a lawsuit from anyone not removing them before eating.) Stick a coriander seed in each hole (these are both edible and healthful), and *Moshe* is ready to float to his destiny.

Eingemacht

Makes about 5 cups

Long before the advent of prepared Passover products, Eastern European housewives used to prepare *Eingemacht,* derived from the Yiddish word *einmachn,* which means "to preserve food," for serving with roasted meats or spreading on matzah, especially on Passover. Beet *eingemacht* was a specialty of Ukrainian Jews, while many Polish grandmothers would make the preserves out of black radishes, turnips, or carrots. Spread on matzah (or after Passover, on bread), *eingemachts* were also used as a relish and spoon sweet.

This glistening version created by our mother really captures that Old World flavor.

2 pounds fresh whole beets (to yield 4 cups tightly packed shredded beets)	1 lemon, very thinly sliced and seeded
1 cup sugar	1 cup blanched slivered almonds
¾ cup water	1 tablespoon minced, peeled fresh gingerroot
1 cup honey	

1. Wash and peel beets and shred with a grater or food processor, or cut into small dice.

2. Bring sugar, water, and honey to a boil in a medium-size saucepan, stirring constantly until sugar is dissolved. Add beets, lower heat to a simmer, and cook, partially covered, for 1 hour.

3. Peel the lemon and cut the rind into thin strips, with as little pith as possible. Discard the pith and thinly slice the lemon. Add both rind and lemon slices to the beets and simmer, covered, 1 hour longer, until jellied and beets are transparent.

4. Add almonds and ginger, stir well, and cook 15 minutes longer. Cool, cover, and store in refrigerator. Keeps at least 3 months.

Several years ago, a reader of my question-and-answer newspaper column wrote in to ask for a recipe for lemon curd, promoting an avalanche of responses from other readers who had come to Israel from Britain. As it turns out, lemon curd is a favorite of British Jews at Passover time, perhaps because most versions of the recipe use egg yolks left over from baking Passover cakes and macaroons.

"When I grew up in England," wrote reader Shifra Tarem, from Israel's seaside town of Ashkelon, "the only food available that was kosher for Passover was matzah, so everything else—biscuits, jam, preserves, and even matzah meal—was made at home. The Jewish community hit on English lemon curd as an ideal spread for matzah. It could keep for weeks, if we didn't eat it all up sooner."

But our dear family friend Cherna Crome, who lives in London, told us that she is amazed how Jews seem to use lemon curd only at Passover, while other people in Britain eat it all year round, and "it is always available in every supermarket." She also told us that "lemon curd dates from the seventeenth century, when it was used as a filling for cheesecakes, little tarts filled with lemon, orange, or apricot curd, or other fruit cheeses seldom made now, except for Damson cheese, which generally has too many pits to serve as a jam."

Here is Cherna's favorite lemon curd recipe. It can be kept in the refrigerator anywhere in the world for four to six weeks.

3 large unwaxed lemons	1 whole egg and 3 yolks (or
½ cup (1 stick) unsalted butter	3 whole eggs, or 4 yolks)
1 cup sugar (preferably	
superfine)	

1. Grate the zest of 2 lemons into a bowl and add the juice of all 3. Leave the mixture to infuse for 2 to 3 hours. Strain.

2. Melt the butter in a double boiler (or in a bowl over a pan of boiling water) and mix in the sugar and the strained juice. When the sugar has completely dissolved, beat the eggs (or egg yolks) and pour a little of the sugar-lemon mixture over them. Return to the double boiler and stir with a wooden spoon, until the mixture coats the back of the spoon. Remove from heat. It will thicken as it cools.

3. Pour into warm dry jars, cover when cool, and refrigerate.

Cherna's Favorite Lemon Curd

Makes about 1½ pounds

He shall come home with shouts of joy,
bringing his sheaves with him.
—Psalm 126:6b

The Omer: Awaiting the Harvest

Mimouna and Lag b'Omer

I f we could rename the Omer, we'd call it "the Season of Winds." It's no wonder that these seven weeks between the second day of Passover and Shavuot filled our ancestors in the land of Israel with trepidation. As they reaped their barley day by day in the mostly mild and lovely spring weather, they faced the possibility of sudden north winds that could be so rainy the fruit trees would be destroyed, or south winds so hot their wheat could be stunted before the harvest, just weeks away.

The weather in Israel during the Omer hasn't changed much since ancient days, but the way we celebrate the Omer certainly has. Once upon a time in early spring, the Greeks and Romans honored their goddesses of the grains, while the farmers of Israel honored God. Believing the weather to be a matter of divine judgment, the farmers followed the biblical law to bring a measure (the meaning of the word *omer*) of their new sheaves of barley to the Temple in Jerusalem to wave as an offering, in the hope that God would control those potentially "injurious winds" and "injurious dews" (Leviticus Rabbah 27:5 and Song of Songs Rabbah, 7:2).

But the farmers' pilgrimage was no longer possible once the Temple fell.

Rather than eliminate the Omer from our calendars, in characteristic fashion the Jews reinterpreted it. In the hills of the Galilee, kabbalists continued to count each of its forty-nine days, but envisioned the whole Omer period as a "season of judgment" that aligned heavenly energy with human character until the climactic fiftieth day, the Festival of Shavuot, when the Torah was revealed at Mount Sinai and heaven and earth "married." The mystics' tradition is still meticulously honored by observant Jews today.

For the Moroccan Jews, on the other hand, the agricultural roots of the season evolved into a grand folk festival, the Mimouna, at the end of Passover, the seventh day of the Omer. Mimouna became a festival of faith (*emunah*) on which both one's personal prosperity (*mamone*) and the bounty of the land—like the old harvest—would be determined. Later a second explanation for the holiday was found: Mimouna was seen as a way to honor the sage Maimonides, who had lived in the city of Fez in the twelfth century. The result today is that wherever in the world Moroccan Jewish communities are found, Mimouna is a time of feasting, dancing, prayer, and song—an opportunity for neighborhood parties, open houses, and picnics.

At home, the tables are laden with an abundance of foods symbolizing fertility and plenty, sweet dishes like couscous topped with pumpkin, zucchini, fried almonds, and raisins, a panoply of sweets like jams and preserves, *zaben*, a candied meringue, *mahiya*, a licorice liqueur, and sweet mint tea in gold-rimmed little glasses. But the queen of the evening is undoubtedly a pile of *muffleta* (page 64), thin crepelike pancakes, waiting to be drenched in butter and honey, with their secret message: May you experience abundance in your life, as abundant as these *muffleta*.

In Morocco the Mimouna was also a time for courting. Engaged couples would be invited to dine at the table of the fiancée's parents, where *muffleta* and grilled fish—symbolizing fertility—would be served. If the couple proved promising, families would sit outside and mingle with one another well into the night.

The origins of the season's second folk festival, Lag b'Omer ("the thirty-third day of the Omer"), are even more shrouded in legend than Mimouna's. The Talmud claims that on the thirty-third day of the Omer a mysterious plague that had caused the deaths of 24,000 students of the sage Rabbi Akiva came to a sudden halt. Some modern historians believe that the so-called "students" were actually Jewish soldiers who had joined the ill-fated Bar Kochba revolt against Rome in 132–135 C.E.

Yet another, very different tradition holds that this was the day that Rabbi

Shimon Bar Yochai, a student of Rabbi Akiva, received the mystical secrets of the Torah, which he laid down in his great kabbalistic work, the Zohar. And still another maintains that the date is the anniversary of Shimon Bar Yochai's death. Because Bar Yochai's last request was to celebrate the day with bonfires, torches, songs, and feasting, Lag b'Omer became a Great Celebration all over the Sephardic and Mizrahi Jewish worlds.

Finally, though not trying to ferret out the holiday's origins, anthropologist Theodore Gaster suggests that Lag b'Omer is parallel to European May Day, an ancient rural festival whose traditions, like those of Lag b'Omer, included going out to the fields and forests to shoot arrows at demons and evil spirits during the season in which when they're believed to be most rampant, and of kindling bonfires to keep away "demons and witches when the cattle are first let out of the barn."

However Lag b'Omer came to be, ever since the sixteenth century, pilgrims have flocked to Bar Yochai's grave on Mount Meron in the Galilee to celebrate with dancing, music, enormous bonfires, and elaborate picnics, many of which include lamb slaughtered and barbecued for the occasion. It's also a major festival among the 2,000-year-old Jewish community of Tunisia's Djerba. In many countries today, the holiday is celebrated with barbecues, picnics, and/or sporting events, and little children are still given pretend bows and arrows like those of Rabbi Akiva's student-soldiers.

Whether you opt for a barbecue, bonfire, or picnic, Lag b'Omer's various traditions and its unique timing during the barley harvest can provide inspiration for a variety of menus and dishes such as Spring Barley Mini-croquettes with Tahini and Fresh Herb Sauce, Grilled Cornish Hens in Lemon and Hot Pepper Sauce, Baked Potato and Sprout Salad with Fresh Parsley Dressing, and Carob Walnut Brownies, recipes for which follow in this chapter.

Recipes for the Omer

Appetizers

Spring Barley Mini-croquettes with Tahini
and Fresh Herb Sauce **D**
Red Lentil Hummus with Olive Oil **P**

Main Courses

Grilled Cornish Hens in Lemon and Hot Pepper Sauce **M**
Yehiel's Famous Kabob **M**

Salads and Accompaniments

Baked Potato and Sprout Salad with Fresh Parsley Dressing **P**

Barley Salad with Lemon and Cilantro **P**

Aromatic Chickpeas **P**

Wilted Cabbage with Mustard Seeds **P**

Cherry Tomatoes, Basil, and Tassos Olives in Olive Oil **P**

Cheese in the Fire **D**

Desserts

Carob Walnut Brownies **D** **P**

Miri's *Muffleta* **D**

Spring Barley Mini-croquettes with Tahini and Fresh Herb Sauce

**Makes about
10 medium or
16 mini-croquettes
(serves 4–6)**

In just this season and probably during these very same days thousands of years ago, the great-grandmother of King David, Ruth, gleaned in the barley fields of Boaz. It was there, under the hot sun, that Boaz first fancied her and—long before perfume or flowers—gave her a gift of "six measures of barley" as a token of his affection.

When she got home, she might have made a variety of these crispy barley croquettes to serve to her mother-in-law.

Serve medium-size croquettes as a vegetarian main dish, or make mini-croquettes to serve as hors d'oeuvres while the barbecue heats up.

1 cup pearl barley
2 cups water
1 teaspoon salt
½ cup whole-wheat flour
1 to 2 garlic cloves, minced or
    pressed
2 teaspoons honey
¾ cup finely grated carrots
½ cup finely chopped onion
Extra flour, for dusting
2 to 4 tablespoons extra-virgin
    olive oil
1 to 2 tablespoons butter or
    Biblical Butter (page 72)

Tahini Sauce
⅔ cup tahini (sesame paste)
½ cup hot water
2 to 3 tablespoons freshly
    squeezed lemon juice
2 garlic cloves, minced
¼ cup finely chopped fresh dill
1 tablespoon finely chopped
    Italian parsley
1 tablespoon finely chopped
    fresh mint (optional)
Salt
Freshly ground black pepper
    to taste

1. Rinse the barley in several changes of water until the water remains clear. Drain well and place in a pot with 2 cups of water. Bring to a boil, skim off the foam, cover, and cook over low heat about 15 to 20 minutes, or until water is absorbed. Barley should be tender, but not mushy. Let cool until easy enough to handle.

2. Transfer barley to a mixing bowl, and add the salt, flour, garlic, honey, and vegetables. Mix well, using your hands to combine the ingredients. Form the mixture into about 10 palm-sized patties, or 16 mini-croquettes, if preferred. Dip on both sides in a light coating of flour and shake off excess.

3. Heat the oil and butter in a large heavy skillet. When hot, add the barley cakes and brown over medium-high heat. Turn and brown on the other side. Lower heat and cook for a few more minutes. Remove from heat, cover, and keep warm.

4. Place the tahini in a small bowl. (Stir the contents of the can or jar before measuring—the tahini usually separates.) Add the hot water gradually while mixing with a spoon until smooth. Add lemon juice, garlic, and herbs. Season with salt and black pepper to taste.

5. Serve as a sauce for the medium croquettes, a dip for the mini-croquettes, or even as a salad dressing. Thin with an extra tablespoon or two of boiling water if necessary.

So Naomi returned, and Ruth the Moabite, her daughter-in-law, with her, from the field of Moab—and they came to Bethlehem in the beginning of the barley harvest.

—**Book of Ruth 1:22**

And First There Was Barley . . .

Barley is the oldest cultivated cereal in both the Middle East and Europe, and may even have come before cultivation of rice in the Far East. In ancient days, it was the most important food grain in the region, eaten as porridge, made into unleavened bread, malted for beer, and used for animal fodder. Low in gluten, it produced a dense, heavy bread, far less desirable than wheat bread. A poor man's food used to feed the masses, it came to symbolize worthlessness and poverty.

And yet, despite its lowly status, barley comes second in the biblical list of the Seven Species, perhaps because it was far more dependable and far less finicky than wheat, surviving heat and drought better and (still) ripening in Israel about a month before wheat. The barley harvest also served as a harbinger of spring, a renewal of hope for nourishment in the year to come, and like wheat, was the inspiration for artistic design on coins, stone reliefs, and even furniture.

Just fifty years ago, an old Arab villager once told us, barley was still used by the poor in Israel to make pita bread, and in ancient Greece and up to the early 1960s in Crete and the Aegean islands, a variety of twice-baked barley biscuits, called *paximadia,* were a basic source of sustenance.

Lower in fiber than other grains, barley is easy to digest, which probably accounts for the age-old remedy of barley water for stomach ailments and as a restorative traditionally given to infants and invalids. A sweetened barley porridge with nuts, called *belila,* is traditionally made by Sephardic Jews to celebrate a baby cutting its first tooth.

The Omer

53

Red Lentil Hummus with Olive Oil

Serves 4 to 8

Like barley, which ripened one month before wheat, lentils also ripened at this time, before their cousin the chickpea. Our ancestors cooked them for soups and stews, and could puree them hummus-style, much like the classic chickpea hummus, still a mainstay in the Middle Eastern diet.

Serve Red Lentil Hummus with hot grilled pita brushed with olive oil and sprinkled with zahtar, as a starter before a barbecued meal or alongside a choice of salads, for a biblically inspired picnic.

Note: Chilled slightly until it thickens, red lentil hummus can also be used to fill phyllo or puff pastry squares.

2 cups red lentils, picked over
2 bay leaves
1½ teaspoons salt
4 to 5 large garlic cloves, pressed
1½ to 2 tablespoons chopped fresh oregano
¼ cup extra-virgin olive oil, plus more for garnish
Freshly ground black pepper to taste
Pinch paprika or cumin (optional)
1 lemon, cut into 4 to 8 sections

Toppings
½ cup chopped fresh cilantro
⅔ cup coarsely chopped sun-dried tomatoes, drained
⅔ cup sliced radishes
⅓ cup chopped scallions, or 1 small red onion, sliced
3 to 4 tablespoons kalamata olives, pitted and chopped

1. Place the lentils in a bowl and cover with water. Swish around with your hand, drain, and repeat process until water is clear. Drain.

2. Put lentils and bay leaves in a large pot with water to cover plus 1½ inches. Bring to a boil and lower heat. Skim off foam that develops on top (it is difficult to get it all, so just remove as much as possible). Cover and cook over low heat for 45 minutes, stirring occasionally. There will be a small amount of water left on top. Remove the bay leaves.

3. Beat the mixture with a tablespoon until it is a smooth mash, and any remaining water is incorporated. In a small bowl, mix the salt, garlic, oregano, and olive oil, and stir briskly into the pot in circular motions. Add black pepper to taste.

4. Smooth the warm puree in an even layer on one large or several small plates. Pour a little extra olive oil on top, and garnish with a pinch of paprika or cumin and a little chopped cilantro. Serve with lemon sections and toppings in separate bowls. (Puree may be prepared in advance and served at room temperature or warmed in the microwave.)

Grilled
Cornish
Hens in
Lemon and
Hot Pepper
Sauce

Serves 6 to 8

Poultry was available in all of the countries in which Jews lived; it's not only versatile, but associated with Sabbath and festive occasions. Our friend Hanoch Bar Shalom, a creative chef who contributed several recipes to this book, serves these hens on grill-toasted pita or lavash, in Middle Eastern style. To accompany them, choose from the variety of salads that follow, including Hanoch's own Cherry Tomatoes, Basil, and Tassos Olives in Olive Oil (page 61).

3 Cornish hens, about 1½ pounds each
Salt
Freshly ground black pepper to taste
8 garlic cloves, crushed
2 medium mildly hot or hot green peppers, like Anaheim or poblano

1 cup freshly squeezed lemon juice
½ cup extra-virgin olive oil
3 bunches of arugula
1 large round pita (lavash) or focaccia

1. Rinse the hens and pat dry. To reduce fat, we like to dip the hens in boiling water and scrape the skin with a knife to remove excess surface fat. Cut each Cornish hen into 4 pieces and season with salt and pepper. Set aside.

2. Slice each hot pepper in half lengthwise and remove the seeds and ribs if a milder taste is preferred. Cut into small dice, and mix with the garlic, lemon juice, and olive oil. Let stand at room temperature while the grill heats.

3. Rinse the arugula well to remove grit, and cut off the roots.

4. Over medium-high coals, grill the Cornish hen pieces for 6 minutes on each side, or until done. Do not overcook or the hen will dry out and burn.

5. Remove the hen pieces and warm the pita for a few minutes on the grill. Put the pita or lavash on a large serving platter, and scatter the arugula on top. Lay the hen pieces on the arugula, pour the sauce over, and serve.

Yehiel's Famous Kabob

**Makes 20 kabobs
(serves 8 to 10)**

When we have a yen for Bulgarian food, we always visit Yehiel Philosof at his Bulgarian restaurant in Jaffa, famous for both its Bulgarian Leek Patties (page 144) and this excellent kabob.

2 thick slices challah, crusts removed

11½ ounces beef (boneless short ribs)

1 pound beef shoulder, cut in cubes

5 ounces lamb fat (ask your butcher)

3 eggs, lightly beaten

1⅔ cups chopped onion (about 2 large onions)

1½ cups finely chopped Italian parsley

1 teaspoon salt

1 teaspoon sweet paprika

½ teaspoon freshly ground black pepper

½ teaspoon ground cumin

1. Soak the challah in water, drain, and squeeze out. Grind together with the meats and the lamb fat (you can ask the butcher to grind it for you). Combine with the eggs, onion, parsley, and seasonings. Mix well, cover, and let stand in the refrigerator for 3 hours to blend flavors.

2. Form 20 patties. Grill on both sides over hot coals, or place on a rack with a drip pan underneath, and broil on high, turning occasionally, until nicely browned.

Inspired by the bonfire-baked potatoes that are traditional fare on Lag b'Omer in Israel, this superb salad can be made at home or around the fire; prebake the potatoes until they're almost done, and throw them into the bonfire (encased in aluminum foil jackets) to add that special smoked scent. Keep the dressing in a separate jar and add just before serving.

1½ pounds new or red thin-
   skinned potatoes
Oil
Salt
Freshly ground black pepper
2 cups fresh bean sprouts
1 cup sliced fresh mushrooms

Dressing

6 tablespoons extra-virgin
   olive oil
6 tablespoons freshly squeezed
   lemon juice
¼ cup chopped fresh Italian
   parsley
1 to 2 tablespoons finely chopped
   onion

1. Preheat the oven to 350°F. Scrub the potatoes, but do not peel. Rub with oil, season with salt and pepper, and pierce in several places with the tines of a fork. Bake in the oven about 1 hour, until tender. Cool slightly, cut the unpeeled potatoes into large chunks, and transfer to a salad bowl. Add the sprouts and mushrooms.

2. In a small bowl, whisk together the ingredients for the dressing. Season with salt and pepper, and pour over the warm potatoes. Stir gently and serve.

Variation

For a spicy touch, add a teaspoon or more of Yemenite *Tzoug* (page 299) to the dressing.

Baked Potato and Sprout Salad with Fresh Parsley Dressing

Serves 6

Barley Salad with Lemon and Cilantro

Serves 4 to 6

Barley salad is another truly delicious way to experience a grain most people assume has only one use—in soup. Cubed avocado may also be added, or the salad may be stuffed into large avocado halves.

1 cup pearl barley
2 cups water
1 cup chopped (unpeeled) English (hothouse) cucumber
½ cup fresh mushrooms, sliced

Dressing
½ cup safflower or extra-virgin olive oil
3 tablespoons freshly squeezed lemon juice

1 garlic clove, minced or pressed
1½ teaspoons honey
1 teaspoon chopped fresh thyme, or ½ teaspoon dried
1 teaspoon grated lemon zest
½ cup finely chopped cilantro or Italian parsley
Salt to taste

1. Rinse the barley in several changes of water until the water remains clear. Drain well and place in a pot with 2 cups of water. Bring to a boil, partially cover, and cook over low heat about 15 to 20 minutes, or until water is absorbed. Rinse under cold water to stop the cooking process, drain, and cool. Add the chopped cucumber and sliced mushrooms.

2. In a small bowl, whisk all of the ingredients for the dressing, except the cilantro, until well blended. Reserve some of the mixture. Stir the cilantro into the larger portion of the dressing and pour over the salad.

3. Let stand a few minutes to blend flavors, or cover tightly with plastic wrap and chill. Refresh the salad with the reserved dressing before serving.

Like barley, fresh lentils, and wheat, fresh chickpeas were a spring crop that could easily be dried and stored by our ancestors for use as daily fare throughout the year. Today, they're great to nibble on throughout the day and evening.

Serves 6 to 8

2 cups (approximately 1 pound) dried chickpeas

1 bay leaf

4 large garlic cloves, minced or pressed

1 teaspoon paprika

½ teaspoon cayenne pepper (or more to taste)

1½ teaspoons salt

½ cup minced fresh Italian parsley

Freshly ground black pepper to taste

3 tablespoons extra-virgin olive oil

1. Sort chickpeas and soak overnight in water to cover. (Or boil for 5 minutes and let soak for 1 to 2 hours.) Drain. Cover with fresh water to cover by 2 inches. Add bay leaf, bring to a boil, and cook over low heat about 1 hour, until chickpeas are tender but not mushy. (Cooking time will depend on size and age of the chickpeas.) Drain, discarding bay leaf. Transfer to a serving bowl.

2. Add remaining ingredients while chickpeas are still hot. Taste and adjust seasoning. Serve warm or at room temperature.

Wilted Cabbage with Mustard Seeds

Serves 4

P

Three kinds of mustard are mentioned in Talmudic literature. A prolific weed the sages cautioned to keep far away from wheat fields, mustard leaves and stems were pickled in brine or vinegar to serve as a vegetable or condiment, and the tiny seeds were used as seasoning, as a unit of measurement, and were pressed for oil. They were even used to feed pigeons.

1 small head cabbage (1 pound)
1 heaping tablespoon coarse or
   kosher salt
⅓ cup finely sliced scallions
¼ cup regular or extra-virgin
   olive oil

1 to 2 tablespoons wine vinegar
   or lemon juice
¾ teaspoon black mustard seeds
   or caraway seeds

1. Cut cabbage in half and remove core. Using a chef's knife, shred cabbage as thinly as possible, or shred thinly in a food processor. (You should have about 4 to 4½ cups.)

2. Place the cabbage in a colander and mix in the salt with your fingers. Let stand about 20 minutes, or until wilted. Squeeze cabbage to expel liquid. Rinse briefly and squeeze again. Place in a bowl and mix with scallions, oil, and vinegar.

3. In a dry skillet, lightly toast mustard or caraway seeds until they pop. Stir into cabbage salad and serve.

This jarful of flavor is lovely to behold. The bright red of the tomatoes echoes the color of the bonfires, the green basil leaves recall the fresh young leaves of spring, the olives hold at their center the promise of fuel (in ancient times they were used for tinder), and the olive oil that covers it all was once a source of light. Easy to carry to any picnic and convenient to serve at a backyard barbecue, this combination created by Hanoch Bar Shalom goes well with grilled chicken, and may also be served alongside stuffed phyllo squares and cheese dishes.

Cherry Tomatoes, Basil, and Tassos Olives in Olive Oil

Serves 6 to 10

For a 1-Quart Jar
1 pound cherry tomatoes
1 cup lightly packed fresh basil
  leaves
1 dried hot pepper
5 ounces Tassos or kalamata
  olives (see Note)

2 garlic cloves, peeled and sliced
4 cups extra-virgin olive oil, or
  more to cover
2 teaspoons coarse sea salt or
  kosher salt

1. Rinse cherry tomatoes and basil leaves and pat dry. Slit open the hot pepper, remove the seeds, and set pod and seeds aside.

2. In a clean quart-size jar, alternate layers of tomatoes, olives, and basil, sprinkling the garlic cloves, dried pepper pod, and seeds between them. Pour olive oil over to cover and add the coarse salt. Cover and let stand for 12 hours before serving. Covered in oil, it will keep up to one week in the refrigerator.

Note: Tassos olives are unpitted black salt-cured olives with an intense flavor. If no Tassos are available, use a good-quality black olive such as the kalamata.

Cheese in
the Fire

Serves 6 to 8

If you're celebrating Lag b'Omer with a bonfire instead of a barbecue, try this delicious combination of melted cheese and nuts that you remove from the fire at intervals and spread on pita, crackers, baguette slices, or vegetable sticks. Our ancestors would no doubt have enjoyed it too, had they had access to aluminum foil.

Two 8-ounce pieces of Swiss,
    Cheddar, or other cheese (or a
    mixture)
1 tablespoon unsalted butter, at
    room temperature

1 cup mixed toasted nuts
Extra-wide heavy-duty
    aluminum foil

1. Place one piece of cheese in the middle of a sheet of foil large enough to enclose it, with an additional few inches on each side. Butter the top of the cheese with half the butter, and spread half the mixed nuts on top. Press down with the palm of the hand so the nuts stick to the cheese.

2. Cover with the second piece of cheese, butter the top with the remaining butter, and press the rest of the nuts on top. Fold two sides of foil over the cheese. Crumple the two remaining sides tightly, and join to form a handle at the top, so that the package may easily be removed from the fire.

3. Place the package in a low fire, or at the edges of the bonfire, for about 8 to 10 minutes. Remove and carefully open the package. Use a knife to spread the outer layer of melted cheese on bread, crackers, or vegetable sticks. Reclose the package, replace in the fire, and repeat the process as long as the cheese lasts.

Legend has it that when Rabbi Shimon Bar Yochai and his son Reb Elazar hid in a cave in the Galilee to escape the Romans, a miracle occurred—a carob tree suddenly appeared and a spring of water burst forth nearby. For twelve or thirteen years they studied Torah together and developed the Zohar, surviving only on the carob pods and water (see page 65). What could be more appropriate than celebrating the holiday with a carob-based confection!

Makes 12

½ cup (1 stick) butter or
   margarine, at room
   temperature
1 cup packed brown sugar
2 teaspoons vanilla extract
3 eggs
3 tablespoons boiling water
6 tablespoons carob powder
2 tablespoons brewed strong
   instant coffee or espresso

½ cup unbleached all-purpose
   white or whole-wheat pastry
   flour
1 teaspoon baking powder
⅛ teaspoon salt
½ cup chopped walnuts
Confectioners' sugar (optional)

1. Preheat the oven to 350°F. Grease and flour an 8-inch square pan, knocking out excess flour, or line the bottom of the pan with parchment paper and lightly grease the sides.

2. Beat butter and brown sugar together in a medium-size bowl. Add vanilla and eggs, and beat well. Set aside.

3. In a small bowl, mix boiling water and carob powder until smooth. Add the coffee, and stir into the butter mixture.

4. Mix flour, baking powder, and salt, and add to the bowl gradually, blending just until incorporated. Stir in the walnuts. Pour into the prepared pan (for more and smaller brownies use an 8-by-12-inch rectangular pan). Bake for 20 minutes, or until a toothpick inserted in the center comes out clean. Cool slightly before cutting into squares. Dust with confectioners' sugar before serving if desired.

Miri's Muffleta

Makes about 15

The centerpiece of the Moroccan Mimouna celebration held on the seventh day of the Omer (as Passover exits), *muffleta* are thin crepe-like fritters that are prepared using copious amounts of oil and fried somewhat unconventionally—in a tall stack. The stack is then pulled apart into individual fritters and served with melted butter and honey or preserves. Guests can spread the melted butter and honey over their own *muffleta* and roll it like a blintz, or the mixture can be poured over the entire stack.

To teach us how to make *muffleta*, my Moroccan neighbor Miri was happy to demonstrate her technique, which we offer here. For those still wary about the traditional method, the fritters can be fried and served individually.

4 cups unbleached all-purpose flour	2 tablespoons vegetable oil, plus more for greasing and frying
¾ tablespoon yeast	½ cup (1 stick) butter
¼ teaspoon salt	¼ cup honey
1½ to 1¾ cups warm water	

1. Generously oil a large baking pan or baking sheet, and keep the container of oil handy for oiling your hands and the skillet. Set aside.

2. In a large bowl, mix the flour and yeast. Stir in the salt. Gradually pour in 1½ cups warm water, stirring to form a soft sticky dough. Add up to an additional ¼ cup water only if the dough seems too dry.

3. Oil hands and work 2 tablespoons oil into the dough. Beat it with a cupped hand until fluffy. Oil hands again, form 10 to 15 balls slightly larger than Ping-Pong balls, and place in the prepared pan.

4. Grease a skillet with a paper towel dipped in oil and heat over medium-low heat. Oil a work surface and your hands. Take one of the *muffleta* balls and use the fingers of both hands to open it into a circle slightly smaller than the size of the skillet. It should be as thin as possible. Don't worry if there are holes in the dough. (Although this step is traditionally done by hand, *muffleta* can be rolled out into a thin circle with an oiled rolling pin.) Place it in the skillet, and while it fries, begin preparing the next.

5. When the *muffleta* is just lightly browned, like the bottom of a crepe, flip it over in the pan and place the uncooked one on top of it.

6. Prepare the third *muffleta*. Flip the first and second ones over together and put the third one on top, and continue with this process until you have a stack of 10 muffletas. Remove the *muffletas* and serve immediately, while you prepare the rest from the remaining dough.

7. To serve, melt the butter and honey in a small saucepan, and stir to blend. Let guests separate the stack (it doesn't have to be a neat job), and dip their *muffleta* in melted butter and honey. Or separate the stack of *muffletas*, roll each one like a cone, and place on a large plate or tray.

8. Pour the melted butter and honey over and serve immediately.

In [the Galilee town of] Peki'in there are Jews, some fifty households, workers of the land and vineyards. . . . And Peki'in is full of good things; nothing is lacking in this area. Springs of water come from the valleys and hills. And there is the huge carob tree of Rabbi Shimon Bar Yochai; it is old now and does not bear fruit, and all the non-Jews regard it as holy, and any branch that falls won't be used for anything, not even for firewood. And a fellow traveler told me that the tree is so large that he sat together with some other men on the top of the tree and they learnt the Kabbalah together!

—*Simcha ben Joshua of Zalazich, 1764*

. . . Honey and milk are under your tongue. . . .
—**Song of Songs 4:11b**

Shavuot

Spring Harvesttime

We'll never forget the scene. It was one of those beautiful sunlit spring days in the hills of Menashe, in the Galilee, many years ago: The wagons rolled in, heaped to the brim with the freshly harvested wheat; baskets overflowing with homegrown fruits and grains were laid out on the table; and the whole community was singing. Even the dairy cows were decorated with wreaths. It was the festival of Shavuot, and the whole kibbutz was celebrating.

Newly arrived in Israel, we stood among the kibbutzniks amazed. This was a world apart from any Shavuot we had ever celebrated in America. Harvest festival? Shavuot for us had always been *Z'man matan Torah*—"the Time of the Giving of the Torah." And then we realized that we were witnessing the Bible brought to life: Israelites, as the book of Exodus commands, "shall hold a festival for the Feast of the Harvest, of the first fruits of your work, of what you sow in the fields" (23:16a).

So how did the spring agricultural harvest festival the Bible describes and the kibbutz celebrated turn into what we knew as "the Time of the Giving of the Torah"?

As with all of the holidays, the key lies in how the rabbis of the Talmud coped with the loss of the Temple and the exile of the people. When the Temple stood, Shavuot, like Passover and Sukkot, was a joyous pilgrimage festival: Thousands of farmers and their families and clans traveled to Jerusalem to offer a basket of their first fruits to God. Then, acting on behalf of the whole nation, the high priest presented the offering unique to Shavuot on the altar: two loaves of bread, baked from the newly harvested wheat.

For having received "the rain, the seed, the sunshine," *from* God, the Israelites reciprocated by offering the bread they had baked *to* God. It was their way of acknowledging the "partnership of human beings with God in giving food to the world," as Arthur Waskow writes in *Seasons of Our Joy.*

But the fall of the Temple meant exile from the land. Refusing to imagine the festival dying, the rabbis of the Talmud infused it with new meaning. Searching through the Bible like determined detectives, they found clues that proved to them that the ancient harvest festival had actually coincided with a crucial "spiritual harvest" too: What the Israelites "reaped" at Shavuot was the Torah. Passover marked the exodus from Egypt, but the real "closing" (*atzeret*) of the holiday came weeks later, in the desert, when the Law was revealed at Mount Sinai. For the rabbis and for the Jews scattered all over the world in the centuries that followed, it was the giving of the Torah that became the "partnership" between God and Israel to be celebrated at Shavuot.

Even the foods we eat at Shavuot show the stamp of the rabbis' influence. For though it was the time of the wheat harvest, it's dairy foods that have become the culinary heart of the holiday. The explanations given are often fanciful: in Hebrew numerology (*gematria*), the word for milk (*halav*) equals 40—the same number of days that Moses lingered on Mount Sinai to receive the Law. Alternatively, Psalm 68 describes the Torah as being given on "a mount of *gavnunim*"—a word that means "many peaks," but was cleverly linked with the Hebrew word for cheese (*gevinah*).

Nature itself, though, provides another explanation. Like the spring holidays of ancient Canaan and Rome, Shavuot occurs in the very season when animals grazing in the lush pastures green from winter rains produce an abundance of milk; cheese-making, too, was part of spring harvest festivals across the world.

And so emerged our special holiday foods. In the dairy regions of late-nineteenth-century Russia, where milk supplies were also plentiful in the spring, the Jews adapted traditional Russian dishes like blini or blintzes, cheese-stuffed kreplach, knishes, and kugels for their Shavuot table. In the Ukraine, *schav* borscht (see our version on page 78), made from tender green spring sorrel leaves enriched with sour cream or egg yolk, was also an early favorite.

Throughout the Sephardic world, cheese-stuffed pastries like *bourekas* (page 76) have graced the Shavuot menu for centuries (though meat was consumed during the holiday as well). And while some Moroccan families continue the tradition of baking challah in the shape of a giant key on Shavuot (to help "open the gates of heaven"), in other Sephardic lands, the challah were shaped to resemble a book, the Torah; a bird, to carry prayers (page 156); and a hand, to evoke the receiving of the Torah.

So when planning a Shavuot meal, keep in mind that in addition to dairy the real meaning of the holiday includes fresh wheat and barley—the latter harvested just weeks before—the tender young greens of spring, and touches of the "first fruits" of the season, primarily those representing the Seven Species.

A delightful custom, evoking those ancient processions of farmers, is to decorate the holiday table and home with green leaves and branches. In medieval times, Jews scattered precious spices and roses on the synagogue floors—echoing the Midrashic tale that when the Torah was given, all herbs, flowers, grasses, and trees vied with one another for a seat on Mount Sinai to witness the revelation of the Law. In keeping with the tradition, you might want to add some fresh herbs, whole spices, and roses as well.

Shavuot Recipes

Shavuot Basics

Biblical Yogurt Cheese **D**
Biblical Cream Cheese **D**
Biblical Butter **D**

Appetizers and Soups

Pistachio-Coriander Cheese Balls **D**
Feta Cheese in Seven-Ingredient Olive Oil Marinade **D** **P**
Cheese and Olive S'Mores **D**
Bourekas b'Milui Badinjan (Short Crust Pastries Stuffed
    with Eggplant and Feta Filling)
Schav and Spinach Borscht with Nutmeg **D**
Taratour with Walnuts **D**

Main Dishes

Spinach-Feta Quiche with Fresh Basil **D**
Hot and Bubbling Semolina and Sage Gnocchi **D**
Ida's Classic Cheese Blintzes **D**

Salads and Accompaniments

Sweet Noodle Kugel **D**

Cabbage Salad with Grapes and Almonds **P**

Zucchini *Fattoush* Salad **P**

Whole Wheatberry Tabbouleh with Biblical Butter **D**

Spring Green Salad with Tangerine and
    Fennel Seed Vinaigrette **P**

Quick Garlic and Chive Rolls **D**

Desserts

Double-Ginger Granola Cheesecake **D**

Lishansky's Famous Halvah Cheesecake **D**

Mom's Famous Buttermilk Pie **D**

Anise-Scented Milk **D**

Biblical Yogurt Cheese

Makes 1½ cups

Yogurt cheese (*labaneh*) was an excellent way for our ancestors to expand the limited repertoire of foods in the biblical diet and prolong the shelf life of yogurt. It could be drained until soft and used as a spread, or left to drain until firm and turned into olive-oil-marinated balls, which could last throughout the year.

1 quart plain thick cow's-, sheep's-, or goat's-milk yogurt, with no stabilizers

Cheesecloth or muslin bag

1. Place a large wire-mesh strainer over a bowl. Cut 3 to 4 layers of cheesecloth into 20-inch squares, dip in cold water, wring out, and line the colander. Spoon in the yogurt, bring up the edges, and squeeze the bottom a little to extract some of the moisture. Twist the corners of the cloth together, and tie the two opposite edges into a knot.

2. Hang the package from the kitchen faucet for several hours or overnight, and let it drip directly into the sink, or leave to drain over the bowl at room temperature until the yogurt is the consistency of cream cheese. Squeeze the package gently from time to time to help the package drain faster. Remove the cheese from the cheesecloth and transfer to a closed container. Store in the refrigerator.

3. To serve, bring the cheese to room temperature and spread on a plate. Garnish with extra-virgin olive oil and chopped olives, capers, and parsley, if desired. Serve with warm earthy bread, pita, or Panfried Scallion Bread (page 236).

Variations

Add ½ cup chopped fresh herbs such as parsley, dill, or mint, or a combination and ½ teaspoon salt to the yogurt in the strainer.

Add 1 to 2 teaspoons black sesame or nigella seeds.

Add coarsely cracked black pepper to taste.

Long before the advent of bagels and lox, goat or sheep cream cheese was a part of our ancestors' diet. Prepared soft, it could be used as a spread or as a first course for dipping in bread, in the same way that hummus or *labaneh* is used today. Allowed to drain slightly longer, it could dry out sufficiently to be made into balls and covered in olive oil and herbs for extended storage, like *labaneh*. It is a superb substitute for regular cream cheese in any recipe. In fact, we even use it for Double-Ginger Granola Cheesecake (page 94).

Use full-fat sour cream that does not contain stabilizers—available in Persian or Middle Eastern stores.

Biblical
Cream
Cheese

Makes 3¼ cups

4 cups (2 pints) dairy sour cream	Cheesecloth or muslin bag
½ teaspoon salt (optional)	

1. Line a strainer or colander with a double layer of cheesecloth and place over a bowl. Pour the sour cream and salt into the strainer and allow to drain for 1 hour. Gather up the edges of the cheesecloth and tie them, lightly squeezing out as much moisture as possible.

2. Hang the bag over the kitchen sink, and leave for several hours or overnight. For a softer-spreading cheese, check after 3 to 4 hours. Refrigerate when the desired consistency is reached.

Biblical Butter

D

The invention of the churn changed the course of culinary history, for it was a first step in the formation of butter—a vital cooking fat. Skimming the fat off of goat's or sheep's milk, placing it in a pot, and cooking it over low heat to remove its milk solids, impurities, and moisture, the ancients could then enjoy a clarified butter (like Indian ghee), which under optimum conditions could last for a year or more.

This "butter," similar to what Bedouin Arabs and Yemenites today call *samneh*, was a richly flavored medium with a burning point higher than regular butter and oils, making it ideal for cooking and frying. Much richer tasting than regular butter (and used in Ayurvedic medicine as a healthful food and a salve), it's worth making a jarful and using it for cooking, frying, or spreading on bread.

1 pound (4 sticks) unsalted butter

1. Melt the butter in a heavy saucepan over lowest possible heat.
2. Simmer just until foam develops on top, skim off, and continue cooking until the milk solids drop to the bottom and form a milky layer of sediment and the top layer is a pure golden yellow.
3. Remove the saucepan from the heat, and let sit for a few minutes to allow the last of the solids to settle to the bottom.
4. Strain through a cheesecloth-lined wire-mesh strainer, and store covered in an earthenware or glass jar in the refrigerator (best used within 3 months) or the freezer (best used within 6 months).

Note: Biblical (clarified) butter varies in flavor and intensity depending on how long you cook it. After the butter has fully separated, the milk solids at the bottom of the saucepan begin to brown and take on a fragrant nutty flavor the French call *beurre noisette*—also known as "brown butter" or "hazelnut butter." But watch carefully—mere seconds exist between a truly memorable brown butter and one that burns and needs to be discarded.

Pistachio-Coriander Cheese Balls

S erve with bread or crackers for breakfast or lunch, or as a party snack.

1 cup firm Biblical Cream
   Cheese (page 71), or a
   commercial variety, chilled
1 tablespoon Black-and-White
   Seasoned Salt (page 298)

2 tablespoons finely chopped or
   ground salted pistachio nuts

Makes about 15

1. If using Biblical Cream Cheese, let drain in the cheesecloth an additional few hours until the cream cheese is rather firm. Oil hands and roll into 1-inch balls.

2. In a small bowl, mix the Black-and-White Seasoned Salt with the chopped pistachio nuts. Roll the cheese balls in the nuts until well covered. Serve immediately, or cover and chill on waxed paper until serving time.

Note: Yogurt cheese may also be used for this recipe.

Feta Cheese in Seven-Ingredient Olive Oil Marinade

Serves 4 to 6

Just as certain foods hold symbolic meaning for the Jewish people, so the number seven is considered to hold special significance in Jewish mysticism. Not only does the first sentence of the Torah have seven words (in Hebrew), but the number is repeated in the number of days in the week and other cycles in Jewish life.

Rich and earthy, this simple dish combines the Shavuot holiday culinary tradition of dairy foods with a seven-ingredient marinade that takes just minutes to prepare. The result, as you'll see, is Seventh Heaven.

Serve the marinated feta cheese for entertaining, a quick snack, or as part of a lunch or dinner. I like to make it just as guests arrive, so the marinade is still hot. Alternately, make it a few hours ahead of time, and let the cheese marinate for several hours to absorb flavors. Serve in a rustic-looking shallow ceramic dish, if you have one.

Those who avoid dairy products can use this recipe with tofu with the addition of salt to taste. Store either variation in an airtight jar in the refrigerator for 3 to 4 days.

Note: This same marinade is delicious over other cheeses as well, such as cubed mozzarella or whole Camembert. It may also be used as a dressing for potato or green salads.

12 ounces feta cheese or the
    equivalent amount of
    firm tofu

Seven-Ingredient Marinade
1½ cups extra-virgin olive oil
6 whole peppercorns, lightly
    cracked
2 bay leaves

2 sprigs fresh thyme, each
    broken in half
1 sprig fresh rosemary, broken
    into pieces
4 garlic cloves, peeled and halved
1 cup lightly packed fresh basil
    leaves, or ½ cup fresh sage
    leaves (or a combination)

1. Cut the cheese or tofu in half lengthwise and then crosswise into ½-inch slices. Place in a serving dish.

2. In a saucepan, heat all the ingredients except the basil until very hot. Remove from heat, add the basil leaves, and pour over the cheese. In late summer or early fall, add pomegranate seeds as a garnish.

ike the chocolate-marshmallow campfire desserts, these snacks are so good that everyone will want some more. They easily can be made in advance, frozen, and baked as necessary. Perfect to nosh on throughout the Shavuot holiday, on the odd chance that they last.

8 ounces grated Muenster or
    Monterey Jack cheese
½ cup (1 stick) butter, at room
    temperature
1 cup unbleached all-purpose
    flour

½ teaspoon salt
1 teaspoon sweet paprika
24 pitted or pimiento-stuffed
    olives
Sesame seeds and/or zahtar

Cheese and Olive S'Mores

Makes 24

1. Preheat the oven to 400°F. Line a baking sheet with parchment paper.

2. In a medium-size bowl, beat the grated cheese and butter together. In a second bowl, mix the flour, salt, and paprika. Add the flour mixture to the butter mixture, and mix well.

3. Take a teaspoon of the mixture and roll it between the palms of your hand to form a ball. Press an olive into the ball with the stuffed side facing up. Repeat the process with the rest of the dough and the olives. After the balls are made, roll them lightly in sesame seeds or zahtar. Place the balls on prepared baking sheet.

4. Bake for 15 minutes, or until golden brown. Serve warm.

Bourekas b'Milui Badinjan

Short-Crust Pastries Stuffed with Eggplant and Feta Filling

Makes about 40 to 50 (recipe can be halved)

The traditional Jerusalemite *bourekas,* served on holidays and special occasions, are made with short-crust pastry dough. There are three basic fillings: cheese, beef (page 186), and *badinjan* (eggplant) mixed with a dry feta-type cheese called *Tzfatit.*

This family recipe is Gil Hovav's, an Israeli cookbook author and television personality who was born in Jerusalem in the 1960s to a Ladino-speaking family that had lived in the Holy City for generations. He remembers that the type of *Tzfatit* popular in Jerusalem was always a very dry and firm kind that in days past was brought to the city from Tzfat (Safed) in the north, and stored in large tin cans for many long weeks. Our closest approximation is feta cheese.

Note: Ideally, the dough should be prepared the night before, or chilled at least 4 hours before using.

Dough
3½ cups unbleached all-purpose flour
1 tablespoon salt
1 cup (2 sticks) butter
2 tablespoons white vinegar
¾ cup yogurt or dairy sour cream

Filling
2 to 2¼ pounds eggplant (about 2 medium)
4 ounces feta cheese, drained
1 teaspoon freshly ground black pepper
1 egg yolk and 1 tablespoon water for brushing
Sesame seeds

1. Place the flour and salt in the bowl of a food processor and drop in cubes of butter until coarse crumbs are formed. Add the vinegar and yogurt and pulse until a ball forms around the blade.

2. Remove, knead briefly, and divide into 3 balls. Cover each with plastic wrap and chill in the refrigerator at least 4 hours or overnight.

3. When ready to prepare *bourekas,* roast the eggplant on all sides (for method see page 142). Place in a paper bag, close, and let sit for 10 minutes before scooping out the flesh with a spoon.

4. Place the eggplant flesh in a wire-mesh strainer and let stand 30 minutes to drain.

5. Mash the eggplant with the feta cheese and black pepper. (Do not use a food processor.) Set aside.

6. Preheat the oven to 350°F. Line 2 cookie sheets with parchment paper.

7. Remove the dough from the refrigerator and let stand until easy to work with (but not too soft). Roll out one ball thinly on a lightly floured surface and use a 2½- to 3-inch-wide glass or pastry cutter to cut out circles. Gather up the remainders and roll out again to form more circles. Repeat with the other balls of dough. You should end up with 40 to 50 circles.

8. Lay the circles on top of the parchment paper. Keep the bowl with the filling and a bowl of cold water to the side. Put a level teaspoon of the filling in the bottom of each circle, and use a finger dipped in water to moisten the edges. Fold over to form a half-moon shape, pinching the edges tightly shut. (Don't be tempted to put too much filling in or the *bourekas* will burst open during baking.) Repeat with the rest of the circles. Beat the egg yolk with the water and brush onto the *bourekas,* then sprinkle with sesame seeds.

9. Bake for 30 minutes, or until golden brown. Serve warm.

Schav and Spinach Borscht with Nutmeg

Serves 10 to 12 (recipe may be halved)

Lemony sorrel, or "sour grass," a perennial plant native to Europe and Asia, grows along roads and damp meadows in spring, right around Shavuot, particularly in the Ukraine, where this soup originated as a holiday specialty. It combines an easily available seasonal ingredient, which was easy for the poor shtetl dwellers to collect or buy in the market, with dairy products (in this case, sour cream), which were traditional and also available in this season. The little leaves were more than just tasty; they provided a good source of protein and minerals that were a boon to a limited diet.

This version uses both sorrel and spinach, but either all *schav* or all spinach can be used.

Serve cold, topped with sour cream, and with little bowls of thinly sliced cucumbers and radishes for guests to add their own.

1½ pounds boiling potatoes
10 cups water
1 pound sorrel
1 pound spinach
¾ cup finely sliced scallions
1 tablespoon salt
½ teaspoon freshly ground
   black pepper

3 to 4 tablespoons sugar
3 eggs
1½ cups dairy sour cream
Freshly squeezed lemon juice
   (optional)

1. Peel the potatoes and cut into small chunks. Place in a large soup pot with the water and bring to a boil. Lower heat and cook 10 minutes.

2. In the meantime, rinse the sorrel and spinach to remove all grit, cut off the stems, and discard. Coarsely chop with a knife and add to the pot with the scallions, salt, and pepper.

3. Return to a boil. Lower heat and cook an additional 20 minutes, or until the potatoes are done. Remove from heat and stir in 3 tablespoons sugar. Cool slightly.

4. In a medium bowl, whisk eggs and sour cream together. Add ½ cup soup at a time, whisking constantly to prevent curdling, until you have added about 3 cups. Pour the mixture into the soup and mix well. Taste and add more salt, pepper, or sugar if necessary. Squeeze in a little lemon juice, if desired. Let cool completely and chill.

This refreshing chilled yogurt soup is a specialty of the Balkan states. There are many varieties, some with scallions or radishes, some with yogurt and sour cream—but we particularly love this recipe, adapted from the Hebrew cookbook *Summer Foods* by Suzi David. Serve very cold.

3 cups plain yogurt
4 tablespoons olive oil
2 tablespoons white wine vinegar
1 English (hothouse) cucumber, finely diced
2 garlic cloves, minced or pressed

Salt to taste
1½ teaspoons sugar (optional)
½ cup lightly packed mixed fresh dill and mint leaves, finely chopped
½ cup coarsely chopped walnuts

1. Whisk together all of the ingredients except walnuts, blending well. Cover and chill thoroughly.

2. Just before serving, stir in most of the walnuts, and save the rest for garnish. Divide among 4 tall glasses, and garnish with the remaining walnuts. Serve immediately.

Taratour with Walnuts

Serves 4

Spinach-Feta Quiche with Fresh Basil

Serves 6

With spinach reminiscent of spring's fresh green leaves, and dairy products traditional to Shavuot, this delicious quiche is suitable cut into small wedges as holiday hors d'oeuvres or into large wedges for lunch or dinner. Serve with Taratour with Walnuts (page 79) and Spring Green Salad with Tangerine and Fennel Seed Vinaigrette (page 92).

Quiche Crust
1¼ cups whole-wheat flour
1 teaspoon salt
¾ cup (1½ sticks) cold butter or margarine
1 egg yolk
⅓ cup plain yogurt

Filling
1 package (10 ounces) frozen chopped spinach
6 small scallions, with 2-inch green tops included, chopped
4 ounces (1 cup) crumbled feta cheese
½ cup cottage cheese
2 tablespoons extra-virgin olive oil
3 tablespoons chopped fresh basil
1 large garlic clove, minced or pressed
½ teaspoon freshly ground black pepper
4 eggs
½ cup milk

1. Preheat the oven to 400°F.

2. Prepare the crust. Put the flour and salt in the bowl of a food processor. Cut the butter into chunks and add to the flour. Process in on/off pulses until coarse crumbs are formed.

3. In a small bowl, beat together the egg yolk and yogurt and add to the flour mixture while the machine is running. Remove and shape into a neat ball. (The dough should not be sticky. If it is, knead it briefly on a floured surface.)

4. Flatten the ball and, using thumbs, press into a 10-inch pie plate, distributing the dough around equally, with no dough buildup around the inner edges. Flute the top. Alternately (but more work), dough may be wrapped in plastic wrap, chilled for 30 minutes, and rolled out.

5. Use a fork to pierce the bottom and sides of the dough, so it will not rise, or weigh the dough down with dry beans (they can be reused) placed on a circle of parchment paper for easy removal. Bake the crust for 10 minutes, or until just lightly browned.

6. Remove from the oven and let cool slightly. Remove the beans and the parchment paper, if using.

7. Prepare the filling: Thaw the spinach, and put in a wire-mesh strainer to drain. Press and squeeze out any excess liquid.

8. In a food processor, chop the scallions and add the rest of the ingredients except for the spinach. Process for 30 seconds, or until blended. Add the spinach and process briefly in on/off pulses.

9. Pour the filling into the partially baked crust and bake 10 minutes.

10. Lower heat to 350°F. Bake an additional 10 to 15 minutes, or until the quiche is set and a toothpick inserted in the center comes out moist but not wet. Serve hot or at room temperature.

Hot and Bubbling Semolina and Sage Gnocchi

Serves 4 to 6

*O*f all the herbs that flourished in the spring in ancient times, sage was probably the most valuable. Not only did it serve our ancestors as a culinary herb, they also chewed on the fresh leaves to promote fertility and longevity, and threw them on a red-hot fire to help keep illness—interpreted as the "evil eye"—away. An eight-branched form of sage (illustrated on the back jacket of this book) may also have been the inspiration for the Hanukkah menorah.

And while early cooks turned their fresh wheat into grain pastes, as the centuries passed and cooking facilities improved, they might have created a semolina dish much like this to grace their Shavuot holiday table.

Serve these gnocchi straight from the oven, with Multicolored Roasted Pepper Salad (page 206) or Spring Green Salad with Tangerine and Fennel Seed Vinaigrette (page 92).

2½ cups milk	2 eggs
1½ teaspoons salt	1 cup freshly grated *Kashkeval*
⅛ teaspoon nutmeg	or Parmesan cheese
1⅓ cups semolina	(4 ounces)
4 teaspoons minced fresh sage	5 tablespoons butter, melted
leaves	A few small (1 inch or less) fresh
Freshly ground black pepper	sage leaves, for garnish

1. Butter a large baking sheet or pan (that will fit into your refrigerator). Set aside.

2. In a heavy-bottomed medium saucepan, bring the milk, salt, and nutmeg to a boil over medium heat. Add the semolina to the pot gradually, stirring constantly with a wooden spoon to avoid lumps.

3. Add the sage and a few grindings of pepper, lower heat slightly, and cook, stirring constantly, until the semolina thickens. It is ready when the spoon will stand, unsupported, in the middle of the pan.

4. In a small bowl, beat the eggs with a wire whisk and add half the cheese. Beat into the semolina with the wooden spoon until incorporated.

5. Pour the mixture onto the prepared sheet, and smooth into an even ⅓-inch-thick layer using a palette knife, dipped in hot water as necessary. Let cool at room temperature, cover with plastic wrap, and chill in the refrigerator at least 1 hour, until firm.

6. Preheat the oven to 400°F. Butter a 9-inch oven-to-table baking dish.

7. Use a 1½-inch-diameter small glass or cookie cutter, dipped in hot water periodically, to cut out small circles of the semolina and transfer them to the dish. Work from the outside in, in a circular slightly overlapping pattern. Tuck in a few small fresh sage leaves here and there between the gnocchi, if desired, for garnish.

8. Brush the tops with the melted butter, and sprinkle with the remaining Parmesan cheese. Bake in the center of the oven for about 12 to 15 minutes, or until crisp, golden, and bubbling. To brown the top, slip under the grill for less than a minute, watching carefully to avoid burning the cheese. Serve right from the oven.

Ida's Classic Cheese Blintzes

Makes about 32

Although blintzes were a traditional Eastern European dessert served at the end of a festive Shavuot meal, everyone loved our mother's blintzes so much that we often had them *as* a meal. She always made them in quantity to keep in the freezer, lest she be caught unprepared when the inevitable guests arrived.

Derived from the Ukrainian word for pancake, blintzes are made like crepes but are slightly thicker.

Note: For best results, make and fill blintzes one at a time. This helps keep the blintzes from drying out.

Blintzes
4 large eggs
1 cup whole milk
¼ cup (½ stick) unsalted butter, melted
¼ teaspoon salt
2 cups unbleached all-purpose flour
½ cup water
Extra butter, for greasing pan

Cheese Filling
1½ pounds farmer cheese
8 ounces cream cheese, at room temperature
2 large egg yolks
1 teaspoon vanilla extract
½ cup turbinado sugar or regular sugar

1. Whisk the eggs until well blended. Add the milk, melted butter, salt, and flour, and continue whisking until there are no lumps and the mixture is smooth. Whisk in the water and blend until smooth. Let the batter stand 30 minutes at room temperature, or several hours in the refrigerator. Whisk again before using.

2. Combine the ingredients for the filling in a medium bowl until well blended. Set aside.

3. Thoroughly grease a 6- or 7-inch omelette or crepe pan with butter. Use a paper towel to coat the surface evenly. Heat over medium-high heat. Use a ¼-cup measure and fill it with 3 tablespoons of the batter. Pour the batter in, starting in the center of the pan and rotating it so that the surface is evenly covered. Cook 2 minutes, or until lightly golden on the bottom. Regrease the pan lightly each time with a paper towel and a dab of softened butter or oil.

4. Turn over onto a work surface. (Mom always turned them over onto a clean old pillowcase or tablecloth used just for that purpose.) While the blintz is still warm, put 1 heaping tablespoon of filling on the cooked side of the blintz, about an inch from the bottom. Fold the bottom "flap" over the filling, then fold both sides in. Roll up from the bottom and transfer to a plate seam side down.

5. Repeat the process, greasing the pan with melted butter before making each blintz, until all the batter is used up. When ready to prepare, fry in a little butter or light vegetable oil until nicely browned. (Uncooked blintzes may be frozen in a covered container for up to 1 month.)

Sweet Noodle Kugel

Serves 12

Kugels have been a part of the Ashkenazic kitchen as long as anyone can remember, and are one of the foods such as cholent that evolved as a response to the biblical injunctions against kindling fires and working on the Sabbath and festival days.

Since there is no prohibition to allowing a fire to burn if it is kindled prior to the start of the Sabbath or a festival, observant Jews developed a variety of seasonal dishes that would not be perishable and could be kept warm for long periods of time.

Kugel originally referred to the type of pan that the kugel was traditionally baked in. Eventually the actual food inside the pan came to be called "kugel" and could refer to noodle kugel, potato kugel, matzah kugel, or various other vegetable kugels. It was the Shavuot tradition of incorporating dairy products into the festival meal that gave birth to the dairy noodle kugel, and especially the sweet noodle kugel—which echoed the theme of the "sweetness" of the Torah.

Although sweet noodle kugel is usually eaten as a dessert, we often snacked on it throughout the Shavuot holiday, starting with breakfast. "It cheers you up," our mother often said, "and is light, not heavy."

1 pound thin noodles
4 large eggs or 6 small, beaten
   with a fork
½ teaspoon salt
8 ounces cottage cheese
8 ounces cream cheese
1 cup dairy sour cream
1 cup sugar
1 teaspoon vanilla extract

1 cup dried apricots, each piece
   quartered
1 cup canned drained or fresh
   pineapple chunkc

Topping
¼ cup sugar
1 teaspoon cinnamon
¼ teaspoon nutmeg

1. Preheat the oven to 350°F. Generously grease a 9-by-12-inch pan with 3 to 4 tablespoons butter.

2. Cook the noodles according to package directions. Pour into a colander and rinse under cold water to stop the cooking process. Let drain and cool thoroughly. Transfer the noodles to a large bowl and mix in the beaten eggs.

3. In a small bowl, mash the cream cheese and cottage cheese with the sour cream and salt, and blend into the noodle mixture. Add the sugar and vanilla. Mix thoroughly, and stir in the apricots and pineapple. Pour the noodle mixture into the prepared pan and smooth the top with a knife.

4. Topping: Mix together sugar, cinnamon, and nutmeg, and sprinkle over the top.

5. Bake for 45 to 50 minutes, or until the kugel is nicely browned on top. Serve warm or cold. (May be frozen for up to 1 month. Defrost before reheating.)

Cabbage Salad with Grapes and Almonds

Colorful and festive, this light slaw is a pleasing addition to the holiday table, and makes a crunchy and flavorful accompaniment to classic cheese blintzes and other Shavuot cheese dishes.

1 small head cabbage, thinly sliced (4 cups)
½ cup thinly sliced scallions, white and tender part of green
1 rib celery, finely chopped
2 cups small green or red seedless grapes (or large, cut in half)
¼ cup sliced blanched almonds

¾ cup thick rich plain yogurt
2 to 3 tablespoons frozen orange juice concentrate, or to taste
1 tablespoon honey
2 ripe but firm pears
Salt
Freshly ground black pepper to taste
1 to 2 tablespoons chopped crystallized ginger

1. In a large bowl, mix cabbage, scallions, celery, and grapes. If not serving immediately, cover tightly and refrigerate until serving time to crisp.

2. Toast the almonds in a dry skillet over low heat until lightly browned. Set aside for garnish.

3. Just before serving, whisk yogurt with orange juice concentrate and honey in a small bowl. Taste and add more orange juice or honey if desired.

4. Peel, halve, core, and thinly slice pears. Add to the yogurt mixture and pour over the salad. Season with salt and pepper to taste. Sprinkle the toasted almonds and crystallized ginger on top and serve.

When a man comes down to his field and sees a ripe fig, or a perfect cluster of grapes, or a beautiful pomegranate, he ties each with a red thread, saying, 'These are bikkurim, the first fruits for the Festival.'

—Babylonian Talmud

Although our friend Erez Komorovsky began his career in his early twenties as a somewhat avant-garde caterer, most people in Israel today know him for the revolution he created in the bread world; his chain of bakeries called Lehem Erez (Erez's Bread) added a new dimension to both the quality and variety of breads previously available.

Not only does he like to bake bread, he loves to find creative ways to use it. As panzanella is to the Italians, so *fattoush* is to the Lebanese and other Middle Eastern peoples. Originally created as a way to use up stale pita, *fattoush* is also delicious with pita lightly sautéed in olive oil. This is Erez's unique version.

Zucchini Fattoush Salad

Serves 4

1 cup watercress
2 cups mustard greens, leaves only (or more watercress)
1 cup fresh Italian parsley leaves
1 cup fresh cilantro leaves
½ cup extra-virgin olive oil
¼ to ⅓ cup freshly squeezed lemon juice
1 teaspoon garlic cloves, minced or pressed
Coarse sea or kosher salt

Coarsely or freshly ground black pepper to taste
2 pita breads, torn into medium to small pieces and lightly sautéed in olive oil
6 to 8 baby zucchini (½ to ¾ pound), cut into very thin lengthwise strips with a vegetable peeler
½ cup minced white onion
Pinch of sumac (optional)

1. Rinse the herbs well and dry thoroughly on a paper towel. Separate the leaves from the stems and measure the required amount. Discard the stems.

2. Prepare the dressing by whisking together olive oil, lemon juice, and garlic. Season to taste with salt and pepper.

3. In a medium bowl, mix sautéed pita pieces and zucchini with the dressing. Top with the herbs and garnish with onion and a sprinkling of sumac, if desired. Serve immediately.

A Land of Wheat and Barley

A land of wheat, and barley and vines and fig trees,
and pomegranates, a land of olive oil and honey.

—Deut. 8:8

Ripening every year at Shavuot, wheat appears first in the biblical list of the Seven Species. Interestingly, in *gematria,* the Jewish form of mystical numerology that studies numerical equivalents and their spiritual significance, the word *wheat* has the same numerical equivalent as the word *backbone.*

If there was plenty of wheat, it was a sign of plenty, an assurance of strength and sustenance in the year to come. And there were so many things to do with it! The famous couscous we still enjoy today is made from semolina, a wheat product, and olive oil–soaked tabbouleh salad is made from bulgar, a parboiled cracked wheat.

But most of all, *wheat* meant *bread.* Bread was so important, it was considered holy, and could substitute for an animal sacrifice in the ancient Temple in Jerusalem. That same bread is represented by the challah today.

Just as the herringbone pattern, inspired by the fish, symbolized fertility to the early artisan, so the wheat sheaf symbolized joyous abundance—and its form was used on ceramics, coins, and jewelry.

With the scent of freshly harvested wheat as his inspiration, Erez Komorovsky celebrates both the whole wheatberry and fresh greens of spring in a salad traditionally devoted to bulgur—tabbouleh. Instead of using just olive oil, as we do in modern times, Erez adds Biblical Butter, or *samneh* (page 72), the clarified butter used in the days of the Bible.

It's best to rinse and soak wheatberries overnight to reduce cooking time, which, depending on their age, can take anywhere from 1 to 2 hours. The wheatberries will never get as soft as rice, but they give the salad a pleasantly chewy taste.

Note: The wheatberries may be cooked, and the greens chopped, somewhat in advance, but this salad should be put together right before serving.

1½ cups whole wheatberries

5 to 6 tablespoons freshly squeezed lemon juice

¼ cup extra-virgin olive oil

¼ cup wildflower honey

½ cup Biblical Butter (page 72), melted

Salt

Coarsely ground white pepper to taste

1 cup finely chopped fresh Italian parsley

1 cup finely chopped fresh mint leaves

1 cup finely chopped fresh basil leaves

1 cup finely chopped fresh dill

1 cup finely chopped fresh cilantro

½ cup finely chopped scallions (white and tender part of green)

1. Rinse and soak the wheatberries overnight, drain, and place in a pot with water to cover. Bring to a boil and cook over medium-low heat for 1 to 2 hours, or until the wheatberries are tender but still slightly chewy. (Cooking time varies according to age of wheatberries.) Drain and rinse under cold water to stop the cooking process.

2. Whisk lemon juice, olive oil, honey, and Biblical Butter in a small bowl. Season with salt and pepper, and pour over the wheatberries. Mix in the parsley, mint, basil, dill, cilantro, and scallions with a fork. Let stand for 5 minutes. Taste, adjust seasoning, and serve immediately.

Whole Wheatberry Tabbouleh with Biblical Butter

Serves 4 to 8

Spring Green Salad with Tangerine and Fennel Seed Vinaigrette

Serves 6 to 8

The first time I visited Israel, I was twelve years old, and when I got off the plane, I was hit by an incredible sweet scent that filled the air. It was amazing, and unrecognizable to me as an urban New Yorker. Does this whole country smell this sweet? I wondered to myself innocently. It was spring, and that sweet fragrance was the scent of orange blossoms, in the orchards surrounding Ben Gurion Airport.

For me, this salad recalls the wondrous scent of orange, pomelo, grapefruit, tangerine, lemon, kumquat, lime, and limequat blossoms that fills the air with sweetness in this season.

Salad

8 ounces mesclun (or a
    combination of greens like
    arugula, radicchio, mâche)
1 pound (1 medium head)
    romaine lettuce
8 ounces fresh asparagus
4 ounces snow peas, tips
    trimmed and strings removed

Vinaigrette

1 cup freshly squeezed tangerine
    juice
½ cup extra-virgin olive oil
1 tablespoon balsamic vinegar
1 teaspoon salt
½ teaspoon freshly ground
    pepper, or more to taste
1 teaspoon fennel seeds

1. Rinse the mesclun and dry thoroughly (any moisture clinging to the leaves will make the salad soggy). Wrap in a paper towel or kitchen towel, place in a plastic bag, and chill until serving time. Remove coarse outer leaves of the romaine and discard. Rinse, dry, wrap, and chill.

2. Remove the stems from the asparagus tips and save for another use. Blanch the tips in just enough boiling lightly salted water for 1 minute. Remove and drain. Trim and blanch the snow peas for 2 minutes. Rinse briefly under cold water to stop the cooking process. Slice the snow peas crosswise in half.

3. In a small bowl, whisk together all the ingredients for the vinaigrette except the fennel seeds. Toast the fennel seeds in a dry skillet until fragrant, and add to the vinaigrette. Taste and adjust seasonings.

4. In a salad bowl, mix the chilled greens and lettuce with the asparagus tips and pea pods. Pour in half the dressing and toss gently to moisten the leaves. Divide among individual serving plates and serve immediately. Pass the remaining dressing.

Variations

Add crumbled Roquefort cheese and walnuts, well-drained mandarin orange segments, slices of fresh fennel, or watercress.

Quick Garlic and Chive Rolls

Makes 12

D

These easy-to-make rolls are perfect for mini-sandwiches or for serving with soups, hard cheeses, and the biblically inspired soft cheeses in this chapter.

1 cup milk
1 egg
3 tablespoons butter, melted
2 to 3 garlic cloves, crushed
2 tablespoons fresh-snipped chives

1 tablespoon sugar
4 teaspoons baking powder
½ teaspoon salt
2 cups sifted unbleached all-purpose flour

1. Preheat the oven to 375°F. Grease a 12-cup muffin pan. Set aside.

2. In a medium-size bowl, mix the milk, egg, melted butter, garlic, and chives.

3. In a separate bowl, sift sugar, baking powder, salt, and flour. Add the dry ingredients to the milk mixture and blend well with a fork. Divide the dough among the prepared muffin cups.

4. Bake in the preheated oven for 15 to 20 minutes, until golden brown. Serve warm or at room temperature.

Double-Ginger Granola Cheesecake

Serves 10 to 12

You must add this to your cheesecake experience! Despite the calories and fat, we were raised to believe that it's better to have a small piece of really good cheesecake than a larger piece of fat-free, low-calorie, artificially sweetened, flavored, and stabilized cheesecake impostor.

Granola Crust
3 cups any favorite granola
1 tablespoon light brown sugar
½ teaspoon cinnamon
1 teaspoon ground ginger
½ cup (1 stick) butter, melted

Filling
2 pounds cream cheese (we love
    Philadelphia), at room
    temperature, or part Biblical
    Cream Cheese (page 71)

2 teaspoons vanilla extract
1 cup sugar
4 eggs
⅔ cup heavy cream

Topping
1 cup dairy sour cream
2 tablespoons sugar
¼ cup finely chopped
    crystallized ginger

1. Position a rack in the upper third of the oven. Preheat oven to 350°F. Cut a circle of parchment paper to line the bottom of a 9- or 10-inch springform pan (the 9-inch pan will result in a higher cake). Affix to the bottom with a little butter or nonstick cooking spray. Cut a 3-inch-wide strip of parchment paper and affix to the side of the pan.

2. In a food processor, finely grind the granola and transfer to a bowl. Add the sugar, cinnamon, ground ginger, and melted butter. Mix well and press evenly into the bottom and halfway up the side of prepared pan. (Use the bottom of a wide glass to press evenly and firmly into the bottom and corners of the pan.) Chill in the refrigerator.

3. In the meantime, in the bowl of a standing electric mixer on low speed, gently beat the cream cheese, vanilla, and sugar until smooth, scraping the bottom and side of the bowl often to make sure cheese is blended. Add eggs one at a time, beating lightly after each addition. Pour in the heavy cream and mix briefly. (Overbeating the filling will make the finished cake crack.) Pour the batter into the chilled crust and level out the top with an offset spatula.

4. Bake in the preheated oven for 60 to 70 minutes, or until a toothpick inserted in the center comes out clean but still slightly moist. Do not overbake. (The center will sink and the cake will shrink slightly from the sides of the pan.) Turn off heat and let cake sit undisturbed in the oven for 20 minutes. Remove and cool to room temperature on a wire rack.

5. Lower oven temperature to 300°F. In a small bowl, beat sour cream and sugar, and pour over the top of the cake. Level with a palette knife or small offset spatula and bake for 5 minutes. Remove from the oven and let cool completely. Sprinkle with the crystallized ginger and chill the cake until firm. Cover with plastic wrap after the top has firmed up, and chill at least 4 hours or, preferably, overnight.

Cheesecake Smarts

Low-fat cream cheese or Neufchâtel cheese may be used, but they will affect the texture of the finished product and give drier results. Baking time will be slightly reduced.

Always remove filling ingredients from the refrigerator 1 hour before making the filling. Avoid drafts when removing the cake from the oven and during the cooling process. Drafts will also cause cracking.

Cool cheesecake completely before refrigerating. Chilling it while it is still warm will make it soggy.

Lishansky's Famous Halvah Cheesecake

Serves 12 to 14

Veteran cookbook author and maker of liqueurs and jams out of every conceivable fruit, herb, and vegetable, Ya'acov Lishansky, who recently passed away in his nineties, was the first (and only) Israeli man to win first prize at the "Queen of the Kitchen" cooking contest. This recipe is adapted from one of his.

Crust
1 cup unbleached all-purpose flour
½ cup sugar
1 egg yolk
1 teaspoon freshly grated lemon zest
¼ cup (½ stick) butter, melted
¼ teaspoon vanilla extract
Cold water

Filling
2½ pounds cream cheese, at room temperature
1¼ cups sugar
1 cup mashed vanilla halvah
3 tablespoons all-purpose flour
¼ teaspoon vanilla extract
6 eggs
¼ cup heavy cream

1. Preheat the oven to 400°F. Prepare a 9- or 10-inch springform pan by cutting a circle of parchment paper to line the bottom (the 9-inch pan will result in a higher cake). Affix to the bottom with a little butter or non-stick cooking spray. Cut a 3-inch-wide strip of parchment paper and affix to the sides of the pan.

2. Mix flour and sugar in a medium bowl. Beat egg yolk, lemon zest, melted butter, and vanilla together with a fork. Make a well in the flour mixture and pour in the liquids, then stir the mixture with a fork, adding just enough cold water to form a ball.

3. Transfer to a lightly floured surface and roll out to ⅛-inch thickness to fit the bottom and side of the prepared pan. (The dough does not have to come all the way up the sides.) Prick the bottom and sides with a fork, or add pie weights or dry beans placed on a circle of parchment paper, and bake for 15 to 20 minutes, until lightly browned. Remove and let cool.

4. Increase oven temperature to 500°F. In the bowl of a standing electric mixer, beat the cream cheese, sugar, halvah, flour, and vanilla together just until smooth. Add the eggs one at a time, blending lightly after each addition, and pour in the cream. Do not overbeat or the cake will crack in the center while baking. Pour the filling into the baked crust.

5. Bake for 12 to 15 minutes. Turn heat down to 200°F and bake 60 to 90 minutes, until a toothpick comes out clean and only slightly moist.

6. Let stand in the oven with the oven door partially open for 1 hour. Remove and cool completely; chill until firm. Cover with plastic wrap after the top has firmed, and refrigerate at least 4 hours or overnight.

What a joy it was to come home and discover that our mom had baked this light, melt-in-your-mouth Shavuot treat for the family! It was so rich tasting, our friends and relations couldn't believe it was made with buttermilk. We love it warm or chilled.

For a 10-Inch Piecrust
1½ cups unbleached all-purpose
   flour
½ teaspoon salt
½ cup (1 stick) cold butter
1 egg yolk beaten with 2
   tablespoons water

Filling
2 cups buttermilk
2 tablespoons butter, melted
2 egg yolks, beaten
2 tablespoons all-purpose flour
½ cup sugar
⅛ teaspoon salt
3 egg whites

1. Sift flour and salt in a medium bowl. Cut in the cold butter with a pastry cutter or two knives (or your fingers, if your mother isn't looking) until coarse crumbs are formed. Mix in the egg yolk and water with a fork. Flour your hands and form a ball. Wrap in plastic wrap and chill for 1 hour.

2. Preheat the oven to 375°F. In a large bowl, using an electric mixer or a wire balloon whisk, blend the buttermilk, melted butter, egg yolks, flour, sugar, and salt until smooth.

3. In a clean, dry bowl, beat the egg whites until soft peaks form. Fold into the buttermilk mixture with a rubber spatula until completely blended.

4. Roll out the dough on a lightly floured board until large enough to fit the bottom and side of a 10-inch pie pan. Pierce it with a fork or weight down with pie weights or dry beans placed on a circle of parchment paper.

5. Bake 10 minutes. Remove from the oven and cool.

6. Raise oven temperature to 400°F. Stir the buttermilk mixture again and pour into the prepared crust. Bake for 10 minutes, then lower heat to 350°F and bake for 25 minutes, until firm and nicely browned in the center.

Anise-Scented Milk

Makes 1 cup

Native to the entire Mediterranean region, anise (*Pimpinella anisum*) has grown profusely in hills and valleys since ancient times. Its leaves are enjoyed in salads and cooked dishes, its seeds in beverages, pickles, and pastries, its roots as a vegetable, and the entire plant as a carminative (relieves intestinal gas) and digestive. This is no doubt the reason it first appeared on *Ka'a'him* (page 173), the little round biscuits served in many Sephardic homes.

Many Mediterranean cultures love the flavor of anise, particularly in beverages—the Arabs in arak, the Greeks in ouzo, the Italians in sambuca, and the French in anisette and Pernod. Chinese cuisine features the flavor of anise in its classic Five Spice Mixture—using star anise, with the same essential oil as the seeds. Warm milk—a soothing beverage in itself—blends perfectly with anise to create a relaxing drink, which also may be frothed to serve with hot coffee.

1 teaspoon aniseed	2 to 3 teaspoons honey
1 cup milk	

Soak the aniseed in the milk for 30 minutes. Strain and heat the mixture slowly until hot, but not boiling, stirring occasionally. Pour into a cup and add honey. (Hot milk may be frothed with an espresso machine, a French press coffeemaker, a blender, or a wire whisk.)

**Curd and honey shall he eat, when he knoweth
to refuse the evil and choose the good.**

—Isa. 7:15

The Festivals
of Summer

*Israel had no days as festive as the
fifteenth of Av and Yom Kippur, when the
maidens of Jerusalem would go out in
white dresses, which they borrowed so as
not to embarrass those who had none. . . .
The maidens would go out and dance in
the vineyards. And what would they say?
"Young men, raise your eyes, and see
whom you choose for yourself!"*
—**BT, Taanit 26b**

Tu b'Av

The Fifteenth of Av's
Little-Known Festival of Love

Summer was high season in the vineyards of the Holy
Land, with the intense heat of day broken only by cool
breezes at sunset. An abundance of grapes promised a
supply of wine and raisins, vinegar and sweet syrup in
the year to come—and the grape leaves themselves could be stuffed or used
in pickling. And Tu b'Av, the fifteenth day of the month of Av (about mid-
August), was the high point of the harvest.

The most romantic day of the biblical Jewish year, this little-known festival, lit by the full moon, was a kind of Jewish Valentine's Day—though with
very different roots, of course. In an age when marriages were most often
arranged, here was a unique opportunity to choose a future spouse by a romantic dash through the vineyards.

Some historians liken it to a virtual Sadie Hawkins Day, when the nubile
young women of Israel dressed in white and danced in those vineyards intent
on choosing their groom. Others insist that it was the men who popped the
question. In either case, the result was the same: the promise of marriage. But
why on Tu b'Av?

One Talmudic rabbi suggested that Tu b'Av courting harks back to tribal times, when it was then and only then that the twelve tribes, including the punished tribe of Benjamin, were permitted to intermarry. A thousand years later, the medieval commentator Rashi suggested that the festivities of Tu b'Av commemorated the day that God again spoke to Moses with love. And yet another explanation is that, as with other Jewish holidays, the rhythms of nature and the seasons played a role.

For it's on the fifteenth of Av—Tu b'Av—that the days grow shorter and the nights longer (just as, in counterpoint, on the January festival day of the fifteenth of Shvat—Tu b'Shvat—the days grow longer and the nights shorter; see page 255). As clouds appear in the sky and mists of dew gather in the mornings, the grape harvest is at its yearly high, olives begin to ripen and fill with oil on the trees, and, finally, amid the rain-deprived summer-brown hills, white squill flowers burst into bloom everywhere in the country at exactly the same time (the only plant in Israel to do so)—a natural inspiration for those Israelite maidens in their white dresses.

And that's how the Talmud came to link Tu b'Av with Yom Kippur, according to botanist Nogah HaReuveni. For after Tu b'Av and by the time Yom Kippur fell, the farmers began to harvest the green olives for food, and the blooms of the squill flowers faded. The season that had begun with Tu b'Av came to an end around Yom Kippur, and on both days, adorned in white, the young women danced!

To help celebrate the day, we've included a few suggestions for both grape- and wine-inspired light but satisfying dishes, and recipes using foods considered throughout history to be aphrodisiacs, such as fresh figs and marinated fish. Since grapevines are mystically associated with inner peace and ripen to "gladden the human heart," we've also included champagne in two guises to reawaken those ancient stirrings in the vineyard.

Tu b'Av Recipes

Appetizers and Soups

Peach Champagne Cocktail **P**
Yellowtail Ceviche in Lemon-Coriander Marinade **P**
Champagne and Melon Soup with Feta Cheese **D**

Main Courses

Ricotta-Stuffed Ravioli with White Wine Sauce **D**
Chicken and Red Grapes with Honey-Mustard Vinaigrette **M**

Salads

Salad of Goat Cheese, Arugula, and Figs Ⓓ

Hearts of Palm Salad Ⓟ

For Breakfast Tu b'Av Morning

Brioche French Toast with Fruit and Honey-Yogurt Sauce Ⓓ

Melt-in-Your-Mouth Breakfast Scones Ⓓ

Desserts

Mango Brûlée Ⓓ

Chocolate Frangelico and Hazelnut Truffles Ⓓ

Aphrodisiacs

Food and sexuality have been connected in Judaism ever since Adam and Eve took a bite of the apple and discovered that they were naked. In fact, throughout human history, certain foods have been considered aphrodisiacs, some purely because of their appearance and others out of human intuition, the validity of which modern science is beginning to substantiate, at least in some cases.

In ancient Greece, Pliny recommended hippopotamus snout and hyena. Ovid extolled pine nuts, and Horace, liver. Others have suggested camels' humps, curry, chutneys, shark's fin and bird's nest soups, elephant and hippopotamus tusks, cocoa and chocolate, not to mention caviar, clams, oysters, lobsters, and swans' genitals.

How did people decide that one food or another is an aphrodisiac? First and foremost by shape. Plants that resemble human sexual organs were considered very desirable, such as eels or bananas or oysters, as well as meat from animals known for their fecundity, such as rabbits, or truffles for their pungent scent. It's true that some foods, such as chili peppers and various other condiments, do stimulate the body, and some foods considered aphrodisiacs might have been so because they increased the feeling of physical or mental well-being.

In the book of Genesis, Leah used the aphrodisiac mandrake root to woo Jacob into spending the night with her. Even the English poet John Donne wrote of it ("Get with child by mandrake root!").

Beer and wine have long been candidates for aphrodisiacs. But so has honey water—the sage Maimonides advised sipping it, along with wine, as a kind of twelfth-century version of Viagra.

Peach Champagne Cocktail

P

Peaches, with their soft fuzzy downlike skin and luscious flavor, have always been considered a sensual fruit and an aphrodisiac. But I never thought of turning them into a cocktail until I tasted this delightful drink one warm summer night at Mika Sharon's Tel Aviv restaurant, Mika.

For each serving

⅔ cup champagne
⅓ cup peaches, peeled, pitted,
    ground in blender, and
    strained (or peach schnapps
    or peach nectar)

Mix champagne and peaches and chill. Just before serving, pour into chilled champagne glasses.

L ike raw (but nonkosher) oysters, marinated raw fish in its various styles, such as carpaccio and ceviche, with their melt-in-your-mouth taste, also yields sensual dishes. At Mika's, this is one of Sharon's signature dishes.

Serve as an appetizer with paper-thin slices of radish, cucumber, and scallion (cut with a mandoline if possible) and broccoli sprouts.

10 ounces fresh boneless
    yellowtail fillet, skin removed

Marinade
2 cups extra-virgin olive oil
½ cup freshly squeezed lemon
    juice
¼ cup freshly squeezed lime
    juice
1 tablespoon coriander seeds,
    crushed
1 small dried red hot pepper
½ teaspoon chopped fresh thyme
    leaves, or ⅛ teaspoon dried
3 tablespoons coarse salt

**Accompaniments
and Garnishes**
½ cup very thinly sliced
    radishes
½ cup finely sliced scallions
½ cup packed chopped broccoli
    or alfalfa sprouts, roots
    removed
½ cup very thinly sliced English
    (hothouse) cucumber
1 tablespoon each chopped fresh
    Italian parsley and cilantro

1. Rinse the fish and pat dry. Mix together the ingredients for the marinade, and pour over the fish. Cover and marinate in the refrigerator overnight.

2. Drain the fillet and place in the freezer for 15 to 20 minutes to firm up, then slice it very thinly, a little thicker than carpaccio and a little thinner than sashimi.

3. On a serving platter or two separate dishes, make layers of radishes, scallions, sprouts, marinated fish slices, and cucumbers. Garnish with fresh Italian parsley and cilantro, and serve with fresh rolls.

Champagne and Melon Soup with Feta Cheese

Serves 2

One of our favorite chefs, Tamar Blai, suggests this summer soup to chill the lips but warm the heart. It goes particularly well with the Yellowtail Ceviche on page 105.

1 medium honeydew melon
   (about 1 to 1½ pounds),
   peeled, deseeded, and cut
   into cubes
5 mint leaves

1 cup champagne, plus ½ cup
   extra to top off soup
6 ounces feta cheese, crumbled,
   plus extra for garnish

1. Place melon, mint leaves, 1 cup champagne, and feta cheese in a blender or food processor and process until smooth. Cover and chill.

2. Pour a ladleful of melon soup into two bowls, and top each with ¼ cup chilled champagne. Garnish with a little crumbled feta cheese and serve immediately.

This dish, evoking the legendary white dresses of the maidens, is easy to make from scratch with the easy-to-work-with dough. Serve with the light white wine sauce, in keeping with the holiday's themes of the grape harvest and the production of wine. It also makes a great dish for Shavuot.

Ricotta-Stuffed Ravioli with White Wine Sauce

Makes about 35 (serves 4)

Ravioli
1¾ cups all-purpose or durum wheat flour
2 large eggs
1 tablespoon olive oil
⅛ teaspoon salt

Filling
8 ounces full-fat or part-skim-milk ricotta cheese
½ cup chopped fresh Italian parsley

⅛ teaspoon salt
⅛ teaspoon freshly ground black pepper

Wine Sauce
1½ cups dry white wine
1½ tablespoons white wine vinegar
6 tablespoons cold butter
⅛ teaspoon salt
Freshly ground black pepper

1. Combine all the ingredients for the ravioli dough in a food processor and process in on/off pulses until a soft, slightly dry dough is obtained. Make a ball, wrap in plastic wrap, and set aside for 20 minutes.

2. Flour a work surface and rolling pin generously, and roll out the dough to ⅛-inch thickness. Use a 2½- to 3-inch-diameter glass to cut out circles. Roll out the dough again and cut additional circles. You should have about 35 circles altogether.

3. In a small bowl, mix together the ingredients for the filling and place a teaspoonful in the center of each circle. Fold the circles in half to form a half-moon shape and pinch gently but firmly to close. If the edges do not stick well, seal with a little water or beaten egg.

4. Pour the wine and vinegar into a small saucepan and cook over medium heat until reduced to 1½ tablespoons. Remove from heat and whisk in the butter, stirring constantly. Season with salt and pepper. (Add a tablespoon or two of any chopped fresh herb like tarragon or thyme if desired.)

5. Cook the ravioli in a large pot of boiling salted water with a tablespoon of olive oil for 5 minutes. Drain, place on a serving platter, and pour over the sauce. Garnish with a sprig or two of fresh herbs and serve. (Ravioli may be prepared in advance and frozen between sheets of plastic wrap sprinkled with flour or cornmeal. Do not defrost, just put immediately in boiling water. Cook an additional 2 to 3 minutes.)

Grapes and Wine in Biblical Times

Bread was for the stomach, but wine was for the soul. Third in the list of the biblical Seven Species, the grape is the only fruit that has its own special blessing. Throughout the ages, the consumption of grape wine has played an integral part in the celebration of the Sabbath and every religious occasion.

To the ancients, the grapevine symbolized security and well-being, peace, quiet, and abundance. So common, popular, and vital was it in the lives of the people that prophets, patriarchs, and psalmists all used it as metaphors, conjuring up life or death.

Our biblical ancestors preferred imbibing wine to water, and often it was safer. Both grape juice and wine vinegars were beverages as well as seasonings, and iron-rich grapes probably made high-energy raisins for Noah and his children, who no doubt saved the vine leaves for pickling and stuffing on their long cruise.

Wine also served as a folk cure for virtually every illness. Wine or vinegar was suggested for headaches. Mixed with oil, it was used as a liniment for injuries or wounds. In pleasure or pain, the "blood of the grape" was inextricably bound up in the lives of the populace, through all the generations of the Bible.

Light but satisfying, this main course salad evokes the taste and color of the lush red grapes that characterized the Tu b'Av grape harvest and the red wine vinegar used for imbibing (as Ruth did in the fields of Boaz), seasoning, and preserving. Suitable for lunch or dinner.

2 butterflied boneless chicken
   breasts
½ cup dry white wine
1 bay leaf
2 whole allspice
¼ teaspoon peppercorns
1 parsley sprig
½ cup sliced celery
¾ cup halved red grapes
⅓ cup pecan halves
4 cups mixed red and green oak
   leaf lettuce

Dressing
1 tablespoon minced shallots
1 garlic clove, minced or pressed
1½ tablespoons honey
1 tablespoon grainy Dijon
   mustard
¼ cup red wine vinegar
1 to 2 tablespoons freshly
   squeezed lemon juice
½ cup extra-virgin olive oil

Chicken and Red Grapes with Honey-Mustard Viniagrette

Serves 2 as a main course, 4 as a side salad

Ⓜ

1. Rinse the chicken breasts and pat dry. Cut each breast in half lengthwise into 2 pieces.

2. Pour enough water into a large skillet to reach 2 inches. Add the wine, bay leaf, allspice, peppercorns, and whole parsley sprig, and bring to a boil. Lower heat and cook 5 minutes.

3. Add the chicken breasts in one layer. They should be covered by the water. If not, add boiling water to cover. Bring to a boil over medium heat and remove from heat. Let stand for 5 to 10 minutes. (The chicken breasts should be ready. If not, cook them on low heat until done.) Cool and cut into pieces or shred. Mix with the celery, grapes, and pecans.

4. Put the lettuces in a large salad bowl or on a serving platter and place the chicken-and-grape mixture on top.

5. To prepare the dressing, put all the ingredients for the dressing in the blender, except for the olive oil. Slowly add the oil with the machine running (keep the top partially on, or pour through an opening in the cover). Alternately, whisk the ingredients for the dressing until emulsified.

6. Pour just enough dressing over the salad to moisten it, and pass the rest. (Dressing may be kept in a covered container in the refrigerator for up to 2 weeks.)

The Voluptuous Fig

Back in biblical times, figs were far more than summer fruits. Unripe fig sap and ripe fig milk took the place of rennet to curdle cheese, and both fresh and dried figs were fermented into beer or cooked down into honey. Easily dried, they were an essential part of the diet, an article of trade, and a source of income. And long before metal weights, single figs, just like carob and mustard seeds, were used as a standard of measurement.

The fig appears early on in the Bible. In the story of Creation, the leaves of its tree prove to be the first dictates of fashion. Some scholars consider the fig tree the Tree of Knowledge, based on the fact that Adam and Eve used fig leaves to clothe themselves moments after eating the forbidden fruit.

Once the basic needs such as grain and wine are met, freed from the pangs of hunger and the ravages of war, one is liberated to turn to sensory pleasure. Perhaps that's why figs appear fourth in the biblical list of the Seven Species. Laden with seeds within and thus an ancient symbol of human and divine fertility, it's no wonder that the voluptuous fig came to be considered an aphrodisiac.

E nriched by sensuous fresh figs, which ripen just around Tu b'Av and were considered an aphrodisiac in ancient times, this remarkably delicious salad can be served warm or cold as a starter, or with warm scones and Cherna's Favorite Lemon Curd (page 47) for breakfast in bed.

Salad of Goat Cheese, Arugula, and Figs

Serves 4

Ⓓ

4 cups arugula leaves
11-ounce long-shaped package of
    Bucheron or other goat cheese
8 large or 12 small fresh ripe figs

Dressing
6 tablespoons olive oil
2 tablespoons balsamic vinegar
2 to 3 teaspoons freshly squeezed
    lemon juice
½ teaspoon grainy Dijon
    mustard
4 to 5 teaspoons honey
Salt
Freshly ground black pepper
½ cup fresh raspberries,
    blackberries, or blueberries
    (optional)

1. Remove the stems of the arugula, rinse well, and pat dry. Divide the leaves among 4 serving plates, or place on one large serving plate.

2. If using large figs, cut them in quarters (leave each two quarters attached at the top). If using smaller figs, cut them in half. Cut the cheese into ⅓- to ½-inch pieces. Divide the figs and cheese among the salad plates.

3. In a small bowl, whisk olive oil, vinegar, lemon juice, mustard, and honey. Season with salt and black pepper, and pour over the individual salads. Serve with a sprinkling of berries on top, if desired. To serve warm, lightly flour the cheese circles and sauté in butter until just lightly browned on both sides. Divide between the serving platters, scatter the figs around, and pour the dressing over.

Hearts of Palm Salad

Serves 4

In the Seychelles, among the most romantic islands in the world, the Millionaire's Salad, made of local hearts of palm, is considered a special treat by the natives. A local root vegetable is also added, but crunchy roots such as kohlrabi or daikon (white) radish or peeled cucumbers can be used instead. To shorten preparation time, substitute two 8-ounce packages of salad mix for the red and green oak leaf lettuces.

1 head red oak leaf curly lettuce
1 head green oak leaf lettuce
1 14- or 15-ounce can palm
    hearts, drained and sliced
    crosswise into ½-inch slices
2 cups thinly sliced kohlrabi, or
    daikon (white) radish, or
    cucumber

¼ cup light vegetable oil
½ cup thinly sliced scallions
1 to 2 tablespoons freshly
    squeezed lemon or lime juice
Coarse sea salt or regular salt
Freshly ground pepper to taste
3 to 4 tablespoons finely chopped
    fresh basil

1. Rinse the lettuces well, paying special attention to remove the grit that accumulates at the bottom of the stems. Remove any tough parts of the stems, and tear into bite-size pieces. Dry thoroughly, wrap in a kitchen towel, and chill until serving time.

2. Put the sliced palm hearts in a bowl. Peel and cut the kohlrabi or daikon into matchstick-size slices. If using cucumber, peel and thinly slice.

3. After adding the oil, scallions, lemon juice, and seasoning, mix the lettuces with the basil leaves, and divide among serving plates. Top with the palm heart mixture and serve.

Brioche
French
Toast with
Fruit and
Honey-
Yogurt
Sauce

Serves 2

Ⓓ

Our friend Mika Sharon learned this breakfast-dessert when she worked at the Tribeca Grill in New York, and adapted it to Israeli flavors. For a romantic breakfast, serve it with a variety of sensuous fresh summer berries.

1 large loaf (1 pound) brioche or
   rich white bread
1 to 2 whole, firm but ripe
   bananas
4 eggs
¼ cup heavy cream

2 tablespoons butter
¾ cup plain yogurt
2 tablespoons honey
2 tablespoons almonds, toasted
Fresh raspberries or cherries for
   garnish (optional)

1. Using a sharp knife, make a "tunnel" in the middle of the brioche from one side or end to the other, and fill with a banana (or two, depending on size of loaf). Slice the brioche (2 slices per person if the loaf is small, 3 slices if large) into 1-inch-thick slices.

2. Mix—but don't blend—the yogurt with the honey, so thin stripes of honey can still be seen in the yogurt.

3. Beat the eggs with the cream and gently dip in the slices one after the other. Melt the butter in a skillet and sauté the slices on both sides until golden.

4. Place 2 to 3 hot brioche slices on a plate, carefully pour some sauce around the toast, and sprinkle the top with almonds. Garnish with fresh raspberries or cherries, which can be briefly marinated in a little sugar and lemon juice, if desired.

Melt-in-Your-Mouth Breakfast Scones

Makes 8

Cut some fresh flowers, place them in a delicate vase, set them on a breakfast tray, and nibble on these warm tasty scones on Tu b'Av morning with your beloved. Serve with butter and exotic fruit jam, or, for added pleasure, crème fraîche or Cherna's Favorite Lemon Curd (page 47).

2 cups all-purpose flour
1 tablespoon baking powder
¼ teaspoon baking soda
2 tablespoons sugar
½ teaspoon salt

½ cup (1 stick) cold butter, cut into cubes
½ cup buttermilk
1 egg, lightly beaten

1. Preheat the oven to 400°F. Line a baking sheet with parchment paper. Set aside.

2. In a food processor or in a bowl using a wooden spoon, mix flour, baking powder, baking soda, sugar, and salt. Gradually add the butter cubes and process in short on/off pulses (or cut in with a pastry cutter) until crumbs are formed. Add the buttermilk and continue to process until a soft flexible dough is formed.

3. Remove and roll out on a lightly floured surface to form a 7½-inch circle, approximately ½-inch thick. Cut the circle into quarters, then cut each quarter in half to form 8 scones. Brush each scone with the beaten egg, then go around and brush again.

4. Place 1 inch apart on prepared baking sheet, and bake for 20 minutes, until golden brown. Serve warm. (Dough may be prepared in advance, formed into scones, covered tightly in plastic wrap, and refrigerated. Brush with beaten egg and bake as above.)

One of the easiest desserts to prepare, this sensuous combination of frozen mango and whipped cream topped with a hot crisp crust of caramelized brown sugar always meets with rave reviews. If it's dinner for two, cut the recipe in half and freeze in individual ramekins.

3 large mangos, peeled and
   sliced
1 cup heavy cream

1½ cups firmly packed brown
   sugar

1. Place the mango slices around a 10-inch round freezer- and oven-proof dish (such as Pyrex) in an even layer. Use a chilled bowl and beaters to whip the cream, and use a metal spatula to distribute it evenly over the mango. Cover with plastic wrap and freeze. (May be prepared up to 3 days in advance.)

2. Before serving, heat the broiler to high, remove the dish from the freezer, and spread an even layer of brown sugar over the frozen whipped cream. Pat down. Let stand 10 minutes at room temperature.

3. Slip the dish into the upper third of the oven and broil for 3 to 4 minutes, or until the sugar is caramelized and the whipped cream layer is the consistency of ice cream. Turn the dish occasionally for even browning. Alternately, caramelize using a blowtorch: Hold flame a few inches away and move it around until sugar is golden brown and bubbly. Serve immediately.

Chocolate Frangelico and Hazelnut Truffles

Makes about 20 to 25

As with kisses, it's hard to stop at one!

¼ cup heavy cream
6 ounces good-quality
bittersweet or milk chocolate
2 tablespoons Frangelico or
Amaretto liqueur
¼ cup (½ stick) butter

½ cup finely chopped toasted
hazelnuts (or almonds if using
Amaretto)
¼ cup unsweetened cocoa
powder

1. In a small saucepan, boil the heavy cream until reduced to 2 tablespoons of liquid. Lower heat to a minimum and add the chocolate and liqueur. Continue cooking on low heat, stirring occasionally, until the chocolate begins to soften. Remove from heat and stir until chocolate is completely dissolved and the mixture is smooth.

2. Beat in the butter until incorporated. Let cool down to warm, then cover with plastic wrap and refrigerate until firm.

3. Using a teaspoon, form 1-inch balls, and roll half in finely chopped hazelnuts or almonds and the other half in cocoa. Place on a plate lined with parchment or waxed paper and chill until serving time.

The Festivals
of Fall

Blow the shofar at the new moon,
At the appointed season, for our feast day.
  —Psalm 81:3

The world was created in Tishri.
  —BT, Rosh Hashanah 8a

Rosh Hashanah

At the greengrocers in Israel, the surest sign that Rosh Hashanah is around the corner is the appearance of the Barhi date, an exotic-looking yellow fruit strung up in clusters to entice passersby. The Barhi has one season and one season only—it suddenly appears just before Rosh Hashanah and just as suddenly disappears at the end of Sukkot. Though many Westerners have yet to taste them, the unique Barhi dates are a particular favorite of Persians, as well as Sephardim with Middle Eastern or North African roots, who regarded them as harbingers of fall and gourmet treats in their countries of origin.

In ancient days just as today, if the winter rains had been plentiful and no pestilence had struck the land, by Rosh Hashanah the earth would be rich with vegetation and the trees laden with fruit ripe for picking. There would be a plentiful harvest of pomegranates, figs, and dates, and in some parts of the country the first olives would be ready for eating and for pressing into oil to be used for everything from cooking, medicine, and lighting to anointing kings.

To express their gratitude to God for these basic foodstuffs, the ancient Hebrews gathered together at the Temple in Jerusalem on the first day of the month of Tishri (September/October) for a joyous feast, calling the holiday *Yom Tru'ah*, the Day for Sounding the Shofar, as the Bible had commanded.

But the precious agricultural sense memory of the festival faded over the centuries after the Temple was destroyed, and the people dispersed to the four corners of the world. The focus of the holiday, along with its rituals, had to find new expression.

Living in Babylonia, where the new year was celebrated in the fall, the rabbis of the Talmud reconceived the festival of *Yom Tru'ah* in Tishri as the beginning of a new year as well, calling it "Rosh Hashanah"—the beginning (or head) of the year. But how were they to reconcile a new year in Tishri with the Hebrew calendar, where the first month was Nisan, in spring? They solved the problem ingeniously: Nisan became the new year for *months* and Tishri the new year for *years*. "The world was created in Tishri," said the sages (BT, Rosh Hashanah 8a), turning the holiday into the birthday of the world.

In ancient Israel, the original feast for the Day of Sounding the Shofar probably included wheat and barley from the Shavuot harvest months before, new wine from the summer grape harvest, and the fruits and vegetables of the season. Today, just as in those days, the new wheat is still used to bake the holiday's breads and pastries, and fresh dates are still pressed into *silan*—the biblical honey—to grace the New Year's table.

Over the centuries, however, the first dinner of what became Rosh Hashanah evolved into a festive meal characterized, like the Passover Seder, by the eating of symbolic foods. Some foods were seen as omens with mystical powers; others, a subtle way of asking God to fulfill our needs. Most dishes were chosen because their names in Yiddish, Hebrew, Aramaic, or even Ladino have connotations suitable to the holiday. For example, the custom of eating tzimmes, a carrot-based vegetable and fruit stew traditionally served by Ashkenazim on Rosh Hashanah, comes from the Yiddish word for carrots, *merren* (called *gezer* in Hebrew), which also means "more" or "increased." The carrots are sliced into coin-shaped pieces, a wish for "more" health and wealth for ourselves and our children.

Another Ashkenazic folk tradition is to avoid eating nuts on this holiday, because the numerical equivalent of the word for nut in Hebrew—*egoz*—is the same as that of the word for sin. And lest you think that Ashkenazim eat kreplach (page 130) on Rosh Hashanah just because they taste good, an ancient mystical tradition suggests that since the new moon is nearly invisible at Rosh Hashanah, some holiday foods should be "covered," or hidden, as well. Just as the clouds cover the new moon, so the dough covers the filling of kreplach. Other sources suggest that Sephardim eat round pasta, and Ashkenazim round kreplach, because their shape symbolizes wholeness.

In both Ashkenazic and Sephardic homes, the first foods of the Rosh

Hashanah dinner are sweet in the hope of a sweet year to come (apples and honey, rose petals cooked in syrup, quince preserves, or pomegranates), and all traditions "break bread" at Rosh Hashanah dinner by dipping challah into honey rather than salt, as is traditional on Shabbat and other holidays. According to Rabbi Yehuda Dov Zinger, the custom derives from the image in Psalm 81: "And He would feed him with the cream of the wheat [challah], and from a rock I would sate you with honey."

You'll still find many Ashkenazic homes serving a more or less standard menu that dates back to the Middle Ages: a first course of cooked freshwater fish like gefilte fish (page 14) or salt herring, soup with noodles, or, more frequently, kreplach, chopped liver (page 132)—originally from goose livers, and today made from chicken or beef livers—boiled beef or goose, kugel, and honey cake (page 150), *lekach* (honey and spice cake), or *teiglach*, a sweet dessert.

In Sephardic homes, the rich and diverse culinary traditions have mostly passed the endurance test. Unlike Ashkenazim, for whom a plentiful supply of fresh vegetables was scarce in Eastern Europe, the Sephardim incorporated a fantastic array of pilafs, omelettes, pies, sweet vegetable fritters, and salads with green and leafy vegetables into their holiday meal, to symbolize a new beginning. Instead of honey cakes, Sephardim often end their meal with fresh dates (like the Barhi), figs, and, especially, pomegranates, which were all in season in their countries of origin; pastries with sesame, anise, or nuts, preserves, and often green tea instead of black coffee, in keeping with tradition that nothing sour, bitter, or even black is served, according to Claudia Roden in *The Book of Jewish Food*.

Seven Blessings

Ashkenazim begin their Rosh Hashanah meal by dipping apples into honey; Sephardim, though, enjoy a unique ceremony called *Sheva Brachot* (Seven Blessings), or simply "Brachot," each for a different food and probably derived from the Talmud, which says, "At the beginning of each year a person should accustom himself to eat gourds, fenugreek, leeks, beets, and dates" (BT, Kritut 6a). Fenugreek is *rubia*—a word close to *yirbu*—"increase"—and its accompanying blessing asks that our merits be multiplied. (This is sometimes translated as "Lubia," or fresh green beans, which are in season at this time.) Leeks, beets, and dates (the biblical honey) all evoke Aramaic puns on what we'd like to happen to our enemies—that they be "cut off," "removed," or "consumed." The number of blessings—seven—also echoes the theme of the holy number seven, and the Seven Species with which the Bible tells us the land of Israel is blessed.

The items for the Seven Blessings vary from country to country, with an increasing number of Ashkenazim adopting the custom. Whatever your background, though, a typical Seven Blessings tray should include

Dates—*Tamar* in Hebrew, like the Aramaic word *yitamu*, meaning "will stop" our enemies and all those who wish us ill. Try to obtain fresh dates if possible.

Lubia—Green beans or black-eyed peas, always cooked—meaning "that you be as plentiful as the bean." Some interpret this as *rubia*, or fresh fenugreek. (See *Lubia* Salad, page 145.)

Leek and/or spinach/Swiss chard patties—From *yikrot* in Hebrew, which means to "cut off"—that is, stop our enemies, sometimes served with powdered sugar on top. (See Bulgarian Leek Patties, page 144.)

Pomegranate seeds—A symbol of fertility—sometimes with the addition of rose water and sugar, so that in the coming year we be as full of mitzvot as the seeds of a pomegranate—which according to legend contains 613 seeds, the same number of mitzvot included in the Torah. (See Roasted Eggplant and Pomegranate Seed Salad, page 142, Bulgur Wheat and Pomegranate Seed Salad, page 207, or serve the seeds in a bowl with a few drops of rose water and a pinch of sugar.)

A sheep or fish head—Vegetarians substituting a head of cabbage, garlic, or broccoli. "That we should be at the head and not at the tail."

A bowl of fresh or cooked beets—From the Hebrew word *selek*, meaning that those who seek destruction should themselves "go away" or "be removed."

A bowl of fresh or cooked carrots—From the Hebrew word *gezer*, which sounds like *gzar dino* (judgment)—that we be judged for our good deeds and our enemies for their bad. (See Moroccan Carrot Salad, page 146.)

On a Seven Blessings tray you'll also find apples and honey with the wish that our year be sweet, from beginning to end.

And at dinner on the second day of the holiday, Jews of various ethnicitiesary to incorporate a new—and, hopefully, a little strange—fruit we haven't eaten before or at least for a long time, thus giving us the chance to say the blessing for beginnings, the *Shehehiyanu*, on the second day, just as we have said it on the first.

Rosh Hashanah Recipes

Appetizers

Round Challah with Seven Seeds (P)

The Ultimate Chicken Soup (*Goldene Yoich*) (M)

Any-Way Kreplach (P)(M)

Vegetarian "Chopped Liver" (P)

Ida's Classic Chopped Liver (M)

Seven-Spice-Infused Meat-Stuffed Dried Fruit (M)

Main Dishes

Cornish Hens Stuffed with Bulgur, Raisins, and Caraway (M)

Georgian Chicken in Pomegranate and Tamarind Sauce (M)

Sweet-and-Sour Bass in the Style of Iraq and Salonika (P)

Side Dishes, Salads, and Items for the Seven Blessings

Adi's Tzimmes (P)

Ida's Baked Sweet Potatoes and Apples (P)

Avas Frescas (Green Beans in Tomato Sauce) (P)

Roasted Eggplant and Pomegranate Seed Salad (P)

Bulgarian Leek Patties (M)(P)

Lubia Salad (Green Beans and Black-eyed Peas) (P)

Moroccan Carrot Salad (P)

Desserts

Quince in Spiced Muscat Wine (P)

Figs Stuffed with Halvah, Nuts, and Honey (P)

The Best Honey Cake Yet (P)

Chocolate Honey Brownies (D)

New Moon Butter Cookies (D)

Round Challah with Seven Seeds

Makes 1 large round loaf or 2 smaller round loaves

Throughout the years and generations, the round challah has come to be the most traditional shape for Rosh Hashanah, representing the cycle of life and the wholeness of the universe. This one includes seeds, which from ancient times and in kabbalistic tradition, have always symbolized fertility and plenty. And why seven? For the Seven Species, symbolizing the land of Israel.

Of all three challah recipes in this book, this is our favorite. Adapted from our mother's famous challah, it is the one we make for Shabbat and most holidays. Rich in flavor and texture (due to the addition of part whole-wheat flour and honey), it stores well for several days. For those who prefer the classic white-bread challah, the "Birds of Prayer" Challah Rolls dough (page 156) may also be used.

3 cups whole-wheat flour

5 cups unbleached all-purpose white flour

2 packages Rapid Rise yeast (¼ ounce each)

½ cup corn oil

½ cup mild flavored honey

2 teaspoons salt

3 large eggs

2 cups very warm (not hot) water

1 cup raisins (optional)

1 egg yolk beaten with 1 teaspoon water

Additional flour, for kneading

½ teaspoon each sesame seeds; poppy seeds; pumpkin seeds; black sesame, nigella, or cumin seeds; sunflower seeds; caraway seeds; and anise seeds

1. In the bowl of a standing electric mixer fitted with a dough hook, stir together 2 cups of whole-wheat flour, 3 cups of white flour, and the yeast.

2. In a small bowl, whisk oil, honey, salt, eggs, and warm water in the order listed, adding the water gradually and whisking constantly to avoid curdling the eggs.

3. Make a well in the center of the flour mixture, and add the contents of the small bowl, mixing on low to medium speed with the dough hook attachment until a thick batter is formed. Scrape down the sides with a spatula.

4. Gradually add the rest of the flours, until the dough leaves the side of the bowl (the dough will still be slightly sticky). Pour the contents of the bowl onto a lightly floured surface and sprinkle a little flour on top. Knead the dough in a clockwise direction, incorporating any additional flour gradually. The dough is ready when it is no longer sticky, but may still be slightly moist. The process should take about 5 minutes.

5. Oil a bowl, and turn the dough over in the bowl so that the surfaces will not dry out. Cover with a kitchen towel and place in a warm spot until the dough rises and doubles in size, about 45 to 60 minutes, depending on room temperature.

6. Punch down the dough and let it rest for 5 minutes. If desired, sprinkle the raisins on top and knead into the dough. Choose the desired shape.

- For two round loaves: Line two baking sheets or 10-inch round pans with parchment paper. (If using round pan, cut out a circle of paper to fit the bottom of the pan, and a strip to fit the sides. Affix with a little nonstick cooking spray.) Cut the dough in two. Using your hands, roll out the first piece into a rope and coil it to make a spiral. Fasten the end under the circle with a gentle pinch. Transfer to the prepared pan. Repeat with the second half of the dough. Brush each challah with beaten egg, and sprinkle each kind of seed separately, starting from the center of the coil moving to the end.

- Braided round: Make one large braided challah, and seal the ends together to form a round. Bake in a well-greased kugelhof pan (a pan with a "pipe" in the middle, a flat-bottomed form of the Bundt pan), or do as Evie Leib does and place on a parchment paper-lined baking sheet with a greased empty tin can in the center. Remove the challah after baking, and serve with a little dish of honey in the center.

- One of the most beautiful shapes is the *bulkelah*, or crown, challah: Grease a 10- or 12-inch springform pan. Form the dough into 2½-inch balls and place these touching each other around the inside rim of the pan. Use the rest of the dough to make larger balls and place them in the center of the pan. Brush with beaten egg mixed with a little water and sprinkle a different garnish on each ball (sesame seeds, cumin seeds, caraway seeds, flax seeds, black sesame or nigella seeds, rosemary, oatmeal, etc.).

Bake the Challah

7. Preheat the oven to 350°F.

8. Cover the challah lightly with a kitchen towel and let rise for an additional 20 minutes in a warm place.

9. Bake in the preheated oven about 30 to 35 minutes, until golden brown. Cool 10 to 15 minutes in the pan, and gently turn out onto a wire rack to finishing cooling.

Tips for Successful Challah Making

- Even if you use a mixer to mix the dough, it's always best to do some of the kneading by hand. Otherwise, you might add too much air to the dough. Besides, part of the magic of challah is the love you put into it while you're kneading.

- Although it is possible to make the dough ahead and freeze it, it is best to make and bake it at the same time. If you'd like to freeze the dough, do so immediately after mixing, before the dough has a chance to rise. Defrost it at room temperature and allow it to rise fully before baking in a preheated oven. The oven must be fully preheated before baking.

- Always grease the pan generously to avoid sticking. Use margarine, lecithin spread (available at health-food stores), or nonstick cooking spray (which is healthiest but doesn't work as well as margarine). If baking on a flat surface, always line it with parchment paper; then you won't need to grease the pan at all.

The History of Challah

One of the time-honored delicacies of the Rosh Hashanah table is the challah, the quintessential Jewish bread baked in memory of the offerings of the High Priest in the Temple of Jerusalem. Though most of the year the challah is usually braided and shaped into a rectangular loaf, on Rosh Hashanah its shape reflects the themes of the holiday. The most widespread version is round, signifying the globe whose creation is being celebrated, and the crown of divine sovereignty in the world. The most common round shape is the single spiral, but the challah may be braided and attached at the ends.

In some parts of Eastern Europe, the Rosh Hashanah challah was shaped like a ladder, or had a ladder shape placed on top of it, to symbolize that with our actions on the holiday we determine whether in the coming year we will be brought low and humbled or ascend and be exalted—like the angels in Jacob's dream of the ladder—and that our prayers will climb to heaven. The challah also may be topped with little hovering birds, inspired by a passage in Isaiah (see "Birds of Prayer" Challah Rolls, page 156). Jews originating in Tripoli traditionally baked challah with caraway seeds, and among Moroccans, raisins, nuts, and anise are mixed in the challah dough and a hard-boiled egg placed on top, as symbols of sweetness and fertility.

Raisins and raisin challah symbolize more than the sweet. One interpretation claims that the Ashkenazic custom of eating raisin challah is based on the story of Avigail, a Jewish heroine. Avigail was married to a sheep farmer who had turned away King David and his army when they asked for food. Avigail placated the king with a gift of one hundred clusters of raisins and two hundred loaves of bread, earning both the gratitude and forgiveness of the king, just as we hope for the divine king's forgiveness during the holiday.

The word *challah* appears in the Bible, where it refers to the portion of the dough consecrated as a gift for God, and given to the priests of the Temple in Jerusalem before every Sabbath. To this day, traditional Jews consider it a mitzvah for women to break off a portion of the ready-to-be-baked challah dough and throw it into the oven flames, as a way of both reenacting the ancient Temple rites and acknowledging that the bread—all physical sustenance—is ultimately a gift of the divine.

Whereas on Shabbat and other festivals we "break bread" by dipping challah into salt, on Rosh Hashanah we dip it into honey, reciting the hope that it may be God's will "to renew us for a year that is good and sweet."

The Ultimate Chicken Soup (*Goldene Yoich*)

Serves 8

Often hailed as the "Jewish penicillin," and certainly one of the most famous of Jewish dishes, chicken soup was prescribed as a remedy for colds and asthma as early as the twelfth century by renowned Jewish physician Moses Maimonides (1135–1204). Yet the wild ancestors of the chicken, native to the Indian subcontinent and Southeast Asia, were unknown to our biblical ancestors, and only mentioned in Talmudic literature. By medieval times, however, it had become a beloved dish of Middle Eastern Jewry, reaching Ashkenazim only a few centuries later.

Staples for the Sabbath, chicken and chicken soup also came to be served by both Sephardim and Ashkenazim for most festival meals, especially Rosh Hashanah and the Yom Kippur. Today, we know that chicken soup is not only delicious, but also that scientific studies have found that the soup acts as an anti-inflammatory, while its steam helps clear up congestion. Another study found that chicken soup contains a substance chemically resembling the drug Acetylcysteine, often prescribed for bronchitis and other respiratory problems.

Of all the chicken soups we've ever tasted, our mother's is the clearest and most golden that we've ever encountered. Part of her secret, she claims, is the way she prepares the chicken before cooking, the instructions for which are outlined below.

Note: For a vegetarian alternative to chicken soup, see Golden Thyme-Scented Vegetable Broth (page 19).

4½- to 5-pound chicken, cut into
  pieces
2 teaspoons salt, or more
  to taste
1 large (½ pound) or 2 medium
  onions, quartered, with some
  of the skin left on
2 cups thickly sliced carrots
4 ribs celery with leaves, cut into
  large pieces

2 small parsnips (about ½
  pound), peeled and leaves
  discarded
½ pound celeriac, peeled and cut
  into chunks (optional)
1 pound butternut squash or
  fresh pumpkin, peeled and cut
  into large chunks
12 sprigs *each* parsley and dill

1. Rinse the chicken well in cold water. Place in a large bowl and cover with boiling water. Let stand for 2 to 3 minutes. Drain and use a sharp knife to scrape the chicken skin all around to remove the surface layer of fat, stray pinfeathers, and the hard skin around the bottom of the legs. Rinse in cold water, transfer to a plate, and pat dry.

2. In a large pot, bring 5 to 6 quarts water to a boil with 2 teaspoons salt. Add the chicken and bring to a boil again on medium-high heat.

3. Skim off the foam that collects on top of the soup, and continue skimming until the soup is perfectly clear. (Mom stands for about 10 to 15 minutes skimming, but you might want to sit on a high stool!) When the soup seems clear, stir up from the bottom to check for any renegade particles.

4. Lower heat and add the vegetables to the pot. (Leaving a little bit of the peel on the onion adds to the soup's color.) Bring to a boil over medium-high heat, lower heat, and partially cover the pot. Cook for 1½ hours, skimming occasionally during the cooking process.

5. Rinse the parsley and dill sprigs well, and place on top of the soup. Cover and cook 2 minutes. Turn off heat and let sit, covered, until the soup reaches room temperature. Strain, discarding all but the chicken and carrots.

6. To serve, reheat the broth. Serve the carrots in the broth or with the chicken. Cover chicken and warm separately in oven or microwave. Closed in separate tight containers, soup and chicken are best used within 3 days. For longer storage, strain soup and freeze. Any leftover chicken can be made into chicken salad.

Any-Way Kreplach

**Makes about
25 small kreplach**

Whenever our parents went on vacation, Bubby Rose, our mother's mother, who lived with us, would begin making kreplach. As soon as our parents were out the door, she would get out the old white tablecloth, cast it over the round kitchen table, and get to work.

These kreplach may be filled with either Ida's Classic Chopped Liver (page 132), Vegetarian "Chopped Liver" (page 131), or "New Age" "Chopped Liver" (page 159). You'll need about 2 cups of filling for this recipe.

2 cups unbleached all-purpose flour	1 tablespoon water
2 large eggs	1½ teaspoons salt
	1 tablespoon vegetable oil

1. Place the flour in a medium bowl. In a small bowl, lightly beat the eggs with the water and ½ teaspoon of the salt, using a fork.

2. Make a well in the flour. Mix the eggs into the flour until the flour is absorbed and a smooth dough is formed that leaves the sides of the bowl. This may be done in the food processor, preferably with a plastic blade.

3. Transfer the dough to a lightly floured board and knead the dough until it is smooth and elastic (at least 5 minutes), adding a little flour as needed. Cover the dough and let it rest on the board for 10 minutes.

4. Roll out the dough to about ⅛-inch thickness, and cut out rounds with a 3-inch glass dipped in flour. Fill the centers with a rounded teaspoon of the desired filling, then fold the round to form a half-moon shape. Pinch the edges tightly together, then pinch the two ends together to form the classic kreplach shape (which is somewhat like that of tortellini).

5. Heat a large pot of boiling water and add 1 teaspoon salt and 1 tablespoon oil. Drop in just enough kreplach so they are not crowded. Wait until they rise to the top, then lower heat and let them simmer gently, uncovered, for 5 minutes. Use a wooden spoon to gently push them down into the water during cooking. Remove with a slotted spoon, transfer to a bowl, and let cool. (The kreplach can be stored in a covered container in the refrigerator for 2 to 3 days. Grease the container to prevent sticking.)

Note: Kreplach may be frozen before or after cooking. Freeze them in a baking pan lined with parchment paper, then transfer to a closed container. They will keep for up to 1 month. Thaw the uncooked kreplach and cook for about 15 minutes. To heat already-cooked frozen kreplach, thaw, and either cook in boiling water for 8 minutes, or place in a greased pan, pour a little oil over the top, and heat in the oven at 350°F until hot.

Although genuine chopped liver holds a special place in the annals of Ashkenazic culinary history, today an increasing number of people are looking for an alternative both for health and humane reasons. Based on onions, eggs, walnuts, and green beans, this recipe has a surprisingly real chopped liver taste.

In all vegetarian chopped liver recipes, the secret to success—in both flavor and color—is the slow stewing-frying of the onions until they are well browned but not burnt. To achieve this requires the patience of cooking over low heat for at least 30 minutes, stirring occasionally. It's worth it. This also makes a great stuffing for kreplach.

For another delicious vegetarian version, see "New Age" "Chopped Liver" (page 159).

Note: Use two 14.5-ounce cans French cut green beans, drained well, instead of fresh or frozen whole green beans, if preferred.

Vegetarian "Chopped Liver"

**Makes 12 servings
as an appetizer,
6 servings as a main
course lunch salad**

1 pound fresh young or frozen whole green beans	Salt
⅓ cup olive oil	White pepper and black pepper to taste
2 cups coarsely chopped onion (about 3 medium onions)	Red leaf lettuce, escarole, chicory, or arugula leaves, and
6 hard-boiled eggs, quartered	halved cherry tomatoes or
1½ cups walnut halves	radish slices

1. If using fresh beans, remove the tops and tails. Steam fresh or frozen beans in a steamer basket or a small amount of boiling salted water, uncovered, until they are crisp but tender. Drain well.

2. Heat the oil in a large skillet over medium heat, lower the heat, and sauté the onion slowly, stirring occasionally, until deeply golden.

3. Mix the beans and onion with the oil remaining in pan. Add to the bowl of a food processor with the eggs and walnuts (or use a food grinder with the medium blade). Process in two batches until finely ground. Blend the contents of both batches together in a bowl and season with salt, white pepper, and black pepper to taste. Cover with plastic wrap and chill at least 1 hour, until firm.

4. To serve, make a bed of red and green lettuces or arugula on individual serving plates and top each with a ball of the mixture (use a lightly oiled ice-cream scoop if you have one). Garnish each serving with halved cherry tomatoes or radish slices.

Ida's Classic Chopped Liver

Serves 8 to 12 as an appetizer

Another classic of Ashkenazic Jewish cuisine is undoubtedly chopped liver, which was created for both economic and practical reasons. But the first chopped liver was probably made with goose liver: In Bohemia, Jews were known to breed and force-feed geese as early as the Middle Ages, and the Jews of Alsace specialized in the breeding of fat geese—the liver of which they chopped into a paste, and out of which a seventeenth-century chef developed pâté de foie gras.

In Galicia, a common Sabbath dish dating back many centuries was chopped hard-boiled eggs and onions, and in the course of time, liver was added to provide a nourishing meal that could be eaten cold and feed more people with fewer provisions. When the chicken became more widespread in Europe, chicken liver was substituted.

Although many people use only chicken livers (and can use all chicken livers in this recipe), we find that our mother's unique combination has a particularly rich flavor and texture. In Eastern Europe goose or chicken fat was used to fry the onions, but most people today prefer the more healthful benefits of olive oil. Though best hand-chopped or put through a food grinder, a food processor may also be used (but carefully, so you don't turn it into a paste!).

1 pound beef liver (or calf's liver)	1 teaspoon salt
1 pound chicken livers	1 teaspoon freshly ground black
2½ cups chopped onion	pepper
½ cup light olive oil	Mixed lettuces or a mixture of
6 hard-boiled eggs	lettuce and arugula leaves

1. Prepare the livers by washing and patting dry with a paper towel.
2. Preheat the broiler.
3. Place the beef liver in a perforated broiler pan to allow juices to escape. Place the pan on the bottom rack of a hot oven and broil under high heat until top is browned. Turn over and cook the other side. Cut a thin strip from the middle to check to be sure that liver is no longer pink. Remove and set aside to cool. Remove all skin and membranes.
4. Broil chicken livers in the same manner. Make an incision in one or two of the livers to check to see that they are done. Remove and set aside to cool. Remove all membranes.

5. In the meantime, put the onion in a deep skillet over medium-high heat and pour the oil over the onion. Cook a minute or two, stirring often, then lower heat slightly and cook, stirring frequently with a wooden spoon, until soft and golden brown. Do not allow the onion to burn. Remove the onion from the pan and set aside to cool. Reserve any oil remaining in the pan.

6. Cut the livers into pieces and halve the eggs. Use the fine (some people like medium) disk of a food grinder to alternately grind the livers, onion, and egg. (If using a food processor, chop the ingredients briefly.) Add any additional oil left in the skillet if the mixture seems too dry. Mix thoroughly and add salt and black pepper. Taste and adjust seasonings.

7. Transfer to a large bowl, smooth the surface, cover with plastic wrap, and chill until serving time. Line serving plates with a bed of mixed lettuces or lettuce and arugula leaves. Keep in a tightly closed container in the refrigerator. Best used within 3 days.

Seven-Spice-Infused Meat-Stuffed Dried Fruit

Serves 8

Dainty spice-infused stuffed dried fruit is traditional in many Sephardic homes during all the month of fall holidays of Tishri, in keeping with the custom of eating both stuffed and sweet foods. This is a fine dish to serve as a first course or appetizer during the rest of the holiday. Perfect for Sukkot and Tu b'Shvat as well.

Fruit and Stuffing

4 cups water

15 large dried figs

15 large dried pitted prunes (not the moist kind)

15 large dried pitted apricots

10 ounces lean ground beef or lamb (or a mixture)

3 tablespoons minced onion

¼ teaspoon *each* turmeric, coarsely ground black pepper, nutmeg, grated peeled fresh gingerroot, cumin, and cinnamon

1 teaspoon salt

3 tablespoons pine nuts (optional)

1 egg, beaten

Cooking Sauce

¼ cup extra-virgin olive oil

2¼ cups finely chopped onion (about 3 large)

2½ cups soaking water

½ cup dry red wine

5 bay leaves

½ cup granulated or turbinado sugar

¼ teaspoon turmeric

1 teaspoon grated peeled fresh gingerroot

1½ tablespoons toasted sesame seeds, for garnish

1. Bring the water to a boil and remove from heat.

2. Rinse the dried fruit to remove traces of sulfur dioxide (used to preserve freshness). Snip off the tips of the figs. Drop figs, prunes, and apricots into the water and let stand about 10 minutes, until they plump. Drain, reserving soaking water and place the fruit on a paper towel. Taking one piece of fruit at a time, use a forefinger to create a little pocket for the meat filling in top of the figs and the sides of the prunes and apricots. Set aside.

3. In a medium-size bowl, mix the ground beef, onion, spices, salt, pine nuts, if using, and egg. Cover and chill for 1 hour.

4. In the meantime, prepare the sauce: Heat the oil in a large skillet with cover and sauté the onion until golden, stirring frequently.

5. Heat $2\frac{1}{2}$ cups of the soaking water to boiling (or heat in the microwave) and add to the onion along with the wine, bay leaves, sugar, and spices. Bring to a boil and continue boiling on medium heat for 10 minutes.

6. Using a teaspoon, fill each fruit pocket with about $\frac{1}{2}$ to 1 teaspoon of the meat mixture, pressing the mixture down slightly with your forefinger. Lower the heat on the sauce to a simmer and carefully place each fruit in the pot. Cover and cook over medium-low heat for 1 hour, or until the meat is done and the sauce has a syrupy consistency, checking occasionally to make sure the sauce has not evaporated. (Both stuffed fruit and sauce may be prepared up to 4 hours in advance, and packed separately in closed containers in the refrigerator. Reheat the sauce and cook the fruit as outlined above.)

The Customs of Rosh Hashanah

From the shores of Salonika to the shtetls in Poland—indeed, throughout the Jewish world—there has always been a flurry of activity leading up to Rosh Hashanah. The new moon of Tishri, the new spiritual year and the themes of purification and renewal, have been echoed in the custom of wearing new clothes and giving gifts to family members, employees, care providers, those in need, as well as any who host us on the New Year. The custom may well have originated from a principle in the Talmud called *Hiddur Mitzvah,* enhancing a mitzvah, a commandment, by taking the time to make it more special.

It's that custom that is behind our setting the holiday table with the finest cloth, plates, and cutlery, and preparing a special kiddush cup, challah tray, and even honey dish for the holiday meals. In years gone by, mothers would teach their daughters the art of needlework on decorative challah cloths for Shabbat and holidays, still an ideal opportunity in our own day for parents and children to create Judaica together.

Because *gemilut hasadim,* acts of generosity, are fundamental to the holiday, many people use the Rosh Hashanah season to make donations of foods and funds. Throughout the Jewish world, many people also visit the graves of their departed loved ones.

Cornish Hens Stuffed with Bulgur, Raisins, and Caraway

Serves 4

This attractive and unusual dish of Middle Eastern flavors blends two of the Seven Species—*hita*, or wheat in the form of bulgur, and *gefen*, or vines in the form of raisins. We like to use the small Cornish hens (about 1 to 1¼ pounds), and serve one per person. If none is available, use the large (1½ to 2½ pounds) and serve each person a half.

Note: The same quantity (1¼ to 2½ teaspoons) of *Baharat* (page 299) may be substituted for the spices for the rub. Add the salt.

4 Cornish hens, each weighing about 1 pound

Rub
¼ to ½ teaspoon *each* nutmeg, sweet paprika, black pepper, cardamom, salt, and sumac

Stuffing
1 tablespoon olive oil
1 cup chopped onion

1 cup medium (#2) bulgur wheat
2 cups boiling water
½ teaspoon caraway seeds, toasted in a dry skillet
¼ teaspoon ground black pepper
1 teaspoon ground cinnamon
¼ teaspoon ground cumin
½ cup raisins or currants
½ cup chopped walnuts (optional)
Salt to taste

1. Rinse the Cornish hens and place in a bowl of boiling water. Let stand 1 minute, then remove and scrape gently to remove excess surface fat and any pinfeathers, especially around the wings and legs. Rinse and pat dry. Mix together the spices for the rub, and rub into the hens on all sides. Place in a baking pan.

2. To prepare the stuffing: Heat the oil in a heavy skillet over medium heat. Gently sauté the onion over medium-low heat about 5 minutes, until translucent, stirring often. Add the bulgur and toasted caraway seeds, stirring frequently, for 2 minutes. Add the water and spices, stir, and cook, covered, over very low heat for 10 to 12 minutes, or until the water is absorbed. Remove from heat, add the raisins, and fluff with a fork. Cover and let stand 5 minutes. Uncover and cool to room temperature.

3. Preheat the oven to 375°F. Using a spoon, stuff the hens with the bulgur mixture and tie the legs together (cover the stomach cavity with a flap of skin). Cover lightly with aluminum foil.

4. Bake for 30 minutes. Lower heat to 350°F. Remove the cover and continue to bake for 15 to 20 minutes, or until the hens are nicely browned.

This richly flavored fragrant chicken dish from Georgia on the Black Sea is traditional among Georgian Jews for Rosh Hashanah and the festival season. We tasted this tempting version of it at Nanuchka, the Georgian restaurant in Tel Aviv.

Traditionally made with chicken thighs, it can also be made with a combination of thighs, legs, and breasts. Serve with plain rice, mashed potatoes, or Barley Salad with Lemon and Cilantro (page 58). Both tamarind paste and pomegranate sauce are available in Middle Eastern groceries.

Georgian Chicken in Pomegranate and Tamarind Sauce

Serves 5 to 6 (or more if using a combination of chicken parts)

10 chicken thighs

2 cups diced onion (about 4 medium)

4 cups diced red onion (about 4 medium)

2 cups chopped fresh cilantro

10 garlic cloves, sliced or pressed

1 teaspoon sweet paprika

1 teaspoon hot paprika or cayenne pepper

1 teaspoon black pepper

3 tablespoons tamarind paste

½ cup pomegranate sauce, diluted in ½ cup water

2 tablespoons tomato paste

1½ teaspoons salt

Seeds of ½ pomegranate, for garnish (optional but spectacular)

1. Remove the skin from the chicken thighs, rinse, and pat dry. Set aside.

2. In a large Dutch oven or pot with cover, mix the diced onions, 1½ cups cilantro, the garlic, and spices. Blend in the tamarind paste, diluted pomegranate sauce, tomato paste, and salt. Add the chicken thighs and ladle the sauce on top. Cover and cook on medium-high heat for 10 minutes, then lower heat and cook for a total of 1 hour and 20 minutes.

3. Transfer the chicken and sauce to a serving platter and garnish with the remaining ½ cup chopped cilantro. Sprinkle the pomegranate seeds on top and serve hot.

Sweet-and-Sour Bass in the Style of Iraq and Salonika

Serves 6

And God said: Let the waters swarm with swarms of living creatures. . . . And God blessed them, saying: Be fruitful and multiply and fill the waters of the sea. . . .

—**Genesis 1:20–22**

Throughout both the Ashkenazic and Sephardic worlds, fish is traditionally included in the Rosh Hashanah meal as a symbol of fertility in the year to come. For Sephardic Jews the choice holds an extra benefit—the fish head is used in the Seven Blessings ceremony (page 121).

This sweet-and-sour fish recipe, which traditionally serves as a first course in Sephardic holiday menus but can be used as a main course for nonmeat eaters as well, was adapted from one given to us by chef Ezra Kedem of the Arcadia restaurant in Jerusalem, whose roots go back to Sephardic families that emigrated from Iraq and Salonika and settled in Jerusalem, many generations ago.

Ground Persian dried lemon is available in Middle Eastern groceries.

6 fillets of Chilean sea bass (4 to 5 ounces each) or halibut, deboned
Salt
White pepper to taste
2 tablespoons freshly squeezed lemon or lime juice
2 tablespoons sugar
1 tablespoon tomato paste
½ teaspoon ground Persian dried lemon (optional)
¼ cup vegetable broth

¼ cup extra-virgin olive oil
¾ cup coarsely chopped onion
¾ cup coarsely chopped red onion
3 to 5 tablespoons mildly hot green pepper, minced (optional)
1 pound ripe tomatoes, peeled, seeded, and coarsely chopped, or 1½ cups finely diced canned plum tomatoes

1. Rinse the fillets and pat dry. Season with salt and white pepper and set aside.

2. Prepare the sauce: In a small saucepan, mix the lemon or lime juice with sugar, tomato paste, ground Persian dried lemon, vegetable broth, and a good pinch of salt. Bring to a boil, lower heat, and simmer for 6 to 7 minutes, stirring occasionally to completely dissolve the sugar. Set aside.

3. For the vegetables: In a heavy cast-iron pan, heat 2 tablespoons of olive oil and sauté the onion and green pepper until softened. Add the tomatoes and season with salt and white pepper. Set aside.

4. Heat the remaining olive oil in a separate skillet and sear the fillets on both sides until opaque. Transfer to the pan with the vegetables, pour over the prepared sauce, cover, and cook over medium heat for 6 to 7 minutes, or until the fish has reached desired doneness.

5. Serve the fish with a spoonful of vegetables and sauce on top.

Although coin-shaped carrot tzimmes is a traditional dish for Rosh Hashanah, I must admit I've never been a great fan. Our friend Adi invented this carrot-free tzimmes for people just like me. It's a different and refreshing take on the traditional version, and a welcome addition to both Rosh Hashanah and Passover menus.

Adi's Tzimmes

Serves 8

2 pounds sweet potatoes, peeled and cut in chunks

1 pound pumpkin or butternut squash, peeled, seeded, and cut in chunks

Salt

½ cup dried cranberries

½ cup dried apricots, each cut in half

½ cup dates, each pitted and cut in half

1 cup freshly squeezed orange juice

⅓ cup brown sugar or honey

1 cinnamon stick

2 tablespoons dry sherry or Calvados or fruit liqueur of your choice

1. Preheat oven to 350°F. Grease a large casserole dish.

2. Cook sweet potatoes and pumpkin in lightly salted boiling water to cover, just until tender. Drain and save the cooking liquid.

3. Transfer the sweet potatoes and pumpkin to prepared casserole. Add dried fruit, orange juice, and brown sugar. Mix well. Place cinnamon stick in the center, cover, and place in the preheated oven. Bake for 1 hour.

4. Lower heat to 200°F. Remove cover and continue to bake for 30 minutes. Remove cinnamon stick and add liqueur 15 minutes before the end of baking. If the tzimmes looks dry, add some of the reserved cooking liquid.

Ida's Baked Sweet Potatoes and Apples

Serves 6

To coax us to eat this when we were little, our mother often used to put marshmallows on top, and bake them until browned.

2 pounds sweet potatoes
1½ pounds Granny Smith or firm
   red apples (about 4)
¼ cup orange marmalade or
   apricot jam

½ cup butter, walnut oil, or
   hazelnut oil
¼ cup honey
1 teaspoon cinnamon
¼ teaspoon nutmeg

1. Scrub sweet potatoes and boil in their jackets until they can be pierced with a fork. Do not overcook. (May also be microwaved: Prick whole sweet potatoes to prevent bursting and put in a microwave-safe dish with ¼ cup water. Cover and cook for 5 minutes. Or cut into 1½-inch pieces and place in a covered dish. Cook 5 minutes.) Let cool. Peel the sweet potatoes, and slice into thick slices or chunks. Peel the apples and slice into eighths.

2. Preheat the oven to 375°F. Grease a baking dish.

3. In the bottom of prepared dish, place a layer of sweet potatoes and top with apple slices and half of the marmalade or jam. Dot with butter (or brush with oil, if using). Repeat for a second layer.

4. Mix the honey with the cinnamon and nutmeg and drizzle over the top. Loosely cover with aluminum foil.

5. Bake for 20 minutes. Lower heat to 300°F. Remove foil and bake an additional 10 minutes, or until apples are tender but still retain their shape.

6. If desired, dot the top with marshmallows and return to the oven for 2 to 3 minutes, until they are browned and gooey.

Green Beans in
Tomato Sauce

Serves 4 to 6

Fresh green beans (some strains called *lubia* in Hebrew) come in all shapes and sizes around Rosh Hashanah time—such as long snake beans, yellow wax beans, and speckled and plain green flat beans—and are the base for this centuries-old Sephardic recipe, traditionally served on Rosh Hashanah and Sukkot. The secret of this dish is not to stir it but to gently shake the pot (with the cover on) so as not to damage the cooked beans, and to cook it on low heat.

2 pounds fresh or frozen whole green beans	1 teaspoon salt
3 tablespoons extra-virgin olive oil	1 teaspoon freshly ground black pepper
1 cup finely chopped onion	1 teaspoon paprika
4 drained canned plum tomatoes, chopped, plus ½ to 1 cup juice from can	1 teaspoon sugar

1. Top and tail the fresh green beans, and remove strings. Cut the beans in half.

2. Heat the oil in a skillet and fry onion until golden. Add the beans, tomatoes, ½ cup tomato liquid, and spices. Cover and cook over low heat for 1 hour (30 minutes if using frozen beans), adding the remaining ½ cup of can liquid if necessary during the cooking process. Do not stir; just shake the pot to mix. Serve warm.

Roasted Eggplant and Pomegranate Seed Salad

Serves 6

One of the finest ways to enjoy eggplant, this version of a centuries-old recipe was taught to me by Ya'acov Lishansky, whose mother prepared it every autumn, when pomegranate season peaked in the Galilee. For winter use, she'd oil the pomegranates and keep them in a cool place, where they would last for months.

Lishansky fondly remembered the fabulous smoky scent of roasted eggplant wafting through the house and claimed that "whoever called roasted eggplant a poor man's caviar obviously knew what the rich were missing!"

For best flavor, char the eggplants directly on a gas burner. If your stovetop is electric, the next-best thing is to broil the eggplants on an oven rack close to the broiler element until blackened, turning occasionally. Place a parchment-lined pan under them to keep the oven clean. Serve with challah, hot pita, toast, or crackers.

4 pounds eggplant (about 3 large)
2 tablespoons freshly squeezed
    lemon juice, or more to taste
Seeds of 1 pomegranate
½ cup extra-virgin olive oil
Salt
Freshly ground black pepper

to taste
1 tablespoon chopped fresh mint
    leaves (optional)
3 to 4 tablespoons chopped
    scallions and/or sliced
    radishes

1. Wash and dry eggplants. Cut a hole in the middle of three large squares of aluminum foil to form "collars" for three stovetop gas burners. (This will help alleviate cleanup.) If you have them, place a rack over each burner to hold the eggplant (cooling racks may also be used).

2. Put an eggplant on each one of the burners and roast over medium heat, turning occasionally, until blackened on all sides. Use two large kitchen spoons to transfer one eggplant at a time to a cutting board. Let cool until easy to handle.

3. Slice each eggplant in half lengthwise and use a spoon to scrape out the insides. Discard the skin. Hand-chop the eggplant flesh with a chopping knife until there are no coarse lumps or strips, then transfer to a bowl. (Don't be tempted to use a blender or food processor for this recipe—they destroy the texture.)

4. Using a fork, mix in the lemon juice and pomegranate seeds, then gently whisk in the olive oil. Season to taste with salt and pepper. Pour onto a large plate and garnish with chopped mint in the middle and chopped scallions or radish slices over the rest.

"... An Orchard of Pomegranates" (Song of Songs 4:13)

Fifth among the Seven Species, the pomegranate refreshed both King Solomon and the Queen of Sheba, and its form inspired generations of weavers, carvers, and other artisans. The scarlet seeds were dried and ground as a seasoning; yellow rinds stained leathers and colored ink; and the pomegranate's tufted crown inspired the shape of the crown adorning the heads of kings as well.

Pomegranate juice was delicious and refreshing, but pomegranate wine was even better—the young woman in the Song of Songs yearns for her lover to drink it "spiced." And her lover, in turn, sees her as a "garden of pomegranates" and even compares her temples to a pomegranate that's been split open. This ancient symbol of fertility, interestingly enough, is now known to contain phytoestrogens.

Bulgarian Leek Patties

**Makes 8 large patties
(serves 4)**

Although leeks also grew in ancient Israel, many generations of ancient Hebrews learned about them during their bondage in Egypt, and it was one of the foods they yearned for during their desert wanderings (Num. 11:5). Although leek patties are a traditional part of the Seven Blessings ceremony (page 121), they hold particular significance at Passover as well. Yehiel Philosof's leek patties, served at his Jaffa restaurant, are famous all year round. They can be made exactly the same way without the meat.

5 leeks
1 cup chopped onion
Rounded ½ cup potato flour
½ teaspoon salt
¼ teaspoon freshly ground
   black pepper

5 ounces ground beef
3 eggs, beaten
½ teaspoon garlic powder
Vegetable oil, for frying

1. Remove the stems and roots from the leeks, and rinse the white part well to remove soil. Slice into strips. Place the leek strips and chopped onion in a pot, add boiling water halfway up the contents of the pot, bring to a boil, and steam 20 minutes, until very soft.

2. Drain the vegetables well, and squeeze out as much moisture as possible. Grind coarsely in a food processor and transfer to a bowl. Mix in the potato flour, salt, pepper, ground beef, beaten eggs, and garlic powder. Oil hands and form 8 patties (if making this recipe without meat, use a ¼ cup measure of the batter each time to make pancakelike patties).

3. Heat ⅛ inch oil in a heavy skillet, and fry the patties on both sides until golden. Drain on paper towels and serve.

Lubia
Salad

**Green Beans
and Black-
eyed Peas**

Serves 6

The word *lubia* in Hebrew refers to both green beans and black-eyed peas, the former indigenous to Central or South America, brought back to the Old World by explorers, and the latter a native of China, probably reaching the Middle East and Mediterranean with Arab traders millennia ago.

Sephardic Jews embraced them both to create a dish that is particularly popular on the Seven Blessings tray, and up to Sukkot, when they are in season.

3 cups fresh snap beans, or frozen green beans, thawed	1 large garlic clove, minced or pressed
2 cups water	Salt
1 cup black-eyed peas	Freshly ground black pepper to taste
1 bay leaf	
¼ cup extra-virgin olive oil	2 tablespoons fresh chopped cilantro or Italian parsley
1 to 2 tablespoons raspberry or red wine vinegar	

1. Rinse the fresh green beans and pat dry. Snip off the tips and tails and cut in half (kitchen shears are helpful in this process). Bring a pot of lightly salted water to a boil, and when it bubbles again add the green beans and blanch for 2 to 3 minutes, until just tender and still bright green. (If using thawed frozen beans, blanch for 1 minute.) Remove the green beans and reserve the cooking water. Rinse under cold running water to stop the cooking process. Drain.

2. Drop the black-eyed peas and the bay leaf into the same cooking water as the green beans, and bring to a boil. Cook for 30 to 40 minutes, until softened tender but not mushy. Drain and rinse in cold water. Drain well.

3. In a serving bowl, mix the green beans with the black-eyed peas and bay leaf. In a small bowl, whisk olive oil, vinegar, and minced garlic clove together, and pour over the beans. Season with salt and pepper, garnish with cilantro or parsley, and let stand for 10 minutes to blend flavors. Taste, adjust seasonings, remove bay leaf, and serve. (To prepare this salad in advance, mix the cooked black-eyed peas and green beans with 2 tablespoons of the olive oil, cover, and chill in the refrigerator. Bring to room temperature and add the remaining ingredients up to 1 hour before serving, or the dressing will fade the color of the green beans.)

Note: To make this a main dish salad, add a small can of drained chunk white tuna, ½ cup thinly sliced red onion, and ¼ cup pitted black olives.

Moroccan Carrot Salad

Serves 4 to 6

One form or another of Moroccan carrot salad is found everywhere in Israel, from holiday buffets to falafel stands. Although it is not sweet, its round coinlike shape makes it just right for any Seven Blessings tray.

Note: Some people like to add lemon juice to this salad, but I prefer it without.

1 pound carrots, sliced into ¼-inch rounds (about 6 carrots)

3 tablespoons extra-virgin olive oil

1 to 2 large garlic cloves, minced or pressed

½ teaspoon cumin

¼ teaspoon salt

Tabasco sauce, red pepper flakes, finely minced green hot pepper, or *Tzoug* (page 299) to taste

2 tablespoons chopped fresh Italian parsley or cilantro

Sumac, for garnish (optional)

1. Steam carrots in a steamer basket or in boiling salted water for 4 minutes, until tender but still brightly colored.

2. Drain and add olive oil, garlic, cumin, salt, and Tabasco sauce while the carrots are still warm. Garnish with Italian parsley and sprinkle with sumac, if desired.

3. Taste and adjust seasoning and serve. (This salad may be prepared in advance and stored in a closed container in the refrigerator. Bring to room temperature, taste, adjust seasonings, and serve.)

W hile Ashkenazic Jews always eat apples and honey on Rosh Hashanah, Sephardim may substitute quince or add quince to the holiday meal. Once highly popular in America, when people still made homemade fruit preserves, the exotic quince is now available only in specialty stores. It's worth trying to find them for this recipe given to us by Ezra Kedem.

4 large quince, unblemished	2 tablespoons cardamom pods
2 cups Muscat dessert wine	1 vanilla bean, sliced in half
1 cup sugar	lengthwise
4 cinnamon sticks	1 cup water

1. Rinse the quince, cut each in eighths, and peel.

2. Mix wine, sugar, cinnamon sticks, and cardamom pods in a large, wide pot. Scrape the seeds from the vanilla bean and add with the pod to the pot. Bring to a boil and lower heat.

3. Arrange the quince slices in the pot and spoon over the wine mixture. If there is not enough to cover the quince, add water just to cover. Cover the pot, bring to a boil, and simmer over low heat for 90 minutes, or until quince slices are amber-colored and soft. Serve chilled with sauce.

Menahem's Tip

Menahem, the sous-chef of Arcadia, one of Jerusalem's top restaurants, makes this same recipe at home, but cooks it for 5 hours on the lowest possible heat. "The color and taste are far richer," he says. Do not stir during cooking, he advises, and if the liquids evaporate, just add more water.

Figs Stuffed with Halvah, Nuts, and Honey

Although we're Ashkenazim, we don't follow the custom of avoiding nuts (page 120) on Rosh Hashanah. Instead, we prefer to use biblical-seasonal inspirations to create holiday fare, like this elegant dessert combining three of the Seven Species—figs, grapes (i.e., wine), and honey—and other traditional Rosh Hashanah elements (dates, wine, rose petals) to make a visually appealing and unusual sweet for the end of the festive meal. Edible dried rose petals, lavender, tahini, and rose water can be found in Middle Eastern and/or health-food stores.

Note: This recipe is much easier to prepare than it looks, but an even easier version can be made by omitting the homemade halvah layer.

Serves 6

12 large unblemished dried figs

Wine Sauce
1 bottle dry red wine (Merlot or Petit Sirah)
4 pitted dates
1 teaspoon dried roses, or ½ teaspoon rose petals or lavender flowers (optional)
2 tablespoons honey
1 teaspoon whole coriander seeds
1 cinnamon stick
¼ teaspoon coarsely ground black pepper or peppercorns

Halvah
¼ cup tahini
1 to 2 tablespoons honey
½ cup ground almonds, more if needed
A few drops rose water

Stuffing
½ cup mixed unsalted toasted whole nuts (pistachios, hazelnuts, almonds, walnuts, pine nuts)
½ cup wildflower honey

1. Rinse the figs and snip the tips off with kitchen shears. Place in a medium saucepan with the wine, dates, dried roses, honey, coriander, cinnamon, and coarsely ground black pepper. Bring to a boil, lower heat, and cook for 15 minutes, or until figs are tender but not too soft. Remove the figs and place on a work surface. Strain and reserve the sauce, discarding spices.

2. Return the sauce to the pot and cook on medium-low heat until reduced by half. (Sauce may be prepared in advance and reheated before serving.) In the meantime, use the forefinger to open the stem end of each fig, pressing the middle equally around the sides to create a rimmed "basket."

3. To make the halvah, stir the tahini, honey, and rose water together in a small bowl until well blended. Add in the ground almonds until the mixture is too thick to stir, and knead into a soft dough, adding more ground nuts if the mixture is too sticky. Set aside.

4. Make the stuffing by mixing the nuts and honey.

5. Place a thin layer of halvah at the bottom of each fig and top with a tablespoon of the honey-nut stuffing. (At this point figs may be placed in a container, surrounded by sauce, covered, and stored for several hours or overnight in the refrigerator. Bring the figs to room temperature before serving.)

6. To serve, remove the figs from the sauce if storing. Heat the sauce and pour a few tablespoons of it in the bottom of each of 6 heated plates. Place two figs on each plate and pour a little of the hot sauce over each.

The Best Honey Cake Yet

Makes one 12-inch loaf or two 9-inch loaves

Doing a survey of all our friends and relations, we found that no one we knew really liked the traditional dark honey cake, whether homemade or store-bought. No one liked the flavor. Challenged, we tried it with espresso. We tried it with brandy. We even tried it with tea. But it always seemed to come out heavy and dry—until this one. Inspired by the Romanian Jewish honey cake—which is light rather than dark—this version is light as a feather and really delicious. It's certainly the best honey cake we've ever tasted.

1 cup walnuts or pecans, chopped
½ cup vegetable oil
1¼ cups honey
6 large eggs, separated
¼ teaspoon cinnamon

¼ teaspoon ground ginger
Pinch of ground cardamom
2 cups unbleached all-purpose flour
1 tablespoon baking powder
½ cup sugar

1. Preheat the oven to 375°F. Lightly grease a 12-inch loaf pan or two 9-inch loaf pans. Line the bottom and sides with parchment paper to facilitate removal after baking. Set aside.

2. Place the chopped nuts in a baking pan and roast in the oven for 10 minutes, shaking the pan occasionally. Remove from the oven and let cool.

3. Lower heat to 300°F.

4. In the bowl of a standing electric mixer, beat the oil, honey, egg yolks, and spices. Sift the flour and baking powder and blend into the honey mixture until smooth.

5. In a separate bowl, beat egg whites until foamy. Add the sugar gradually, continuing to beat until the egg whites are stiff. Fold a small amount of the egg whites into the honey mixture, then fold in the rest gradually, mixing gently each time until incorporated. Stir in the nuts.

6. Carefully pour the batter into the prepared pan(s). Bake on the middle shelf of the preheated oven for 60 to 75 minutes, or until a toothpick inserted in the center pulls out almost dry (it will have fine crumbs stuck to it). Place baking pan(s) on a wire rack and let cool for 20 minutes before turning out on a rack to finish cooling.

Variations

Add ⅓ cup finely chopped crystallized ginger to the batter instead of the nuts.

Add ½ cup finely chopped candied citron to the batter instead of or in addition to the nuts.

Fill your holiday quota of honey with these delicious brownies.

½ cup butter

6 ounces bittersweet chocolate

4 eggs

½ teaspoons salt

¾ cup turbinado sugar or packed brown sugar

½ cup honey

1 teaspoon vanilla extract

1 cup unbleached all-purpose flour

1 cup chopped pecans or walnuts

Makes 16 squares

Ⓓ

1. Preheat oven to 325°F. Grease and flour a 9-inch square baking pan (or use nonstick cooking spray or parchment paper). Set aside.

2. Melt butter and chocolate in a heavy saucepan over low heat. Set aside to cool. In a medium bowl, beat eggs and salt until fluffy. Add sugar and honey gradually, beating until the mixture is smooth and light. Add the melted chocolate mixture and vanilla. Stir in flour and nuts. Pour into the prepared pan.

3. Bake for 45 to 55 minutes, or until a toothpick inserted in the center comes out clean. Cut into squares when cool.

New Moon Butter Cookies

Makes about 40

These melt-in-your-mouth crescent-shaped cookies are reminiscent of the new moon of Tishri, which falls exactly on Rosh Hashanah. To capture the look of the "changing of the moon," dip the inside edges are dipped in varying amounts of melted chocolate.

1 cup blanched sliced almonds
1 cup (2 sticks) cold butter, cut in small cubes
2¾ to 3 cups unbleached all-purpose flour
¾ cup confectioners' sugar, plus extra for dusting

1 teaspoon cinnamon
2 teaspoons vanilla extract
3½ ounces milk or bittersweet chocolate, melted with 2 tablespoons butter (optional)

1. In a food processor, grind the almonds to a fine powder. Add the butter, 2¾ cups flour, confectioners' sugar, cinnamon, and vanilla. Process until a dough forms around the blade. Add the remaining ¼ cup flour only if the dough is very sticky.

2. Remove and shape it into a ball, wrap in plastic wrap, and refrigerate for 1 hour.

3. Preheat the oven to 350°F. Line a baking sheet with parchment paper. Divide the dough into 1-inch-diameter balls, and form them into little crescent-shaped cookies.

4. Bake for 15 minutes, or until the cookies are golden at the edges. Cool on the baking sheet and dust with confectioners' sugar passed through a wire-mesh strainer, or dip in chocolate: Melt the chocolate and butter in a small microwave-safe bowl, and stir until smooth. Dip in or brush on varying amounts of the mixture on the inner surface of the cookies. Place on a wire rack until fully dry.

Yom Kippur

The Day of Atonement

Long before sunset on Erev Yom Kippur, a sudden quiet descends on the cities, towns, and villages of Israel, from Metulla to the Negev. It is an astounding calm, an almost thundering quiet, profoundly different from the noisy hustle and bustle of everyday life. You can hear the birds sing. The skies of Jerusalem seem to glow with a new intensity behind the clouds. You can't help feeling that Yom Kippur really *is* the Sabbath of Sabbaths, as the Bible tells us.

Yom Kippur, when we fast from sundown to sundown (plus one hour), arrives after the somber Ten Days of Repentance following Rosh Hashanah. For many Jews, it is most vividly associated with the chanting of the Kol Nidre, a stirring prayer whose ancient legal formula, recited ever since the eighth century, annuls all vows, promises, obligations, and oaths to God.

A time to let go of the flotsom and jetsam of our character both as a people and as individuals, Yom Kippur, also known as *Yom HaDin*, the Day of Judgment, was a time of anxiety for our ancestors in the days the Temple stood in Jerusalem. With their agricultural future a matter of life and death, they wondered: Would the people's repentance and righteous deeds allow the coming year to be a good one? Would the harvest be plentiful? Would enough rain fall in the coming winter to nourish new crops?

With great pageantry, the High Priest carried out a solemn ritual of purification to prepare for the new season. "May it be Your will," he would pray, "that no exile come upon us . . . that this year be a year when prices are low, a year of plenty . . . a year of rain . . . that your people Israel may not be in need of one another's help . . . and that they do not rise to rule over one another" (JT, Yoma 5).

Traditionally, a festive meal is eaten the day before Yom Kippur, with many observant Jews considering it a mitzvah to feast the entire day, so that when we feel the pangs of hunger during the fast, we are more acutely aware of how difficult it is to atone for our sins. The final meal before the fast (seudah hamafseqet) is eaten before sundown.

Whatever your ethnic derivation, there's a good chance your family's tradition included eating chicken, most often in the form of soup, at their pre-fast Yom Kippur dinner. The tradition probably dates back to the Ashkenazic Kapparot ceremony on the eve of Yom Kippur: A live chicken was grabbed by the legs and swung around the head of a man, woman, or child, with a prayer that the chicken absorb the person's sins. Rather than waste it, the same sinful chicken was subsequently eaten for dinner—sort of like eating a humble chicken pie. The custom also became popular among Sephardic Jews who lived in the Turkish Empire after their expulsion from Spain in 1492.

While the pre-fast dinner might be particularly bland and almost always contains chicken soup, the first food to break the fast differs among Jews around the world. For Polish and Russian Jews, it might be a sweet cake, like a babka; for those Romanian Jews who still remember the tradition, it might be sweet tea and lemon with a white honey cake, rather than the more usual dark one (similar to The Best Honey Cake Yet, page 150). Syrian and Iraqi Jews often munch on Ka'a'him (page 173), little round biscuits like mini-bagels with sesame seeds and spices, to soothe the stomach, along with a cup of sweetened tea. Iraqi Jews sip hariri, a sweetened almond milk (also quite easy to digest), along with some kind of sweet or savory pastries. And some Turkish, Bulgarian, and Greek Jews still break their fast with pepitada, a sweetened drink made with melon seeds, together with bourekas (like Bourekas b'Milui Badinjan, pages 76–77).

For the break-the-fast dinner, many people eat leftovers from the previous night, including chicken soup and kreplach among the Ashkenazim, while others, especially in America, prefer to start with a dairy meal, including bagels and assorted pickled or smoked fish. Many Sephardic Jews break their fast with a dairy meal at sundown, and wait several hours before consuming a heavier meat meal, possibly because throughout the warm Sephardic world the custom was to stay up longer into the night and dine later, compared to their Eastern European counterparts for whom the autumn was chilly. And while chicken is a preferred dish among North African Jews, they also might plunge into a bowl of *harirah*—a thick beef, chickpea, and vegetable soup they learned from their Muslim neighbors, who consume it to break the fast of Ramadan, which sometimes falls at approximately the same time.

Yom Kippur Recipes

Yom Kippur Challah and Rolls

"Birds of Prayer" Challah Rolls **P**
"Hands in Blessing" Spiral Challah **P**

Appetizers

"New Age" "Chopped Liver" **P**
Poached Halibut Salad **D**
Autumn Salad with Avocado Vinaigrette **P**
Daniel's Schmaltz Herring Salad in Sour Cream and Apples **D**
Avocado Spread **P**
Mozzarella and Sun-dried Tomato Topping **D**

Soups

Two-Mushroom Lentil-Barley Soup with Thyme **P**
Seven-Spice Vegetable Soup **P**
Raisin and Pine Nut Couscous **P**

Main Courses

Fragrant Chicken with Figs **M**
Herbed Rice with Seasoned Currants **P**
Roasted Chicken Thighs with Honey, Olives, and Oregano **M**
Rainbow Trout Stuffed with Tomatoes and Honey-Basil Pesto **P**

To Break-the-Fast and Desserts

Ka'a'him (Sephardic Sesame Seed Rings) **D**
Festive Mandelbrot **P**
Little Almond Cookies **P**
Sutlage (Jerusalem Star of David Rice Pudding) **D**
Honey-Sautéed Pineapple **P**

"Birds of Prayer" Challah Rolls

Makes 10

These touching and yet whimsical "birds" are inspired by one of the oldest challah-baking traditions of the Days of Awe, whose source is the verse from Isaiah. But instead of placing little hovering birds on a spiral challah, I've turned this recipe into whimsical little rolls, perfect for both the pre- and post-fast Yom Kippur meals. Perched on a nest of bay leaves, they almost seem as if they're resting just before carrying our prayers up to the heavens.

The recipe for this classic basic challah dough, excellent for sculpting, comes from Rita Romano, who together with her family runs a store and catering business called Rita's Kitchen in the seaside town of Nof Yam. The secret of the texture, Rita says, is the addition of semolina (or Cream of Wheat) to the dough.

Though the process of creating the little birds may seem complicated at first, once you get the hang of it, you'll be able to hatch them out in minutes, if you carefully follow the directions. And as for decorating them—let your imagination soar.

Note: "Birds of Prayer" Challah Rolls are a natural accompaniment to any of the appetizers in this book, and perfect for a break-the-fast meal. You might want to try them with Avocado Spread (page 163) and Mozzarella and Sun-dried Tomato Topping (page 164). The dough may also be used for regular challah.

6½ to 7 cups unbleached all-purpose flour (plus extra for kneading)

2 tablespoons semolina or Cream of Wheat

1½ teaspoons salt

2 tablespoons yeast

1 tablespoon sugar or honey

2 cups warm water

6 tablespoons vegetable oil

1 egg, beaten

Yellow or black mustard seeds, coriander seeds, or whole cloves (for the eyes)

1 large egg, beaten with 1 teaspoon water

Bay leaves (for the nest)

1. In a large bowl, or the bowl of a mixer outfitted with a dough hook, mix 6 cups flour with semolina or Cream of Wheat and the salt.

2. In a small bowl, mix the yeast, sugar, and ½ cup of the water. Set aside until bubbly. In another small bowl, use a fork to beat the oil and egg with the remaining warm water.

3. Make a well in the center of the flour and pour in the proofed-yeast and oil-egg-water mixtures. Mix with a wooden spoon or dough hook until the dough starts to form a ball, then transfer it to a lightly floured work surface and knead until a smooth dough is formed. Add a little extra flour as necessary.

4. Make a ball of the dough and turn over in an oiled bowl, to coat all sides. Cover and let rise 30 minutes.

5. Punch down the dough and cut in 10 pieces. Roll out the first piece into a 10-inch-long rope. Now pretend you're about to tie a knot. Take the tip of the rope on the left side, and cross it over the right side and pull it under and through the hole, as you would if you were tying your shoes.

6. If you pull the knot tighter, this left tip becomes the head, and the right tip becomes the tail. Use a knife to cut slashes in the right tip to form a feathered tail.

7. With your fingers, shape the left tip into a bird's head with a beak. Poke two holes with the tip of a whole clove, one on each side of the head," and press in yellow or black mustard seeds, coriander seeds, or cloves as "eyes." (I like to use cloves best, because of the color contrast. The edges of the cloves also look like eyelashes. But cloves are recommended only if you tell your guests not to swallow them.) Repeat with the remaining dough. You see, it wasn't that hard after all.

8. Gently brush the top and undersides of the birds with the beaten oil-egg-water mixture, and place on a parchment-paper-lined baking sheet. Soak bay leaves in water for 15 minutes and pat dry. Stick enough bay leaves around the bases of the birds (you'll need 6 to 8 leaves per bird) to give the appearance of nests.

9. Cover gently and let rise in a warm place for 30 minutes.

10. Preheat the oven to 350°F.

11. Bake the birds for 30 to 40 minutes, or until they are a light golden brown. Serve warm, or reheat briefly in the oven just before serving.

"Hands in Blessing" Spiral Challah

Makes two loaves

Like most of the holidays—except Passover—Yom Kippur was inspiration for bakers in centuries past to develop symbolic forms for their holiday challah. According to Galia Gavish, the curator of the Isaac Kaplan Old Yishuv Court Museum in the Jewish Quarter of Jerusalem's Old City and a collector of challot from different traditions, designs included spiral challah with dough formed into keys (to open up the gates of heaven), birds (to carry our prayers aloft), and hands (either in prayer or in blessing).

For Yom Kippur, we've chosen the "Hands in Blessing" on a spiral challah, symbolic of the High Priest's prayer as described in the Talmud.

Round Challah with Seven Seeds dough (page 124)
Lightly beaten egg or egg yolk mixed with 1 teaspoon water

Poppy or sesame seeds

1. Once the dough has risen for the first time, slice in two. (Remove a small amount of dough from each one and set aside, to form the hands.) Roll out each piece into a rope and coil it to make a flat spiral. Fasten the end under the circle with a gentle pinch. Transfer to a greased or lined baking pan or sheet. Repeat with the second half of the dough.

2. With the remaining dough, form four little circles, each 2 to 2½ inches in diameter, and cut out right- and left-hand shapes from each one using a small knife or scissors. Shape each hand with ring finger and pinky touching, and index and third finger touching (forming a V between the two sets of fingers), and thumbs spread wide apart, touching one another at the tips. Oil the "hands" (so they don't "melt" into the challah) and place them on top of the challot.

3. Preheat the oven to 350°F.

4. Brush each challah with a beaten egg or egg yolk mixed with 1 teaspoon water, and sprinkle with sesame or a variety of seeds, starting from around the hands outward. Cover and let rise in a warm (not hot) place for 15 minutes.

5. Bake the challot for 25 to 30 minutes, until well browned. Remove from the oven and cool on a wire rack. (Challot may be frozen. Cool to room temperature, wrap tightly, and freeze. Best used within 1 month.)

Most Jewish homes in Eastern Europe wouldn't think of a pre-fast Yom Kippur dinner without a chopped liver *forspeis* (appetizer), in keeping with the custom of eating chopped or "beaten" foods, symbolizing how we "beat" our breasts to atone for our sins.

Although I've already given a vegetarian alternative to chopped liver (page 131) in addition to the familiar classic kind (page 132), I've also decided to include this very authentic-tasting version that I discovered—and have made often—in recent years. It is based on tempeh, a fermented soy product considered an excellent source of protein, with all the many health benefits of soy. Tempeh even contains vitamin B^{12}, which is almost impossible to find in the vegetarian kingdom. Sold frozen or chilled in 8-ounce cakes in health-food stores, it looks and seems strange at first, but is actually easy to work with. Like all types of chopped liver, the secret to success is slow-cooking the onions until they are a deep golden brown.

⅓ cup canola oil	Salt to taste
1⅔ cups chopped onion (about 2 large)	White pepper and black pepper to taste
8-ounce package tempeh	Ruby looseleaf, escarole, chicory, or arugula leaves
2 hard-boiled eggs	Snipped chives
½ teaspoon soy sauce	

1. Heat the oil in a large skillet and cook the onion on medium-low heat about 20 to 30 minutes, until deep golden brown, stirring often. Strain the onion, but reserve the oil.

2. In the meantime, steam the tempeh for 15 to 20 minutes in a steamer basket. (If no steamer basket is available, cut the tempeh into large pieces and place in a wire-mesh strainer above a pot of boiling water. Cover while steaming.) Cool.

3. In a food grinder or food processor, place drained cooked onion, tempeh, hard-boiled eggs, and soy sauce, and process until smooth. Season with salt and pepper, and add reserved oil as necessary if the mixture seems dry.

4. Transfer to a bowl, cover with plastic wrap, and chill in the refrigerator at least 1 hour, until firm.

5. To serve, line individual plates with lettuce or arugula leaves. Use an ice-cream scoop to form balls of the mixture and divide among the plates. Sprinkle each with a teaspoon of snipped chives and serve. (May be stored in the refrigerator. Best used within 24 to 48 hours.)

Poached Halibut Salad

Serves 6 to 8

Light and tasty, Poached Halibut Salad can be served as a first course for a dairy pre-fast dinner or as part of a break-the-fast meal. To serve, make a mound of halibut salad in the middle of a large, round plate and surround it with thinly sliced radishes, hothouse cucumbers, finely diced scallions, and green and black olives. You can also serve it on a bed of mixed greens, along with challah or "Birds of Prayer" Challah Rolls (page 156).

Note: Best prepared a day before serving.

2 pounds fresh halibut

Broth
2 medium onions, sliced
1 medium carrot, sliced
½ cup semidry white wine
2 teaspoons salt
½ teaspoon coarsely ground
   black pepper

Salad
¾ cup dairy sour cream
½ cup mayonnaise
2 teaspoons dried tarragon

1. Rinse the halibut, pat dry, and set aside.

2. In a wide saucepan or skillet with cover, mix the onions, carrot, wine, salt, and pepper. Add water to cover the vegetables plus 1 inch. (If using frozen halibut, add water just to cover the vegetables.) Bring to a boil, lower heat to medium, and cook 10 minutes. Taste and adjust seasoning.

3. Place fish on top of broth and cook for 10 minutes. Turn pieces over and cook another 10 minutes. Remove from heat and let cool in the fish broth.

4. Remove the fish with a slotted spoon and place on a platter. Use a fork to carefully flake the fish and remove any bones. Transfer flaked fish to a bowl and cool thoroughly.

5. Mix in the sour cream, mayonnaise, and tarragon. Cover and refrigerate until serving time. Just before serving, taste and add additional salt and pepper only if necessary.

Inspired by the autumn harvest, this salad can be served as a first course for dinner or along with a break-the-fast meal.

1 small head romaine lettuce
1 head butter lettuce
1 head Belgian endive
1½ cups cauliflower florets
1½ cups broccoli florets
1½ cups fresh topped and tailed green beans
1 cup grated carrot (about 2 medium)
¼ cup toasted sunflower seeds, for garnish (optional)

Vinaigrette
1 ripe avocado, peeled
2 tablespoons grainy Dijon mustard
2 to 3 tablespoons freshly squeezed lemon juice
2 tablespoons raspberry vinegar (or 1 tablespoon raspberry vinegar, 1 tablespoon balsamic vinegar)
6 tablespoons extra-virgin or regular olive oil

1. Remove the tough outer leaves of the romaine lettuce, and separate romaine, butter lettuce, and endive into leaves. Rinse well to remove grit. Drain well and dry thoroughly. (If not using immediately, wrap in a paper or kitchen towel and place in a plastic bag in the refrigerator to chill. If chilling more than 2 hours, dribble a few drops of water on the towel.)

2. Bring a medium saucepan filled with 3 inches of lightly salted water to a boil, and blanch the cauliflower, broccoli, and green beans separately for 1 to 2 minutes each. Remove with a slotted spoon (cooking water may be saved for soups). Drain the vegetables and let dry in a colander. (If preparing in advance, cover with plastic wrap and chill.)

3. Puree the avocado in a blender or food processor with the remaining vinaigrette ingredients and blend well. Transfer to a small container, cover, and chill for 1 hour.

4. Tear the lettuce and endive leaves into bite-size pieces and place in a salad bowl. Mix in the grated carrot. Coat the blanched vegetables with a little avocado vinaigrette, and place on top. Garnish with the sunflower seeds if desired and toss at the table. Pass the remaining dressing. (Leftover dressing may be stored in a closed container in the refrigerator for up to 2 days.)

Daniel's Schmaltz Herring Salad in Sour Cream and Apples

Serves 4 to 6

Although our mother never liked herring, for Dad it was almost as important as breathing. When we closed our eyes and breathed in the fragrance of this wonderful salad by chef Daniel Zach, we were catapulted back to our childhood, when our dad, Harry, would come home grinning ear to ear from the local Jewish bakery and "delicacies" shop, laden with fresh loaves of sliced seeded rye, old-fashioned Russian pumpernickel bread, smoked fish, and—if we had already devoured the homemade jars of our grandmother's—lots and lots of herring.

We like to serve this salad with bagels or homemade challah as part of a post-fast meal.

Salad
4 cleaned fillets of "Schmaltz" herring, preserved in oil
¼ cup chopped red onion
1 teaspoon capers, chopped
2 Granny Smith apples, peeled, cored, and thinly sliced
2 tablespoons chopped fresh Italian parsley

Dressing
2 to 3 tablespoons freshly squeezed lemon juice
1 tablespoon mayonnaise
Scant ½ cup dairy sour cream
¼ to ½ cup toasted walnuts or hazelnuts, chopped
Salt
Coarsely ground black pepper

1. Cut the herring into medium dice and set aside.

2. In a serving bowl, mix the onion, capers, apples, and parsley.

3. In a small bowl, whisk together the lemon juice, mayonnaise, and sour cream, and add to the onion mixture. Gently blend in the diced herring and toasted walnuts, cover, and let stand 1 hour at room temperature. Season with salt and pepper to taste before serving. (Or prepare the day before, store in a closed container in the refrigerator, and bring to room temperature before serving.)

Herring—A Jewish Tradition

Herring is a centuries-old tradition among Eastern European Jewish people, playing a significant part in the daily diet, both because it was cheap and because, before the advent of refrigeration, it stored well in so many forms.

By the 1920s Polish Jews consumed an average of one herring a day, most often as our American-born father loved to eat it: with boiled potatoes and black bread. Herring could also be baked, stewed, pickled, smoked, fried, or simply soaked and made into a salad.

Avocado Spread

Serves 3 to 4

Avocados, among the healthiest foods on earth, are revitalizing, and a good choice to add to a post-fast menu. Serve on challah, bagels, or "Birds of Prayer" Challah Rolls (page 156).

Note: Using yogurt in place of mayonnaise will render this dish dairy.

2 large ripe avocados, peeled and pitted
2 tablespoons mayonnaise or plain yogurt (or 1 tablespoon each)
⅓ cup finely chopped scallions
½ teaspoon salt
⅛ teaspoon freshly ground black pepper
1 to 2 teaspoons freshly squeezed lemon juice

Mash the avocados with a fork and mix in the mayonnaise and scallions. Season with salt, pepper, and lemon juice to taste. Cover with plastic wrap and store in the refrigerator.

Mozzarella and Sun-dried Tomato Topping

Serves 4 to 6

Instead of just making spreads for a bagel buffet, I often prepare this combination to serve as a topping. It's easy to make and also delicious with scrambled eggs or on pasta.

8 ounces mozzarella cheese
¼ cup finely chopped oil-packed
    sun-dried tomatoes

4 tablespoons snipped chives
2 tablespoons extra-virgin
    olive oil

Cut the mozzarella into very small dice and mix with the tomatoes and chives. Cover and let sit at room temperature for several hours, or chill overnight in the refrigerator. To prepare, add the olive oil. To serve, place a few tablespoons of the mixture on a toasted bagel or roll.

Nourishing and satisfying, a form of lentil-barley soup was made by our ancestors during this season thousands of years ago. Serve this stomach-soothing soup before the fast with Roasted Chicken Thighs with Honey, Olives, and Oregano (page 170), or at a post-fast meal.

1 cup pearl barley	4 sprigs fresh thyme
¼ cup lentils	3 quarts (12 cups) water
6 dried shiitake mushrooms	1 cup sliced fresh mushrooms
2 cups boiling water	⅔ cup finely chopped celery
2 bay leaves	⅔ cup grated carrot
1½ tablespoons sea salt	1 tablespoon extra-virgin
1 teaspoon pepper	olive oil (optional)

1. Pour the barley into a bowl and cover with water. Swish with your hand or a wooden spoon until the water is cloudy. Drain and repeat the process until the water stays clear. Pick over and rinse the lentils. Rinse shiitake mushrooms and soak in 2 cups boiling water until softened.

2. Place barley, lentils, bay leaves, salt, pepper, 2 sprigs of the thyme, and 12 cups water in a large soup pot and bring to a boil. Partially cover and cook over low heat for 30 minutes. Skim off any foam that develops on top.

3. Drain the shiitake but reserve the soaking water. Discard the hard stems and cut the caps into strips. Add to the soup pot along with the fresh mushrooms, celery, and remaining thyme sprigs. Cover and cook on low heat for an additional 30 minutes. Add the soaking water if the soup is too thick.

4. Off heat, stir in the grated carrot, cover, and let stand undisturbed for 5 minutes. Remove the bay leaves and thyme sprigs before serving. (To freeze, pack into 2 to 3 freezer containers, filled almost up to the top—ice crystals will develop if there is too much airspace—and freeze. Best used within 1 month.)

Two-Mushroom Lentil-Barley Soup with Thyme

Serves 12 to 14

Seven-Spice Vegetable Soup

Serves 6 to 8

This recipe, inspired by the very old Sephardic tradition of serving seven-vegetable couscous during the High Holidays to remind us of that mystical number, uses seven spices instead. It also contains a wealth of vitamins and minerals, carbohydrates, and complementary proteins to help nourish and sustain us through the long fast.

Serve with Raisin and Pine Nut Couscous (recipe follows) as a first course or vegetarian main course for a pre-fast meal, or as soup without couscous. If serving without couscous, dice or chop the vegetables.

8 cups water

3½ cups (6 medium, 1 pound) carrot, scraped or peeled, and thickly sliced

3 medium onions (1 pound), quartered

2 medium turnips (10 ounces), peeled and quartered

2 ribs celery, with leaves, cut into ½-inch slices

2 medium potatoes (10 ounces), peeled and cut into 6 pieces each

2 sticks cinnamon, or 1 teaspoon ground cinnamon

1 teaspoon ground cumin

½ teaspoon ground turmeric

2 bay leaves

3 allspice berries

1 tablespoon coarse sea salt, or to taste

½ teaspoon freshly ground black pepper, or more to taste

1 pound butternut squash, peeled and cut into 2-inch chunks

3 medium zucchini, sliced

1 pound cabbage, shredded (4½ cups)

2 cups cooked or canned chickpeas

2 sprigs cilantro or Italian parsley, plus chopped fresh cilantro or parsley for garnish

1. Bring the water to a boil in a large pot. Add carrots, onions, turnips, celery, celery leaves, potatoes, seasonings, and parsley or cilantro sprigs. Return to a boil, cover, and simmer over low heat for 30 to 40 minutes, until vegetables are tender.

2. Add the butternut squash, zucchini, cabbage, chickpeas, and cilantro or parsley. Press the vegetables down under the broth, and cook just until the butternut squash is tender, about 15 to 20 minutes. Do not overcook, or the squash will disintegrate. Remove the cilantro sprigs, celery leaves, and whole spices, if desired.

3. If serving with couscous, spoon the couscous onto a large deep-sided platter or onto individual serving plates. Make a well in the center and fill a few ladlefuls of vegetables. Pour a cup or two of hot stock over the couscous, garnish with chopped cilantro or parsley, and serve immediately.

Although traditional couscous made of semolina is tricky to prepare, instant couscous can be made in minutes. The addition of cinnamon, lemon juice, pine nuts, and golden raisins gives this side dish a special flair.

Serve with Seven-Spice Vegetable Soup (page 166) for a pre-fast meal, as a side dish, or even as a cold salad after the fast with the addition of chopped mint, baby peas, and finely chopped tomatoes. Add your favorite vinaigrette to taste.

Raisin and Pine Nut Couscous

Serves 6 to 8

1 pound (about 2½ cups) instant couscous
2½ cups boiling water
3 to 4 tablespoons freshly squeezed lemon juice
2 garlic cloves, sliced
¼ cup extra-virgin olive oil

1½ teaspoons cinnamon
½ cup pine nuts, toasted in a dry skillet until golden
1 cup golden raisins
1 teaspoon salt
¼ teaspoon freshly ground black pepper

1. Place the couscous in a bowl.

2. In a medium saucepan, combine water, lemon juice, garlic, oil, and cinnamon. Bring to a boil and simmer 1 minute.

3. Remove from heat and pour over the couscous. Cover and let stand about 5 minutes, until water is absorbed. Fluff with a fork. Mix in toasted pine nuts and raisins, cover, and let stand 5 minutes longer. Fluff the couscous again and season with salt and pepper and additional cinnamon or lemon juice if desired. (Couscous may be made ahead and stored in a covered container in the refrigerator. Reheat in the microwave.)

The Celery of the Bible

While for some of us celery conjures up images of the firm green ribs so at home in Waldorf salad, in biblical times it meant a different plant altogether. The celery, or *karpas*, of the Bible was *Gossypium herbaceum L.*, a very special member of the cotton family used for making delicate woven fabric—and inedible. While some Mishnaic commentators later identified the *karpas* of their time as parsley, others insisted that it was celery, or *Apium graveolens*. Whether it was the celery of the Waldorf salad, or its similar-tasting cousin, the celeriac, is anybody's guess.

Yom Kippur

167

Fragrant Chicken with Figs

6 servings

So simple yet so special, this dish combines three of the biblical Seven Species—figs, olive oil, and honey—to create nuances of flavor that are appealing, satisfying, and a delight to the senses. A nice accompaniment is Herbed Rice with Seasoned Currants (recipe follows).

1 3½- to 4-pound chicken, cut into pieces
12 dried figs
1½ cups Muscat wine (preferably Golan Moscato)
4 tablespoons honey
1 teaspoon cinnamon
1 teaspoon ground coriander
1 teaspoon salt, or to taste
½ teaspoon freshly ground pepper
2 bay leaves

1. Rinse the chicken and place in a bowl. Pour boiling water over to cover and let stand for 2 to 3 minutes. Using a sharp knife, scrape the skin to remove excess surface fat. Pat dry and set aside.

2. Rinse the figs and snip off the tops with a scissors. Place chicken and figs in a single layer in a large roasting pan.

3. In a small bowl, mix wine, honey, cinnamon, coriander, salt, pepper, and bay leaves, and pour over chicken. Cover and marinate for 1 to 4 hours in the refrigerator, turning occasionally.

4. Preheat oven to 375°F.

5. Roast, basting and turning occasionally, about 1 hour, until chicken is tender and brown. Serve chicken and figs with a little pan juice poured on top. (May be prepared several hours in advance and reheated in the oven. Leftovers may be reheated the next day in the microwave.)

Rice, the millennia-old symbol of fertility in many cultures, seems eminently appropriate for a meal that captures our desires for a good and productive year to come. The seasoned currants may be made days before, and refreshed with a little olive oil when needed, and the herbed rice is best served within 1 to 2 hours of preparation.

Note: Although you'll be using only a few tablespoons of the seasoned currants for this recipe, you can easily store the remainder in a closed container in the refrigerator, and add them as a garnish for salads, vegetable dishes, and meats in the weeks to come.

Seasoned Currants
(Makes about 1 cup)

1 cup currants, rinsed and dried
4 tablespoons extra-virgin
    olive oil
1 tablespoon balsamic vinegar
1½ tablespoons chopped fresh
    thyme
2 garlic cloves, pressed
Freshly ground black pepper

Rice

3 tablespoons extra-virgin
    olive oil
¾ cup finely chopped onion
    (about 1 large)
2 cups long-grain rice
3 cups boiling water
¼ teaspoon cinnamon
2 teaspoons salt
½ teaspoon freshly ground black
    pepper to taste
¼ cup pine nuts
¼ cup finely chopped fresh mint
¼ cup finely chopped fresh
    Italian parsley
3 to 4 tablespoons seasoned
    currants, for garnish

1. Prepare the seasoned currants first, so they'll have a chance to marinate. Mix the currants with the oil, vinegar, thyme, and garlic. Season with a generous amount of coarsely ground black pepper. Let stand at least 4 hours before serving.

2. To prepare the rice, heat 2 tablespoons of oil in a saucepan and sauté the onion on medium heat until golden, stirring occasionally. Add the rice and sauté for 1 to 2 minutes, until the grains are coated in oil. Pour in the boiling water. Season with cinnamon, salt, and black pepper and bring to a boil. Cover and simmer over low heat for about 15 to 20 minutes, or until water is absorbed. Remove from heat and let sit undisturbed for 10 minutes.

3. In a small pan, heat the remaining tablespoon of oil and sauté the pine nuts until golden. Using a fork, stir the pine nuts, mint, and parsley into the rice. Transfer to a serving bowl or platter and garnish with seasoned currants.

Roasted Chicken Thighs with Honey, Olives, and Oregano

Serves 6

All these ingredients could have been found in a biblical kitchen except, curiously enough, the chicken, which arrived in the Holy Land from India around Talmudic times, spreading from East Asia and the Mediterranean to the rest of the world. Over the centuries, it has become one of the most beloved foods in Israel.

This easy dish, adapted from a recipe from Hanoch Bar Shalom, derives its fabulous flavor not only from the unique combination of ingredients, but also from marinating overnight in the refrigerator.

12 chicken thighs

Marinade
½ cup red wine vinegar
¼ cup extra-virgin olive oil
1 tablespoon capers in brine,
   drained and coarsely chopped
6 garlic cloves, minced or
   pressed

2 tablespoons dried oregano
10 ounces pitted green olives
Salt
Freshly ground pepper to taste
½ cup flavorful honey (not clover)
½ cup dry white wine

1. Rinse the chicken thighs and place in a bowl. Pour boiling water over to cover and let stand for 2 to 3 minutes. Using a sharp knife, scrape the skin to remove excess surface fat. Dry and place in a nonreactive ovenproof dish.

2. In a bowl, mix all the ingredients for the marinade, except for the honey and wine. Pour over chicken. Cover and refrigerate for at least 8 hours, or overnight, turning occasionally.

3. Preheat the oven to 375°F. Turn all the chicken thighs skin side up, and pour the wine over. Brush the thighs generously with honey, and cover the pan with aluminum foil. Bake for 1 hour, remove cover, and continue baking till the tops are golden brown. (May be prepared several hours in advance and reheated in the oven. Leftovers may be reheated the next day in the microwave.)

In this dish, talented young chef Jeki Dabah has combined the tradition of eating fish at festive meals with a little sweetness to help us through the fast ahead.

Ask the fishmonger to debone the fish but leave it whole. If you're squeamish about seeing the fish head on the plate, ask the fishmonger to remove it as well.

Note: The pesto may also be used as a spread for sandwiches, or with cream as a topping for pasta.

Rainbow Trout Stuffed with Tomatoes and Honey-Basil Pesto

Serves 4

1¼ cups sliced blanched almonds

Honey-Basil Pesto
Leaves from 10 sprigs fresh basil, stems removed
¼ cup pine nuts, toasted in a dry skillet
2 tablespoons honey
½ cup extra-virgin olive oil
Salt
Freshly ground black pepper

Fish and Stuffing
2 cups peeled, seeded, and diced fresh or canned tomatoes
4 teaspoons minced or pressed garlic
4 rainbow or other trout, each approximately 10 ounces
Salt
Coarsely ground black pepper

Freshly squeezed lemon or orange juice
Fresh basil or Italian parsley, for garnish

1. Preheat the oven to 400°F. Place the sliced almonds on a baking sheet and toast for 10 minutes. Remove and set aside.

2. Make the Honey-Basil Pesto by grinding the basil leaves, pine nuts, ¼ cup of the toasted almonds, and honey together in a food processor. Add the oil through the feed tube and blend until a pastelike (pesto) consistency. Season with a little salt and pepper, and set aside. (May be prepared up to 1 day in advance and stored in a covered container in the refrigerator.)

3. Prepare the tomatoes for the stuffing: If using fresh tomatoes, remove the skin by dropping them into a pot of boiling water for 1 minute. Peel off the skin, cut off a slice from the top, discard the pulp (or use for soups or stews), and dice. If using canned tomatoes, drain well, slit open the tomatoes, remove the pulp, and dice. Mix the diced tomatoes and the garlic and set aside. (May be prepared an hour or two before using. Cover tightly and store in the refrigerator. Drain off any liquid that may accumulate at the bottom before using.)

4. Preheat the oven to 500°F. Line a large baking pan with parchment paper. Oil the paper.

5. Turn the fish over on their backs and rub the insides of each with ¼ of the pesto mixture. Stuff each fish with ¼ of the tomato-garlic mixture and ¼ cup of the remaining almonds. Season with salt and pepper. Press the sides of the fish together to close the opening. Place in the prepared pan, facing upright. Make a gentle incision along the width of each fish, just under the head (to make it easy to peel off the skin after baking).

6. Bake for 15 minutes. Remove from the oven, peel off the skin, and squeeze a little fresh lemon or orange juice on top of each fish. Garnish with thin strips of basil or chopped parsley and serve immediately on a bed of rice or couscous.

R ich in cumin, coriander, anise, and sesame seeds, four vitamin-and-mineral-packed spices that symbolize our prayers for a fertile year to come, these little rings are a traditional break-the-fast item among Jews from Syria, Libya, and Morocco. The addition of cumin, coriander, and anise is not unintentional, however, and probably comes from the ancient knowledge that these spices help appease the stomach.

Made in advance and stored in a closed jar at room temperature, they are best used within 1 week.

1 cup (2 sticks) unsalted butter or margarine, at room temperature	2 teaspoons *each* cumin seeds, small coriander seeds, and aniseeds
2 tablespoons vegetable oil	½ cup water
4 cups all-purpose flour	1 egg beaten with 1 teaspoon water, for brushing
1 tablespoon baking powder	Sesame seeds
1 teaspoon salt	

1. Preheat the oven to 350°F. Line a baking sheet with parchment paper or lightly grease the sheet.

2. In the bowl of an electric mixer on low speed, or using a wooden spoon, blend the butter or margarine with the oil. Add the flour, baking powder, salt, and spices. Gradually pour in the water to form a smooth dough. Do not beat.

3. To make the rings, form pieces of the dough into 4-inch-long cylinders, and seal the ends of each cylinder together. Brush with the beaten egg and dip in sesame seeds. Place 1½ inches apart on the prepared baking sheet, and bake until just golden, not browned. Remove from the oven and cool completely on a wire rack. Store in a tightly covered container.

Festive Mandelbrot

Makes 40

Mandelbrot was the first thing our family ate to break the fast. But the truth is, our mother baked it so often that there was always mandelbrot in the freezer to enjoy throughout the year.

Though *mandelbrot* actually means "almond bread" in Yiddish, there are many versions of it in Jewish homes; some are baked twice like a Jewish biscotti, while others, like our mother's, are stuffed with a delicious filling and baked once.

4 to 5 cups unbleached all-
    purpose flour
3 teaspoons baking powder
1 teaspoon salt
4 eggs
1 cup sugar
1 cup corn or safflower oil

Filling
½ cup sugar
1 tablespoon cinnamon
2 tablespoons unsweetened
    cocoa powder
1 cup finely chopped walnuts,
    pecans, or hazelnuts
½ cup apricot jam or orange
    marmalade

1. Sift together 4 cups flour, the baking powder, and salt, and set aside.

2. In the bowl of a mixer, beat eggs until thick. Add sugar gradually. Beat in oil. Gradually beat in flour mixture until dough is smooth and firm, adding more flour as necessary, until the dough leaves the side of the bowl. Make into a ball, cover with plastic wrap, and chill for 1 to 2 hours.

3. Preheat the oven to 375°F. Line a baking sheet with parchment paper. Lightly grease paper.

4. Remove the dough from the refrigerator, and transfer to a lightly floured work surface. The dough will still be slightly sticky. Knead in a little more flour until easy to work with. Divide the dough in half.

5. Lightly flour a rolling pin and roll out half the dough to form a 12-by-16-inch rectangle, a little more than ⅛ inch thick.

6. For the filling, mix together sugar, cinnamon, and cocoa.

7. Sprinkle the dough with half the cinnamon-sugar mixture and half the nuts and dot one of the long sides of the rectangle with jam, about 1 inch away from the bottom. Roll up from the long side (so the jam is in the center), pinch the edges closed, and place the roll seam side down on the prepared baking sheet. Tuck the edges under. Repeat with the other half of the dough.

8. Bake for about 30 to 35 minutes, until lightly browned. Cool and cut into ½- to ⅓-inch slices. Store in a covered cookie jar or freeze for up to 3 weeks.

Food writer Elinoar Rabin always keeps these delicate festive little almond cookies tucked away in the freezer, and serves them straight to the table with no defrosting necessary. They may be used to break the fast or as a dessert at a pre-fast meal. Mix these cookies with a fork—no mixer required.

½ cup egg whites (from 2 large eggs)
½ cup sugar
½ teaspoon vanilla extract or 1 teaspoon Amaretto

½ pound sliced blanched almonds (about 2⅔ cups)

1. Preheat the oven to 350°F. Line a baking sheet with parchment paper.

2. In a bowl, whisk the egg whites lightly with a wire whisk (do not beat), then mix in the rest of the ingredients. Transfer teaspoonfuls of the mixture to the prepared sheet, leaving 1½ inches between cookies. Flatten with the back of a spoon or a fork.

3. Bake about 8 minutes, or just until the cookies are golden and firm in the center. Let cool just slightly on the baking sheet, then carefully remove and store in a tightly sealed container or in the freezer.

Sutlage

Jerusalem Star of David Rice Pudding

Serves 8 to 10

Ⓓ

Rice pudding has always been considered a comforting dish, and is a wonderful dessert and gentle way to break the fast. A beloved part of Jerusalem's Sephardic cuisine, long-cooked creamy *sutlage* is not only rice pudding, but rice pudding decorated with the Star of David on the top. Perhaps that's the reason that during the siege of Jerusalem in 1948, Jerusalemites were so determined to make it, they used dry milk powder.

There are different recipes for *sutlage*—some with rice flour, some with rose water, some even with jam—but real Jerusalem *sutlage*, according to Gil Hovav, who gave us his grandmother's recipe, "will always be decorated with a Star of David made of cinnamon. That's the most important thing."

Sutlage may be made the day before (without the Star of David on top) and reheated. Decorate with the Star of David just before serving.

1 cup risotto or short-grain rice	1 to 2 tablespoons grated orange zest, or ½ tablespoon grated lemon zest
1½ cups water	
5 cups milk	
2 cups heavy cream	Cinnamon
½ cup sugar	

1. Place the rice and 1½ cups water in a medium saucepan. Bring to a boil, lower heat, cover, and cook over low heat for 20 minutes, or until the water is absorbed.

2. In the meantime, mix the milk and heavy cream in a separate saucepan, and heat but do not boil.

3. Boil water in the bottom of a double boiler. Transfer the cooked rice, milk mixture, sugar, and orange zest to the top of the double boiler. Mix well. (If there is not enough room for the milk and heavy cream, do not fill the pot up to the top. The remaining liquids can be added as the liquids in the pan evaporate.) Cook, partially covered, for 1½ hours, stirring occasionally. If the liquids in the pan evaporate, add more hot milk and cream.

4. After 1½ hours, when the mixture has achieved a pudding-type consistency, cover and turn off the heat. Keep over the bottom of the double boiler. Let the pot stand covered another hour (the rice will continue to cook and absorb liquids during this time).

5. Transfer to small individual bowls or goblets, cover with plastic wrap (the wrap should not touch the pudding itself), and let chill in the refrigerator at least 4 hours, or overnight.

In the meantime, make a Star of David stencil: Use a ruler to draw two hollowed-out triangles, and glue them one atop the other in opposite directions to form the classic Star of David shape. (The Star of David should be small enough to fit within the circumference of the individual bowls or goblets.)

6. Just before serving, hold the stencil over the rim of each bowl and sprinkle cinnamon through it to make a Star of David. Serve immediately.

Honey-
Sautéed
Pineapple

Serves 6

Sometimes even master chefs appreciate something simple. We got this idea from Yonatan Roshfeld, who suggested it as an easy refreshing dessert for a pre– or post–Yom Kippur meal.

3 large fresh pineapples, peeled
6 star anise
1 cup wildflower honey

4 to 6 tablespoons freshly
    squeezed lemon juice
Coarse salt

1. Cut the pineapples lengthwise into quarters. Trim the cores if desired.

2. Heat a large nonstick skillet and toast the star anise for 1 minute. Add the honey, lemon juice, and pineapple. Cook over medium heat for 5 minutes, adding a pinch of salt just before the end of cooking time.

3. Transfer the pineapple to a serving platter or divide among 6 individual dishes, and pour the sauce (including the star anise) over the top. Serve immediately.

. . . hold the festival for your God for seven days . . .
for God will bless your crops and all your undertakings,
and you shall have Nothing but joy.
    —**Deut. 16:15**

Send rain . . . to nurture flowers and plants, . . .
renew the earth and bless its produce. Hosanna!
    —**From the *Hoshana Rabbah* liturgy**

Sukkot

The Season of Our Rejoicing

The very evening after Yom Kippur ends, the blunt sounds of the tap-tap-tap of the hammer begin to fill the air in Jewish neighborhoods all over the world. For the coming of Sukkot, when Jews from all over ancient Israel made a pilgrimage to the Temple in Jerusalem, is heralded with the building of every conceivable version of that famous biblical hut known as the sukkah, bursting into bloom in the days before the holiday like a strange new plant.

The lovely sukkot of our own day, with their trellised roofs covered with palm fronds, are still constructed and decorated much the way they were over a thousand years ago: "With handmade carpets and tapestries, nuts, almonds, peaches, pomegranates, branches of grape vines, oil, wreaths of ears of corn," as the Talmud says. Yet they had very humble and functional origins. In ancient times, farmers lived in the little huts out in the fields while they harvested their crops, and Sukkot, what is traditionally referred to as "the Festival of the Ingathering," was held once the crops were in, the grapes and figs dried under the summer sun, and the last of the first fruits brought to the Temple.

What's a Sukkah?

A hut? A tabernacle? A holy dwelling? It's nearly impossible to translate the word *sukkah* because it encompasses a host of meanings at once. The simplest definition is "hut," just like the little temporary shelters that farmworkers construct in the fields for rest, eating, and shade during harvest time. But for Jewish people around the world, that is only the beginning of the story of the sukkah.

The Bible instructs us to construct the sukkah to commemorate the protective shelters that God provided for the Israelites during their years of wandering in the desert (Lev. 23:43). For the mystics, though, the sukkah was not merely a flimsy shelter. For them it was a holy tabernacle where the Divine Presence dwelt, hovering in clouds of glory. The ultimate sukkah, they believed, would be a place of peace in which the righteous dwell, safe from all the cataclysms engulfing the world, feasting on the meat of that most massive of magical creatures, the Leviathan. And according to the Zohar, a kabbalistic text attributed to Rabbi Shimon Bar Yochai, the person who sits in this ultimate sukkah "inherits freedom for himself and for his children forever" (III: 103a).

In the sukkot we build, we also create a sacred space by the unique tradition of inviting *ushpizim,* "holy guests," from the ancient past. The Zohar sees each of the holy guests has embodying a different emanation of God. The patriarch Abraham embodies Loving-kindness; Isaac, Strength; Jacob, Beauty; Joseph, Foundations; Moses, Victory; Aaron, Acknowledgment, and King David, Sovereignty. Today, though, many people also invite the biblical matriarchs, personal heroes, and friends and relatives who are sorely missed.

Although most people fill the (crowded) space in their sukkah with a table and chairs, our family looks forward each year to sitting in the sukkah as their ancestors did—cross-legged on the floor. The space is decorated with rugs and extra-large pillows, the lighting comes from a lamp and many candles, and the food is served on a large wooden plank that runs down the center. (Just in case, there are even a few chairs for any unexpected friend or *ushpizim* that may come along.)

Arriving on the heels of Yom Kippur, which meant that the nation had cleaned its spiritual house, Sukkot—known as *HaHag*, The Festival—was the true end of the Judgment period, a time to begin to pray for rain in the winter to come. For unlike Egypt, where water for crops came from the Nile, ancient Israel depended upon plentiful rainfall to refill the rivers and streams, to irrigate the crops, and, most important of all, to drink. And while some scholars have likened the festival to even earlier rites intended to rekindle the sun at the autumn equinox, for the ancient Israelites, in thanksgiving for their bounty, it was the season of rejoicing before God.

The guideline in planning a Sukkot menu is convenience—dishes that can easily be transported from home to hut without much ado, such as a hearty soup or casserole made with vegetables that reflect the autumn harvest. Stuffed foods made with a chopped or "beaten" filling are traditional fare on Sukkot (when we "beat" willow branches in our prayer for rain), as they are on Yom Kippur (when we "beat" our breasts to acknowledge our sins) and Purim (when we "beat" our feet at the mention of Haman's name). This chapter offers many varieties of meat- and grain-stuffed foods to choose from.

Sukkot Recipes

Appetizers

Ladder Challah **P**
Sesame-and-Herb-Stuffed Grape Leaves **P**
Pastelikos b'Milui Gomo (Little Meat-and-Pine-Nut-Stuffed
    Puff Pastries) **M**
Mushrooms Stuffed with Wheat Germ, Sunflower Seeds,
    and Fresh Herbs **D**

Soups

Spiced Butternut Squash Soup **D**
Bubby Rose's Old World Cabbage Borscht with Ida's Vegetarian
    Option **M** **P**
Albondigas Soup with Jerusalem Artichokes **M**

Main Dishes

Chicken with Olives and Sumac **M**
Chicken with Dates, Olive Oil, and Twelve Garlic Cloves **M**
Sweet-and-Sour Stuffed Cabbage (*Prakkes* or *Holishkes*) **M**
Ran Shmueli's Lamb Stew with Chickpeas, Pomegranates,
    Squash, and Cilantro **M**
The Balaban Family's *Vareniki* **P**

Vegetarian Main Dishes or Side Dishes

Cumin-Scented Stew of Red Lentils, Chickpeas, and Pumpkin **P**

Fresh Corn Casserole **D**

Green Lentils and Barley with Tomatoes and Rosemary **P**

Back-to-the-Roots Casserole **P**

Salads

Multicolored Roasted Pepper Salad **P**

Bulgur and Pomegranate Seed Salad **P**

Sweet-and-Sour Cabbage and Carrot Slaw **P**

Jerusalem Artichoke Salad with Crispy Garlic and Rosemary **P**

Desserts

Pears in Red Wine and Spices **P**

Phyllis's Famous Carrot Cake **D** **P**

Zucchini Tea Cake with Cinnamon and Nutmeg **P** **D**

Cranberry Apple Crumb Pie **D**

Tofu Brownies **P**

The ladder shape was once a recurring theme in Jewish holiday challah baking, particularly in Poland and Central Europe. Symbolizing the hope that our prayers would "climb to heaven" or would "ascend and be exalted" like the angels in Jacob's dream, ladder challot could appear on the first or second day of Rosh Hashanah, Yom Kippur, or Sukkot. Some versions had an entire challah shaped like a ladder, and others a little ladder shape placed on top of a spiral challah.

And although no exact number of rungs was customary, those of a mystical bent often made seven, symbolizing the kabbalistic belief that God passed through seven spheres in the creation of the world, which was in this very same month of Tishri.

Ladder Challah

Makes 1 challah

Round Challah with Seven Seeds dough (page 124) or "Birds of Prayer" Challah Rolls dough (page 156)

Lightly beaten egg mixed with 1 teaspoon water

Poppy seeds or sesame seeds

1. To make the Ladder Challah, use the Rosh Hashanah challah recipe, which contains both white and whole-wheat flours, or the "Birds of Prayer" Challah Rolls, a dough made with white flour only that is somewhat easier to sculpt into delicate shapes.

2. Divide the dough in three parts—two for the sides of the ladder and the third for the rungs. Line a large baking sheet with parchment paper, and lightly grease.

3. Roll the two side pieces into logs, about 2 to 2½ inches thick and almost the length of the baking sheet, and place them about 6 inches apart. Divide the remaining dough into seven pieces, and roll seven smaller logs for rungs (make fewer rungs if you like). Arrange the rungs equidistant along the "ladder," tuck the edges underneath, and pinch them in place. Secure with a little beaten egg if the dough seems dry. Brush the dough with an egg wash, and sprinkle with poppy or sesame seeds. We like to let the children decorate each rung with a different topping, like sunflower, poppy, pumpkin or sesame seeds, poppy seeds, dried rosemary, rolled oats, black sesame seeds, or even zahtar. Not only is it fun and breathtakingly beautiful, but it also gives each rung a different color and taste. Bake according to the instructions for the dough you have chosen.

Sesame-and-Herb-Stuffed Grape Leaves

Serves 6 to 10

At the beginning of the grape harvest in late summer, when the grape leaves were still young, tender, and bright green, our ancestors pickled them in brine, in order to store them for stuffing and seasoning in the months to come. I've bought just-picked fresh grape leaves in the souk (pronounced *shuk* in Hebrew) in Israel in summer, and carefully blanched them individually in boiling salted water, in order to freeze them—until taught by my dear Arab friend Laila Tukhi of Jaffa to simply freeze in bundles and drop in boiling water for a few seconds to clean and defrost. Since most urbanites don't have access to fresh grape leaves, the pickled variety found in appetizing stores and supermarkets are a fine substitute.

It may seem like a time-consuming process, but your guests will tell you that nothing can compare with these homemade rice-stuffed grape leaves and their unique combination of fresh herbs and sesame seeds, simmering in a lemon-olive broth. But I had never rolled so *many* grape leaves until preparing for the bat mitzvah of my oldest daughter, Yarden. My sister Miriyam and I took bowls of my filling over to Laila's, who brought out frozen grape leaves that had been picked from her own garden, and enlisted the aid of her sister. By the end of the evening we had rolled more than two hundred, which were later consumed in minutes. Stuffing and rolling grape leaves together made the cultural differences between us fade, as we worked joyously toward a common goal.

½ pound pickled grape leaves

Filling
Scant 3 cups water
1 teaspoon salt
1½ cups long-grain white or
    brown rice
2 teaspoons canola or corn oil
1 tablespoon extra-virgin
    olive oil
⅓ cup finely chopped onion
1 garlic clove, minced
¼ cup chopped fresh Italian
    parsley
¼ cup chopped fresh dill

2 tablespoons chopped fresh
    mint
¼ teaspoon ground turmeric
1 tablespoon sesame seeds,
    toasted
Salt
Freshly ground black pepper
    to taste

Cooking Sauce
½ cup water
½ cup extra-virgin olive oil
⅓ cup freshly squeezed lemon
    juice

1. Drain the pickled grape leaves and rinse in batches under cold water. Transfer to a large bowl and gently separate the leaves. Cover with cold water and soak for 15 minutes to help remove some of the salt.

2. Bring a scant 3 cups water to a boil with 1 teaspoon salt. Add the rice and canola oil. (If using brown rice, rinse in a colander before cooking.) Stir once with a fork, then cover and cook over low heat according to package directions or until water is absorbed. The rice should be just tender and not mushy. Check toward the end of cooking to make sure the water has not evaporated completely and the bottom is not sticking. Transfer to a colander and rinse under cold water to stop the cooking process. Drain well.

3. Heat 1 tablespoon olive oil over medium-low heat and add the onion and garlic. Cook, stirring occasionally, until tender. Off heat, stir in the cooked rice, parsley, dill, mint, turmeric, and sesame seeds, and mix well. Season with salt and black pepper. (Don't oversalt, because the grape leaves are still somewhat salty.)

4. Place one leaf at a time on a clean surface with the veins facing up. (There are often torn or damaged leaves among the good ones; set these aside.) Clip off the stem with kitchen shears or a knife. Place a heaping tablespoon of the rice mixture in a line at the center bottom of the leaf, fold in the sides, and roll up tightly from the bottom. Place seam side down on a plate. Repeat with the other leaves and the rest of the filling.

5. Mix together ½ cup water, ½ cup extra-virgin olive oil, and ⅓ cup lemon juice. Pour a tablespoon or two of the mixture in the bottom of a wide, shallow pot. Line the bottom with any torn grape leaves. Place the stuffed grape leaves in the pot seam side down, packing them tightly one next to the other in a circular pattern, starting from the edge of the pot and working inward. If there is another layer, separate the layers with torn grape leaves.

6. Pour the remaining cooking sauce over equally. Set a heatproof plate on top to keep the grape leaves in place during cooking. Bring to a boil on medium heat, then cover and simmer for 20 to 25 minutes, or until the leaves are tender but not soft. Make additional cooking sauce if necessary and add to the pot as needed. Serve warm or at room temperature.

7. Store the stuffed grape leaves in a tightly covered container in the refrigerator. Pour a little olive oil over them if they look dry. They are best eaten within 3 to 4 days.

Pastelikos b'Milui Gomo

Little Meat-and-Pine-Nut-Stuffed Puff Pastries

Makes about 25

*P*astelikos are stuffed pastries made with puff pastry, and there are as many varieties as ways to prepare them. There are several types of fillings as well, but *Pastelikos b'Milui Gomo* is considered the most festive of all. An age-old Jerusalem pastry, this recipe was given us by food writer Gil Hovav, who was born and grew up in that city. Not only are they in keeping with the theme of eating stuffed foods on Sukkot, but are also wonderful to snack on while spending time in the sukkah.

12 ounces frozen puff pastry

Filling
5 tablespoons vegetable oil
2½ cups finely chopped onion
8 ounces ground beef
1 egg yolk, beaten
⅓ cup pine nuts

½ teaspoon salt, or more to taste
½ teaspoon freshly ground pepper
⅓ cup hot water

1 egg beaten with 1 tablespoon water
Sesame seeds, for sprinkling

1. Remove the pastry sheets from the freezer package and separate. (Wrap unused sheets in plastic wrap and return to the freezer.) Thaw in the refrigerator for 4 hours for individual sheets and 6 hours for an entire package. Alternately, cover each sheet with a piece of plastic wrap and thaw at room temperature for 30 minutes.

2. Make *gomo* filling: Heat the oil in a large skillet and cook the onion on medium heat until golden, stirring frequently. Add the meat, salt, and pepper, and continue to cook, breaking the meat up with a fork, over medium-low heat for 10 minutes, until the meat is no longer red.

3. Add the hot water, cover, and cook over low heat for 30 minutes, or until the meat is tender.

4. Remove the cover and continue to cook until all the liquids evaporate. This may take 35 to 40 minutes, and Gil advises patience. Stir occasionally. The result should be little crumbs of meat and onions. Keep the heat at medium-low or the meat will burn. Remove from heat and let stand 15 minutes. If the meat is still oily, drain it in a wire-mesh colander. Add the beaten yolk and the pine nuts, and mix well.

5. Roll out one sheet of pastry at a time to a ¼-inch thickness on a lightly floured board. Keep the rest of the dough in the refrigerator. If the dough has become too soft to work with, chill it in the refrigerator again for a few minutes. Cut out 3-inch circles from half the dough with a 3-inch round cookie cutter or a glass, and cut out the same number of 2-inch circles from the rest of the dough.

6. Preheat the oven to 350°F. Line a baking sheet with parchment paper. One at a time, place a 3-inch circle in the palm of a slightly cupped hand, closer to the fingers, forming a little cup with the dough. Use the other hand to stuff the cup with 1 or 2 teaspoons of filling, and place a smaller circle on top. Pinch the edges tightly and turn it over, cap facing down, on the prepared baking sheet. Repeat with the rest of the dough. Brush the finished *pastelikos* with the beaten egg, and sprinkle with sesame seeds.

7. Bake about 40 minutes, or until the *pastelikos* are golden brown. Serve hot or at room temperature with a vegetable salad cut into as tiny dice as possible.

Mushrooms Stuffed with Wheat Germ, Sunflower Seeds, and Fresh Herbs

Makes 16

Healthy and winning, these superb stuffed mushrooms, reflecting the Sukkot tradition of stuffed foods (page 181), have received rave reviews as hors d'oeuvres, appetizers, and even as a vegetarian main course. We make them with whole toasted sunflower seeds, which may be chopped if you prefer.

16 large mushrooms
3 tablespoons grated Parmesan, Cheddar, or Monterey Jack cheese
1 large garlic clove, minced
⅓ cup finely chopped onion
1 tablespoon sunflower seeds, toasted
1 cup toasted wheat germ
1 tablespoon chopped fresh Italian parsley
1 teaspoon chopped fresh oregano or basil
2 tablespoons butter, melted
Salt
Freshly ground black pepper
6 tablespoons extra-virgin olive oil (or olive oil mixed with other oil)

1. Preheat the oven to 350°F. Grease a large oven-to-table casserole or baking pan with 2 tablespoons olive oil. Set aside.

2. Rinse or clean mushrooms and gently remove the stems. (Set aside the stems for use in a soup or an omelette.) In a small bowl, mix together the remaining ingredients, except for the olive oil. Use a spoon to pack the filling into the mushroom caps and the back of the spoon to press it down.

3. Place the stuffed mushrooms in the prepared pan. Pour the remaining oil equally over the top.

4. Bake for 20 minutes, or until golden. Serve warm.

This deep orange autumn soup with its creamy light texture is a delicious way to start a holiday meal. Vary the recipe by substituting pumpkin or sweet potatoes for the squash, or mix them if desired.

4½ pounds butternut squash, pumpkin, or sweet potatoes

3 tablespoons extra-virgin olive or other oil

⅔ cup chopped red onion

5 garlic cloves, minced

1 teaspoon sweet paprika

1 teaspoon *Baharat* (page 299) or ground allspice

½ teaspoon chili pepper (optional)

2 teaspoons salt

6 cups water (or more to cover)

½ cup crème fraîche, yogurt, dairy sour cream, sweet cream, or half-and-half

⅓ cup mixed fresh finely chopped cilantro and Italian parsley, or all parsley

1. Scrub butternut squash well and cut off the stem end. Slice in half lengthwise and remove the seeds and strands. Peel and cut into cubes.

2. In a large soup pot with cover, heat the oil and sauté the onion over medium heat, stirring occasionally, until transparent and lightly golden. Add the garlic and sauté 1 minute. Add the butternut squash cubes, paprika, *Baharat,* chili pepper, and salt. Add 6 cups water (or just enough to cover the squash), and bring to a boil. Cover and cook over medium-low heat about 30 to 40 minutes, until squash is fork-tender.

3. Remove from heat and puree in batches in a blender or food processor. Return to the pot and cook an additional 5 minutes (or reheat gently just before serving). Divide among bowls, and garnish each with a tablespoon of crème fraîche, yogurt, sour cream, or a zigzag pattern of cream, and garnish each with 1½ teaspoons of the cilantro-parsley mixture, or pass small bowls of different toppings and let guests garnish their own.

Bubby Rose's Old World Cabbage Borscht with Ida's Vegetarian Option

Serves 16 to 20

Beets were a basic foodstuff in the diet of Russian, Lithuanian, Ukrainian, and Polish Jews, along with cabbage and sorrel (*schav*). Those who came from the Pale of Settlement (an area of formerly Polish territory delineated by Catherine II in 1791 as the only place in the Russian Empire in which Jews would be allowed to live) grew these easily stored vegetables in the patches of land in front of their homes, harvested them in autumn, and stored them in a cold cellar for use throughout the winter months. An inexpensive commodity, beets were more often than not made into borscht, brined into *russel* (a vinegar substitute for Passover), and made into *Eingemacht* (page 46), a sweet preserve that graced the Passover table.

A popular Sukkot food among many Jews of Russian and Polish heritage, borscht is a hot and nourishing meal-in-a-bowl, made with beets, cabbage, and a *shtikele fleisch* (piece of meat) when you have one. The rich taste and fragrance of Bubby's borscht still linger in our memories.

3 pounds flanken, trimmed of fat, or 2 pound boneless beef chuck (from the chuck end of the short ribs)

1 pound marrow bones (or other bones)

4 quarts water

1 tablespoon salt

1½ cups chopped onion

3 cups coarsely grated beets

1 large cabbage, cut in half, cored, and thinly sliced or chunked (about 8 cups)

6 to 8 small potatoes, peeled and quartered

1 28-ounce can crushed tomatoes

1 6-ounce can tomato paste

½ cup packed brown sugar

1 head of garlic, peeled and minced or pressed

Pinch of salt

1 teaspoon freshly ground black pepper

1. Wash meat and bones thoroughly and remove excess surface fat. In a large pot, mix 4 quarts water with 1 tablespoon salt, and bring to a boil. Place meat and bones in the pot and cook over medium heat about 15 minutes, skimming off any foam that appears on top. Lower flame, cover, and simmer for 30 minutes.

2. Remove the cover, and add the onion, beets, cabbage, potatoes, tomatoes, and tomato paste, stirring after each addition. Add sugar, and pepper, partially cover, and cook on a medium flame for 1 hour. Stir all the ingredients again, taste the borscht, and adjust seasoning. Keep the water level as was at the beginning, adding boiling water as necessary to maintain the level. Remove the cover and simmer for another hour.

3. Remove and slice meat, and serve either in the borscht or on a serving platter.

4. Mix the minced or pressed garlic with a pinch of salt and ½ to 1 teaspoon of black pepper. Pass the dish around and let guests add garlic as desired.

For Ida's Vegetarian Option

Eliminate meat and bones. Instead of using raw onion, sauté the 1½ cups chopped onion in ¼ cup olive oil about 15 to 20 minutes, until golden brown. Add to 4 quarts of lightly salted water along with the rest of the ingredients, and cook, partially covered, for 1½ hours. Do not add additional water if the broth diminishes.

The Four Species and the Jewish Rain Dance

Bless with rain those who pour their hearts like water
Open the earth to Your blessing of water.

—from the *Hoshana Rabbah* liturgy

To try to assure that rain will fall in the coming season, the Talmud describes a unique ritual done on Sukkot, based on the "four species" described in the Bible: "And you shall take for yourselves on the first day the fruit of the goodly tree, branches of palm trees, the boughs of leafy trees, and willows of the brook and you shall rejoice before the Lord your God seven days" (Lev. 23:40).

The "fruit of the goodly tree" has been defined as the citron, or *etrog;* the branch, or *lulav,* as the frond of the date palm; the "leafy tree" as the myrtle, and the "willows" as . . . the willow. But how are they connected to rain?

One interpretation came from the sage Maimonides, who believed that the four species commemorated the joy of the Israelites in leaving the desert, "where neither fig, grape, nor pomegranate could grow, and where there was no water to drink," and in entering a fertile land "of fruit-bearing trees and rivers."

Sukkot worshipers still wave the four species in an elaborate pattern in six different directions, as if to every nation of the world and every corner of the universe. Making circuits around the synagogue—seven circuits on the festival's seventh day called "The Great Hosanah" (*Hoshana Rabbah*)—the congregation pleads that rainfall will not be withheld, thirst will be satisfied, the soil will be saved from "curses . . . crops from destruction, flocks from disease, and souls from terror." Though those words were written thousands of years ago, how apt they still are today.

Albondigas Soup with Jerusalem Artichokes

Serves 8

*A*lbondigas means "little meatballs" in Ladino, and they are the highlights of this classic Jerusalemite poor person's soup. Easy and inexpensive to prepare and very filling, the soup has a lemony hot-and-sour broth, Jerusalem artichokes (or potatoes), and little meatballs made of lamb. According to Gil Hovav, who gave us this recipe, every Jerusalemite has his own fond memories of *albondigas* soup. He remembers it as one of the attractions on his family's Sukkot table.

Soup

¼ cup olive oil

4 cups water

2 cups chicken broth

4 heaping cups large-cubed peeled Jerusalem artichokes (or potatoes)

½ cup chopped fresh Italian parsley

1 tablespoon coarsely ground black pepper, plus more to taste

Juice of 1½ to 2 lemons

Albondigas

2 slices plain white bread, crusts removed

8 ounces lean ground lamb

Salt to taste

½ cup chopped fresh Italian parsley

1 egg yolk beaten with juice of ½ lemon, plus more to taste

Cooked white rice, for garnish (optional)

1. Heat the olive oil in a large skillet and carefully add the water and chicken broth (the liquids may spatter). Add the cubed Jerusalem artichokes, parsley, black pepper, and lemon juice. Mix well and bring to a boil.

2. Prepare the *albondigas:* Wet the bread under running water, squeeze out, and grate into a bowl. Add the lamb, salt, and parsley, and mix well. Form Ping-Pong–size balls.

3. When the soup is boiling and the artichokes are partially cooked, gently slip in the meatballs. Make sure that the soup is constantly boiling, or the *albondigas* will fall apart. When all the meatballs are in the soup, continue to cook for 2 minutes. Lower heat, cover, and cook on a gentle boil for 20 minutes, until the artichokes are soft but have not fallen apart.

4. Remove from the heat and quickly stir in the beaten egg and lemon juice. (The soup will change color.) Taste and add additional lemon juice or black pepper (the soup should be hot and sour). Serve immediately with 2 tablespoons cooked rice in every bowl, if desired.

The berries of the sumac plant ripen in fall just before the first of the olives, and have been dried and stored in Israel since biblical times to impart a lemonlike flavor and slight red tinge to foods. Today sumac is popular throughout the Middle East, especially in zahtar, an ancient blend of sumac, sesame seeds, salt, and hyssop (a relative of wild marjoram), often sprinkled on bread, cheeses, and salads.

Note: Both sumac and zahtar are available in Middle Eastern groceries.

Chicken with Olives and Sumac

Serves 4 to 6

1 chicken (3½ to 4 pounds), cut in 6 to 8 pieces

⅓ cup all-purpose flour

¾ teaspoon each ground cumin and ground coriander

¼ teaspoon *each* ground ginger and garlic salt

1 teaspoon turmeric

Freshly ground black or white pepper to taste

½ cup canola or extra-virgin olive oil

2 to 3 tablespoons extra-virgin olive oil

2 large red onions, halved and thinly sliced (2 cups)

3 to 3½ teaspoons ground sumac

2 cups boiling water

2 cups pitted green olives

1. Rinse the chicken and place in a large bowl. Cover with boiling water and let stand 2 to 3 minutes. Drain. Using a knife, scrape the skin to remove excess fat and pinfeathers (especially around the wings and legs). Rinse and pat dry with a paper towel.

2. In a small bowl, mix the flour, cumin, coriander, ginger, garlic salt, turmeric, and pepper, and pour onto a plate. Dip each chicken piece in the flour mixture, shaking lightly to remove excess flour.

3. Heat the ½ cup oil in a large skillet and sauté half the chicken pieces until golden brown on both sides. Remove and place on a paper towel. Strain the oil and sauté the second batch of chicken. Set aside while preparing the onion.

4. In a Dutch oven or a large, wide pot with cover, heat 2 to 3 tablespoons olive oil and sauté the onion on medium heat until golden brown, stirring occasionally. Sprinkle 2 teaspoons of the sumac over the onion and mix well. Place the chicken on top, add boiling water and olives, and bring to a boil.

5. Cover and cook over medium-low heat for 1 hour, or until the chicken is tender. Remove the cover, sprinkle the top with the remaining sumac, and serve.

A Weave of Dates

We never much liked packaged dates when we were growing up in America. They always seemed too mushy, dark, and gloomy in comparison with Good & Plenty or a jawbreaker. It wasn't until we tasted fresh dates for the first time—in Israel—that we were mesmerized. From the crunchy round yellow dates at Rosh Hashanah to the plump, elongated, and tender shiny brown fresh dates of Sukkot, this was a new date experience to be reckoned with, and in the years to come, mounds of fresh dates at the open-air market would make us salivate.

Famed for its towering grandeur, its feathery foliage, and, most of all, for its delectable fruit, the date palm (*tamar*) was cultivated in ancient Israel at least as early as 1600 B.C.E. Its form also inspired artists and coin makers of old, and the Book of Kings describes the Holy Temple in Jerusalem as being carved with "cherubim and palm trees and open flowers." Women of the Bible even bore the name Tamar, as did the daughter of King David. The prophet and judge Deborah gave the tree even more prominence when she turned the shade of a palm tree into her official courthouse.

But the date palm was far more than a source of the fast food of ancient times. Its leaves and fibers were interwoven for rooftops, dwellings, mats, baskets (like that of Moses in the bulrushes), animal traps, and mattresses, and the pits of its fruit were used as fuel or ground for fodder. Whether fresh, dried into hard cakes, or made into honeylike syrup or beer (a favorite drink in Babylonia), dates provided basic sustenance, particularly in areas where the desert sands, or last winter's drought, provided little else to eat. A good source of calcium, potassium, and niacin, along with a range of other vitamins and minerals, dates were also an important source of calories for our ancestors.

Yet dates didn't always flourish in the Holy Land. During the thirteenth-century Mameluke Conquest, invading armies ravished the trees, and after successive wars and neglect in the centuries that followed, almost all natural date trees in Israel had become extinct.

All that changed when brave Ben-Zion Yisraeli from Kibbutz Kinneret risked his life in the 1930s and 1940s to return the date palm to its natural habitat. On a secret mission to Kurdistan, Iran, Egypt, and Iraq—and with the help of Jews from those countries—he managed to (illegally) collect saplings of date trees, carry them on tortuous roads to the Holy Land, and plant them from the Kinneret (the Sea of Galilee) in the north to Yotvata in the south. Thanks to his courage and determination, we have glorious dates in Israel today.

Chicken with Dates, Olive Oil, and Twelve Garlic Cloves

Serves 4 to 6

M

Autumn is the harvesttime for pomegranates and figs, and also the season for fresh dates that could be made into a syrup that most Jewish scholars agree was what the Bible meant by "honey." The date palm holds special significance for Muslims as well, who believe that the Divine Hand created it from the dust remaining after He created human beings.

Whether you've liked them in the past or not, you're bound to begin a romance with the date after eating it in this tempting combination. Use large Medjool dates if they are available, and if not, use a drier type of date rather than the soft pitted kind, which tends to fall apart with long cooking.

1 chicken (3½ to 4 pounds), cut into 6 to 8 serving pieces
1 cup extra-virgin olive oil
12 large garlic cloves, unpeeled
1 cup thinly sliced onion, separated into rings
1½ cups whole, pitted Medjool dates, packed
½ cup honey
3 tablespoons red wine vinegar
1 tablespoon balsamic vinegar
1 cup dry red wine
Coarse salt
Freshly ground black pepper to taste
2 sprigs fresh thyme
2 sprigs fresh rosemary

1. Rinse the chicken and place in a bowl. Cover with boiling water and let stand for 1 to 2 minutes. Using a sharp knife, scrape the skin to remove excess surface fat. Dry and place in a nonaluminum roasting pan.

2. Mix together the rest of the ingredients except for the thyme and rosemary, and pour over the chicken. Break the thyme and rosemary sprigs into large pieces and spread over the chicken. Cover tightly with plastic wrap and marinate in the refrigerator for at least 4 hours, or overnight, turning occasionally.

3. Preheat the oven to 350°F. Turn the chicken skin side up in the roasting pan.

4. Bake, covered, for 45 minutes, turning once. Remove the cover and continue baking about 15 minutes, until golden brown on both sides. Serve with long-grain rice or couscous, tinged with turmeric for a golden-yellow color.

Sweet-and-Sour Stuffed Cabbage

Prakkes *or* Holishkes

Makes about 24

In Jewish culinary tradition, any dish incorporating the harvest of one's own region is appropriate for Sukkot, particularly those featuring a number of ingredients within, since they symbolize the plenty with which we are blessed, and for which we hope in the new year to come. Made with vegetables available in that season, stuffed cabbage, with its chopped ("beaten") filling recalling the ceremonial beating of the willow branches (page 181), is a centuries-old Ashkenazic dish served on Sukkot.

Prakkes (a.k.a. *holishkes, golubtzes*) is possibly the oldest Yiddish name for stuffed cabbage, and probably derives from the Greek name *yaprak* for stuffed grape leaves. One of the best-known dishes in the traditional Jewish repertoire, *prakkes* come in different styles: In Hungary, Slovakia, and Romania they are made with a savory sauce, usually with the addition of fresh sauerkraut and lots of garlic (the tomato arrived quite late in Hungary). Our mother always made the Russian version: "No onions in the meat, no ginger, bay leaves, and certainly no sauerkraut."

1 very large or 2 medium heads
   cabbage
1 cup cooked rice

Cooking Sauce
¼ cup vegetable oil
1½ cups thinly sliced onion
1 28-ounce can crushed tomatoes
3 cups boiling water
1 teaspoon paprika
2 teaspoons salt
½ teaspoon freshly ground
   black pepper

Juice of 1 lemon
1 Granny Smith apple, peeled,
   cored, and chopped
¼ cup honey
½ cup raisins

Stuffing
2 pounds lean ground beef
1½ teaspoons salt
½ teaspoon freshly ground
   black pepper
2 eggs

1. Rinse and remove center core of the cabbage using a sharp knife. There are two ways to prepare the cabbage leaves for cooking:

- Drop the cored head of cabbage into a large pot of boiling lightly salted water, cover, reduce heat, and cook about 10 minutes, until the outer leaves are tender. Stick a large fork or knife in the hollowed-out center of the cabbage to steady it and gradually remove the softened outer leaves one by one, and place in a deep bowl. Continue to cook the cabbages repeating the process until there are about 24 softened leaves. (Avoid trying to stuff the smaller leaves near the center. Chop and save these and any torn leaves for the bottom of the pot. If there are fewer than 24, no matter. The rest of the stuffing can be used to make meatballs, which seem to go over better with children than the stuffed cabbage does.) Coarsely chop the remaining part of the cabbage and save for the sauce.

- Wrap and freeze the cored cabbage at least 24 hours and thoroughly defrost. (The leaves should be tender when thawed.) Whichever method is used, use a sharp knife to cut off part of the hard rib on the back of the leaves, so they may be easily folded.

2. Soak rice in boiling water to cover for 15 minutes and drain.

3. While rice is soaking, make the sauce: Heat the oil in the bottom of a large pot, and sauté the onion on medium heat until golden. Top with the coarsely chopped cabbage. Add the remaining sauce ingredients. Bring to a boil, lower heat, and simmer, covered, while you prepare the stuffing.

4. In a large bowl, mix the ground beef with the drained rice and the remaining stuffing ingredients. Stir the mixture thoroughly.

5. Place a leaf, rib side down, on a work surface or in the palm of your hand, and fill with a heaping tablespoon of the stuffing mixture. Roll the bottom "flap" over the stuffing, fold the sides toward the center, and roll up firmly from the bottom. Repeat with the rest of the leaves and stuffing.

6. Drop the stuffed cabbage seam side down in the pot, in layers, sprinkling the raisins in between. If there is any stuffing left, form meatballs and tuck them around and on top of the stuffed cabbage leaves. The sauce should just cover the top layer; if not, add a 6-ounce can of tomato sauce and an equal amount of water.

7. Bring to a boil, cover, and cook over medium-low heat for 1 hour. Taste and adjust seasonings, and continue to cook for an additional hour. Place on a platter, or divide among individual plates, and ladle some of the sauce on top.

Ran Shmueli's Lamb Stew with Chickpeas, Pomegranates, Squash, and Cilantro

Serves 6

A well-known culinary personality in Israel, Chef Ran Shmueli thinks Sukkot is a grand time for a sumptuous stew, particularly when it contains both the flavors and colors of the season. In Israel he makes this same casserole with lamb shanks, and serves it with Jerusalem Artichoke Salad with Crispy Garlic and Rosemary (page 208) and Pears in Red Wine and Spices (page 211) for dessert.

2¾ pounds shoulder of lamb, cut into cubes, or 3¼ pounds shoulder of lamb with bone, cut in 1½-inch slices

½ cup olive oil, or more if needed

2 cups sliced leeks

2 cups thickly sliced carrots

2½ cups peeled and chunked celeriac (about 1 medium)

½ cup chickpeas, soaked overnight (see Note)

10 garlic cloves

1½ cups dry red wine

⅓ cup pomegranate syrup (pomegranate molasses)

Salt

Coarsely ground black pepper

2 bay leaves

1½ pounds butternut squash, peeled and cut into chunks

⅔ cup chopped fresh cilantro

Couscous or white rice

Seeds of 2 pomegranates, for garnish

1. Rinse the lamb chunks or slices, and pat dry. Cut away excess fat and discard.

2. Heat the olive oil in a large skillet and sauté the lamb until browned (use more olive oil if necessary). Remove from the pan and set aside.

Add the leeks, carrots, and celeriac to the same pan, and sauté to a golden color.

3. Add the uncooked chickpeas and 2 of the whole garlic cloves, and sauté an additional 5 minutes. Pour in the wine and pomegranate concentrate, and continue to cook for 10 minutes. Season with salt and black pepper.

4. Add the bay leaves, remaining garlic cloves, and lamb, and stir gently to blend. Add boiling water to cover the meat. Cover and cook over medium-low heat for about 1 hour for chunks and up to 1½ hours for slices, or until tender. Stir occasionally.

5. Add the squash and cilantro, and cook 10 minutes longer. Serve hot on a bed of couscous or white rice and garnish with the pomegranate seeds.

Note: If using canned chickpeas, drain and add them with the butternut squash.

Bay Leaves in the Biblical Kitchen

He plants a bay tree, and the rain nourishes it.

—Isa. 44:14

Our ancestors were fond of the easily accessible fragrant bay leaves, which kept so well when dried, and undoubtedly used them in soups, stews, and grain dishes. Even the fruit of the bay tree, the drupe, was utilized to season wine.

Medicinally, bay tree fruits and leaves were made into an infusion for use as a carminative, and to expel intestinal worms. Today we can use them not only in cooking, but also to preserve food; a dried leaf or two in a canister of grains, legumes, or flour will help prevent infestation.

The Balaban Family's Vareniki

Makes 45

*V*areniki might be called the Ukrainian version of ravioli, since they are a stuffed pasta usually made with an egg dough. The filling may vary from potatoes and meat to cheese or fruit. The Yiddish author Mendele Mocher Sforim (1836–1917), the grandfather of modern Yiddish literature and the father of modern Hebrew literature, records that dairy *vareniki* were popular at Hanukkah, while our dear friend Nissan Balaban, of Russian heritage, recalls that they were always on the Sukkot table. He remembers: "When I was little, my family would always hold a competition on Sukkot. My mother would make between eighty and one hundred *vareniki* at a shot, and then my father and the three Balaban sons, and sometimes my friend David, would compete to see who could eat the most." Needless to say, none of the Balaban sons grew up to be skinny!

2 pounds potatoes
9 tablespoons vegetable oil
1 cup finely chopped onion
1 teaspoon salt
½ teaspoon freshly ground
    black pepper

3½ cups unbleached all-purpose
    flour
4 eggs
Generous pinch of salt

1. The traditional way to boil potatoes is by cooking them in lightly salted boiling water until tender. While this method is certainly handy, it does result in extensive vitamin loss. If you're not going to use the cooking water in bread baking (always make sure the yeast is well mixed into the flour, or the salt in the water might kill it), you might want to try another method:

2. Steam potatoes in a steamer basket or add the potatoes to 2 inches of boiling water in the bottom of a pot, cover, and steam on medium-low heat for 30 minutes, or until all the potatoes are tender. Check the water level occasionally, and add more boiling water if necessary. Stir from time to time for more even cooking. Cool slightly, then peel. (To microwave: Place potatoes in a covered microwave-safe casserole with ¼ cup water. Cook on high for 10 to 12 minutes, stopping after 6 minutes to stir the potatoes.) Drain, cool slightly, and put through a ricer or mash with a fork. Do not use the food processor.

3. Heat 6 tablespoons of the oil in a skillet and sauté the onion, stirring occasionally, until nicely browned but not burned. Add the onion and the oil the onion was sautéed in to the mashed potatoes, and season with salt and pepper. Mix well.

4. In a food processor, mix the flour, 2 tablespoons of the oil, eggs, and pinch of salt. Process using on/off pulses until the mixture forms a dough around the blade. Remove, roll into a ball, and wrap in plastic wrap. Let rest 20 minutes.

5. Using a lightly floured board and rolling pin, roll the dough to $1/8$-inch thickness. Use a 3-inch-diameter cup or pastry cutter to cut circles, and fill each one with 1 heaping teaspoon of the filling. Fold over to form a semicircle and pinch closed. (The pinch marks create a decorative edge.)

6. Bring a large pot of lightly salted water to a boil and add the remaining 1 tablespoon oil. Drop in half the *vareniki* and cook for 5 minutes. Carefully remove with a slotted spoon and transfer to a buttered plate. Cook the remaining *vareniki* in the same manner.

7. If not serving immediately, mix in a little oil or butter so they don't stick together. Store covered in a lightly greased bowl in the refrigerator for up to 3 days. Reheat in a covered container in the microwave with a little broth, water, or butter.

Cumin-Scented Stew of Red Lentils, Chickpeas, and Pumpkin

Serves 4

To the mystic mind, the lentil symbolizes wholeness, and the red lentil recalls the biblical stew that was so fragrant and tempting that it won Jacob his birthright. For a meal-in-a-bowl with complementary protein, serve atop steamed white or brown basmati rice.

1 cup red lentils, picked over and washed
3 cups water
1 cup thinly sliced carrots
⅔ cup onion, coarsely chopped
2 cups cubed pumpkin or butternut squash (see Note)
½ teaspoon salt, or more to taste
1½ teaspoons ground cumin
3 garlic cloves, pressed
½ teaspoon ground turmeric
½ teaspoon freshly ground black pepper
2 teaspoons freshly grated, peeled gingerroot, or ¾ teaspoon ground ginger
1 15-ounce can chickpeas (garbanzos), drained
⅓ cup chopped fresh Italian parsley or cilantro, for garnish

1. Place the lentils in a pot and cover with water. Swish them around, drain, and cover with fresh water. Repeat until the water remains clear. Transfer to a pot with 3 cups of water and bring to a boil. Partially cover, and cook over low heat for 15 minutes, stirring occasionally.

2. Add the vegetables, spices, and chickpeas. Partially cover, and cook 30 minutes, or until the stew is thick. (If it is too thick, or if serving over rice, add boiling water and thin to desired consistency. Let cook 5 minutes longer. If it is too thin, remove the cover and slightly raise the heat to evaporate excess water.) Stir gently from time to time during the cooking process. Divide among bowls and garnish with parsley or cilantro.

Note: To facilitate peeling the pumpkin or butternut squash, make a few slits in a large piece of pumpkin (or the bottom bulb of the squash) and place in the microwave for 2 to 3 minutes, or until just soft enough to peel. Cool slightly, remove seeds, peel, and cut into chunks.

The word *corn* is used frequently in English translations of the Bible, leading many people to believe that it grew in Israel in biblical times. Although (cold) canned corn is a staple at every Israeli school, scout, and family outing, and hot ears of corn are sold at every soccer and basketball game, this vegetable was a gift of the New World to the Old, born in the Americas and reaching Israel only in the modern era. The biblical *corn* is actually a centuries-old word for grain.

One of our favorite family dishes, this corn casserole is easily assembled and may be prepared in advance and frozen if desired. For a spicy version, use green *Tzoug*, a fiery cilantro-hot pepper condiment found in the refrigerator section of stores selling Middle Eastern items, or serve the casserole with a chopped tomato-cilantro salsa laced with balsamic vinegar and garnished with capers.

Fresh Corn Casserole

Serves 12

4 cups fresh or frozen corn
    kernels
1 cup (2 sticks) butter, melted
1 cup cornmeal
2 cups dairy sour cream or plain
    yogurt
2 teaspoons salt

4 eggs
4 tablespoons mildly hot *Tzoug*
    (page 299) or Tabasco sauce
    (optional)
2 cups diced Monterey Jack or
    Swiss cheese

1. Preheat the oven to 350°F. Grease a 13-by-9-by-2-inch baking pan.

2. If using fresh corn, start at the tip of the ear and run a sharp knife straight down to the stem, leaving just a bit of pulp behind on the cob to prevent detaching tough cob fibers as well.

3. Place 2 cups fresh or frozen corn kernels, melted butter, cornmeal, sour cream, salt, eggs, and *Tzoug* in the food processor and process until almost smooth. Fold in remaining corn and diced cheese and pour into the prepared pan.

4. Bake for 40 to 45 minutes, or until golden brown and a toothpick inserted in the center comes out clean. Do not overbake.

5. Serve immediately, or bring to room temperature, cover tightly, and refrigerate or freeze.

Variation

Substitute 1 to 2 cups frozen mixed vegetables, thawed and drained, for an equal amount of the corn. Grind half with the corn in the food processor, and fold the other half in with the diced cheese.

Green Lentils and Barley with Tomatoes and Rosemary

Serves 6

*C*ooking up a pot of lentils and barley stored from the spring harvest, our biblical ancestors might have seasoned their stew with rosemary growing wild in the hills. It's a shame they never got to taste it with tomatoes, however, since these were only introduced to the Old World from the Americas in the sixteenth century.

A tasty side dish, this also makes a satisfying vegetarian main dish with or without grated cheese sprinkled on top. (This recipe is adapted from the 1971 edition of *The New York Times Natural Foods Cookbook,* by Jean Hewitt.)

½ cup French green (or regular green) lentils
⅓ cup pearled barley
¼ cup extra-virgin olive oil
½ cup chopped onion
½ cup chopped celery
2½ cups drained canned whole tomatoes, cut into pieces

1¾ cups water
2 tablespoons honey
Salt
Freshly ground black pepper
⅛ teaspoon dried rosemary (optional)
½ cup shredded carrots

1. Place the lentils and barley in a pot and cover with water. Swish them around, drain, and cover with fresh water. Repeat until the water remains clear.

2. Heat the olive oil in a medium-size pot and sauté the onion until tender. Add celery and cook 5 minutes longer. Add remaining ingredients except the carrots. Bring to a boil, cover, and simmer for 25 minutes, stirring occasionally.

3. Remove cover, stir in the carrots, and cook 5 minutes longer, or until lentils and barley are tender. Serve hot.

Soothing and delicious, this is one of the easiest recipes to make (once you've prepared the vegetables), and one of the healthiest to eat. Even finicky children, like my daughter Zohar, like it!

2 cups sliced carrots

1 cup chopped onion

2 cups cubed peeled celeriac

1 cup diced peeled turnip

1½ cups cubed unpeeled new
   potatoes

1 cup cubed peeled sweet potato

2 cups water

2 bay leaves

3 to 4 tablespoons Dijon mustard
   (with seeds, if possible)

2 garlic cloves, crushed

2 to 3 tablespoons extra-virgin
   olive oil

Salt

Coarsely ground black pepper
   to taste

Fresh Italian parsley, cilantro, or
   dill, for garnish

1. In a medium-large pot, mix the vegetables with the water and bay leaves and bring to a boil. Cover and cook on low heat for 20 minutes, or until the vegetables begin to soften. Stir gently during cooking, adding a little boiling water if necessary.

2. Stir in the mustard and garlic and cook an additional 10 minutes, or until the vegetables are done. Remove from heat and stir in the olive oil and seasonings. Sprinkle with the desired herb just before serving.

Multicolored Roasted Pepper Salad

Serves 4

This recipe combines colorful peppers with the fruit of the olive and life-renewing seeds to create a fitting accompaniment to a Sukkot meal. Orange, red, and yellow peppers not only reflect autumn colors, but they are also excellent sources of vitamin A. Although peppers were gifts from the New World, they have assimilated so well into Israeli cuisine you would swear they were Sabras.

While most roasted pepper salads may seem labor-intensive and time-consuming, this one is especially quick and easy. It is best made fresh and served without previous refrigeration, but may be prepared several hours ahead and stored in an airtight container in the refrigerator, brought to room temperature, and refreshed with a little olive oil. Add seeds just before serving.

Note: Recipe can be easily doubled or tripled. You may want to use less salt and pepper for greater quantities. For a spicy version, add ½ to 1 teaspoon *Tzoug* (page 299) to the olive oil.

8 assorted bell peppers: red, green, yellow, and orange
¼ cup extra-virgin olive oil
4 garlic cloves, thinly sliced or pressed
1 to 2 tablespoons fresh oregano, basil, or cilantro leaves

¼ teaspoon salt
½ teaspoon coarsely ground black pepper
Lightly toasted sunflower, sesame, or pumpkin seeds (or a combination), for garnish

1. Preheat the broiler and line a baking sheet with parchment paper. Cut the peppers in half and remove the stems, seeds, and white ribs. Place cut side down on the baking sheet.

2. Place under the broiler, close to the heating element. Broil until black spots appear on the peppers. Shift the peppers on the baking sheet occasionally if some are browning faster than others. (It is unnecessary to either turn the peppers or blacken them completely.)

3. Turn off the heat, and let sit a few minutes until cool enough to peel. Peel off only the blackened parts (peeling off all the skin will make them soggy). Cut into 1½-inch squares and place in a bowl.

4. Mix the rest of the ingredients together and gently stir into the peppers. Garnish with the seeds just before serving.

Bulgur and Pomegranate Seed Salad

W heat symbolizes basic sustenance, and the pomegranate both physical and creative fertility—among our most fervent wishes for the New Year.

Serves 4

1½ cups fine or medium bulgur wheat

1½ to 2 cups boiling water

1 to 1½ cups finely chopped fresh Italian parsley

¼ to ⅓ cup finely chopped fresh mint (optional)

¼ cup extra-virgin olive oil

1 tablespoon freshly squeezed lemon juice, or more to taste

Salt to taste

Seeds from 1 medium pomegranate

1. Place the bulgur in a bowl. Cover with 1½ cups boiling water and let stand, covered, until the bulgur is softened. (If using medium bulgur, you may find that it is still a little hard. Add the extra ½ cup of boiling water only if necessary, cover, and let stand an additional 10 minutes.) Fluff with a fork. Blend in the parsley and mint.

2. In a small bowl, whisk together olive oil, lemon juice, and a generous pinch of salt. Pour over the salad, and mix in the pomegranate seeds (save some to garnish the top) with a fork. Serve on a large serving plate or divide among smaller plates. Garnish with additional pomegranate seeds and serve.

The pomegranate i᛫ as we all know a beautiful tree, valued for its fruit and flowers; it is also a fortunate tree, having power against evil spirits, and none need fear to sleep beneath its boughs.

—**Grace M. Crowfoot,**
From Cedar to Hyssop: A Study in the Folklore of Plants in Palestine, **1932**

Jerusalem Artichoke Salad with Crispy Garlic and Rosemary

Serves 6

Although Jerusalem artichokes are a native American food, many Jerusalemites would swear they had a Jewish incarnation, since they have been used in that city for as long as anyone can remember. For Ran Shmueli, who gave us this recipe, it makes a perfect complement to the Lamb Stew with Chickpeas, Pomegranates, Squash, and Cilantro (page 198) he serves every Sukkot.

The key to success in this recipe is not overcooking the chokes; cook until just tender, and sauté chokes briefly, mixing with tongs rather than a spoon.

4½ pounds Jerusalem artichokes
2 heads fresh garlic, separated
   into cloves
¾ cup extra-virgin olive oil
4 to 5 sprigs fresh thyme, broken
   into small sprigs
1½ teaspoons yellow mustard
   seeds, toasted in a dry skillet

Coarse (kosher) salt
Coarsely ground black pepper
   to taste
2 to 3 tablespoons freshly
   squeezed lemon juice

1. Peel the Jerusalem artichokes, and as you do, drop them into a bowl of cold acidulated water to prevent them from discoloring. Steam the chokes in a steamer basket, or bring a large pot of lightly salted water to a boil. Drop in the artichokes and lower heat. Cook until they are almost tender but still slightly firm. (Do not overcook, or the finished dish will be mushy.)

2. Chokes may also be cooked, one pound at a time, in a covered dish in the microwave. Cook 5 minutes on maximum heat and check several for doneness (they do not cook evenly). Drain well, pat dry, and transfer to a bowl. Cover with plastic wrap and chill thoroughly.

3. In the meantime, peel the garlic and slice lengthwise. Heat ½ cup olive oil in a small skillet and sauté garlic until the slices are golden and crispy, stirring frequently to prevent burning. Remove with a slotted spoon, and place on a paper towel to absorb excess oil. Place the broken thyme sprigs in a small dish and cover with the oil left in the pan. Set aside.

4. Cut the chilled chokes lengthwise into long slices. Heat 1 tablespoon olive oil in a heavy skillet over medium-high heat. Sear chokes quickly in batches until browned and crispy, adding the remaining 3 tablespoons olive oil as needed.

5. Transfer the sautéed chokes to a serving plate, and combine with marinated thyme and olive oil mixture, toasted mustard seeds, and salt and pepper to taste. Mix gently with a wooden spoon to avoid mashing the chokes.

6. Let stand 30 minutes, and then add the lemon juice. Mix gently, garnish with the crispy garlic, and serve.

Simhat Beit Ha-Shoeva: The Great Water Festival

He who has not seen the rejoicing at the place of the
water-drawing has never seen rejoicing in his life.

—BT, Sukkah 50a

It's on Sukkot, says the Talmud, that the world is "judged for water" (BT, Rosh Hashanah 16a), and in the days of the Second Temple, the most ecstatic event of the Sukkot holiday was the seven-day "water-drawing festival," illuminating every courtyard and corner of Jerusalem with huge candelabras and glowing torches.

According to the Mishnah, a golden flagon was filled with water from the freshwater spring of Siloam, south of the city, and carried to the southern "water" gate that led to the vast expanse of the Temple Mount. As the shofar resounded, the Levites filled the plaza, singing psalms and playing trumpets and flutes, harps and cymbals, for five of the festival's days.

Even the imposing sages of the Talmud are described as having a mighty good time—singing, dancing the night away, and juggling wineglasses, eggs, and even lit torches. "He who has never seen the rejoicing of the water festival," says one ancient commentator, "has never seen rejoicing in his life."

This festival of fire and water has echoes in ancient rites all over the world. Theodore Gaster believes it was originally a magical rite whose purpose was to rekindle the sun at the time of the autumn equinox and hail it when it rose at dawn. A vivid parallel is the 1,200-year-old Buddhist fire-and-water festival known as Omizutori—"water-drawing"—still enacted each year at the Todaiji Temple in Nara, Japan.

Sweet-and-Sour Cabbage and Carrot Slaw

Serves 6

Simple but winning, this salad lasts for several days in the refrigerator, and may also be served on Purim, when, as for Sukkot, sweet-and-sour foods are traditional. The custom may actually derive from the fact that to help preserve festive autumn and winter dishes, such as Bubby Rose's Old World Cabbage Borscht (page 190) and Sweet-and-Sour Stuffed Cabbage (page 196), vinegar was often added, and raisins or other sweeteners were used to help counterbalance the acidity.

Easy to transport, this slaw also makes a tasty addition to a Lag b'Omer picnic as an alternative to a mayonnaise-based salad.

Salad
1 medium head cabbage, thinly
    sliced
2 cups coarsely grated carrots
3 garlic cloves, crushed
¾ cup minced scallions (white
    and tender part of green)
1 red bell pepper, seeded and
    thinly sliced

Dressing
1 cup apple cider or champagne
    vinegar
½ cup sugar
¾ cup canola oil
1 teaspoon salt
¼ teaspoon freshly ground
    black pepper

1. Mix the ingredients for the salad in a large glass or nonreactive bowl.

2. Place all the ingredients for the dressing in a saucepan, and bring to a boil. Boil for 1 minute and pour over the salad.

3. Let marinate, covered, at room temperature for at least 2 hours before serving. Store covered in the refrigerator for up to 1 week.

The beautiful burgundy color of these delicious pears reminds us of the amazing colors of autumn in Massachusetts. Light but deeply flavorful, they make a perfect dessert for almost any holiday meal.

This superb recipe was given to us by Ran Shmueli, who also makes it with quince, and who suggests serving either fruit with a tart sorbet.

Serves 6 to 8

6 to 8 large ripe but firm pears
2 cups sugar
1 small lemon
1 small orange
1 bottle (750 ml) dry red wine
½ cup honey
15 whole cloves
4 cinnamon sticks
8 star anise
10 cardamom pods
1 to 2 tablespoons brandy
 (optional)
1 cup walnuts, coarsely
 chopped

1. Put the sugar in a wide pot with shallow sides.

2. Peel the pears, cut in half, and core. Place in the pot with the sugar and stir to coat over low heat.

3. Cut the lemon and orange in half, squeeze in half of their juice, then cut unpeeled fruit into small chunks and add to the pot. Stir in the wine, honey, and spices.

4. Bring to a boil, cover, and cook over low heat until the pears are tender, basting them occasionally with the sauce during cooking. They should be a deep burgundy color.

5. Remove the pears from the sauce, increase the heat to high, and reduce the liquid until thickened into a light syrup, stirring occasionally. Remove from heat and strain. Taste and add brandy to taste. Cover and keep warm.

6. To serve, place two pear halves on each serving plate, pour over the warm syrup, and garnish with a tablespoon of chopped walnuts.

Phyllis's Famous Carrot Cake

Makes one 10-inch cake (serves 8 to 10 nongreedy people)

It seems that I was actually the first person to popularize the carrot cake in Israel when I published an earlier version of this recipe in my first (Hebrew) cookbook, *Vegetarian Feast,* in 1981. Today it is one of the most popular cakes served at the Carmel Forest Spa, and versions of it are sold commercially. The original is still the best, but for a new flavor dimension, you might want to substitute Yemenite Hawaiij for sweets (page 300) instead of the cinnamon.

Though carrot cake seems eminently appropriate for harvesttime, it is also suitable for Purim, Tu b'Shvat, and Shavuot.

Note: Without the topping, this carrot cake will stay fresh and tasty without refrigeration for 3 to 4 days. Refrigerate if using the topping: Chill the cake in the refrigerator until the topping is firm, then cover and keep in the refrigerator for up to 5 days. Cake can also be frozen. Bring to room temperature before serving.

4 medium carrots (to yield 3 cups grated)
1¼ cups safflower or canola oil
2 cups turbinado sugar, or 1 cup granulated sugar and 1 cup packed light brown sugar
4 eggs
1 cup whole-wheat flour
1 cup unbleached all-purpose flour
2 teaspoons ground cinnamon
2 teaspoons baking powder
1 teaspoon baking soda

Topping Ⓓ
1 8-ounce package cream cheese, at room temperature
1 to 2 tablespoons honey
1 teaspoon vanilla extract
1 to 2 tablespoons plain yogurt (optional)

1. Preheat the oven to 350°F. Cut a circle and a 3-inch-wide strip of parchment paper to fit the bottom and sides of a 10-inch springform pan. Affix with a dab of of butter or oil. (If no parchment paper is available, grease the pan well with butter or margarine.)

2. In a food processor using the medium disk, shred the carrots, remove, measure, and set aside.

3. Wipe out the bowl with a paper towel. Change to the metal mixing blade and blend the oil, sugars, and eggs. Sift the dry ingredients together and add to oil mixture. Process for a minute or two, until smooth. Return the carrots to the processor and blend briefly, so they don't lose their character altogether. Pour into the prepared pan.

4. Bake for about 45 to 55 minutes, or until a toothpick inserted in the center comes out clean. Transfer to a wire rack and let cool in the pan before carefully removing the outer ring. Slip a knife under the cake, to help detach it from the metal bottom. Remove the parchment paper if it sticks to the bottom of the cake, and place on a serving plate.

5. In a bowl, blend the cream cheese with honey to taste and vanilla. Use a little yogurt to thin it out if necessary. Spread mixture on top of the cake.

Variation

For a rich, sinfully good topping, bring 4 ounces cream cheese and ¼ cup (½ stick) butter to room temperature, and blend in a bowl. Beat in 1½ cups sifted confectioners' sugar and a few drops of vanilla extract, blending well. Spread over the top of the cake. Chill for 5 minutes to slightly firm up the sauce, and serve.

Zucchini Tea Cake with Cinnamon and Nutmeg

Makes one 16-by-5-by-4-inch loaf or 20 to 24 cupcakes

A sweet way to enjoy the end of the autumn harvest, this cake is somewhat denser than carrot cake, and makes a perfect accompaniment to an afternoon cup of coffee or tea.

Bake in a loaf pan and sprinkle with confectioners' sugar, or make as cupcakes and spread with Quick Chocolate Frosting (recipe below).

4 medium zucchini (to yield 3 cups grated zucchini)
1½ cups unbleached all-purpose flour
1½ cups whole-wheat pastry flour
1 teaspoon baking soda
¼ teaspoon ground nutmeg
2 teaspoons ground cinnamon

1 cup vegetable oil
2 eggs
1 cup packed dark brown sugar
1 cup packed light brown sugar or granulated sugar
1 tablespoon vanilla extract
1 cup chopped walnuts
Confectioners' sugar, for dusting

1. Preheat the oven to 350°F. Grease and flour a 16-by-5-by-4-inch loaf pan, knocking out excess flour, or line the bottom and sides with parchment paper, and affix with a little butter or oil. For cupcakes, line two 12-cup muffin pans with paper baking liners.

2. Grate the zucchini coarsely (you should have 3 cups). Put in a strainer placed over a bowl and press with the back of a wooden spoon, to remove excess moisture. Let stand 10 minutes. Sift the flours, soda, and spices together.

3. In the bowl of an electric mixer or food processor, blend the oil, eggs, sugars, and vanilla until combined. Add the flour mixture and blend well. Mix in the grated zucchini and nuts, and pour into the prepared pan.

4. Bake for 45 to 55 minutes (about 18 to 25 minutes for cupcakes), or until a toothpick inserted in the center comes out clean. Let cool slightly and sprinkle the top with a light dusting of confectioners' sugar passed through a strainer. Slice and serve warm, at room temperature, or toasted.

Quick Chocolate Frosting D

Place 7 ounces milk or bittersweet chocolate, broken into pieces, in a microwave-safe dish with 3 tablespoons butter. Cook for 1 to 2 minutes, until the chocolate is softened but not melted. Remove from the microwave, stir quickly to blend chocolate and butter, and spread on the cupcakes.

Apples and cranberries, so reminiscent of autumn flavors in America, were the inspiration for this recipe sent to my newspaper column in Israel one Sukkot by reader Elana Dror. Delicious—and easier than pie to make.

6 large apples (Granny Smith are best)

½ cup canned whole-berry cranberry sauce

½ teaspoon ground cinnamon

½ cup unbleached all-purpose flour

½ cup packed light brown sugar

½ cup rolled oats

½ cup (1 stick) cold butter, cut into cubes

1. Preheat the oven to 400°F. Grease a 9-inch pie pan with butter or margarine.

2. Peel, core, and dice the apples, or cut into eighths. Combine with the cranberry sauce and cinnamon. Pour mixture into the prepared pan.

3. In a small bowl, mix the flour, brown sugar, oats, and cold butter between fingers to form crumbs. Sprinkle evenly over the apples.

4. Bake for 35 to 40 minutes, or until golden brown on top.

5. Serve warm or cold with a fine vanilla ice cream, if desired.

Cranberry Apple Crumb Pie

Serves 6

Tofu Brownies

Makes 12

We've included these brownies in the Sukkot chapter because they're both a delicious (and pareve) dessert and a welcome snack for any *ushpizim* that happen to drop by. While the idea of brownies made with tofu may sound icky, these are actually rich, full of protein, and contain no cholesterol or saturated fat. They keep fresh for several days, but usually don't last that long!

We've tried these brownies both with the nuts inside (crunchier) and sprinkled on top (prettier). The choice is yours.

⅓ cup plus 1 cup unbleached all-purpose flour
⅔ cup water
½ pound tofu
1 cup packed dark brown sugar
1 cup granulated sugar
1 teaspoon salt

2 teaspoons vanilla extract
¾ cup unsweetened cocoa powder
½ cup corn or safflower oil
½ cup whole-wheat pastry flour
1 teaspoon baking powder
½ cup chopped walnuts

1. Preheat oven to 350°F. Line an 8-by-12-inch baking pan with parchment paper and grease the sides with oil or nonstick cooking spray.

2. In a blender or food processor, blend ⅓ cup all-purpose flour, water, and tofu until smooth. Pour into a large saucepan and heat over low heat, stirring constantly until thickened. Let cool to room temperature, then transfer to the bowl of a mixer or food processor. Beat in sugars, salt, and vanilla.

3. In a separate bowl, mix cocoa powder and oil. Add to the tofu mixture and blend well.

4. Sift remaining all-purpose flour, whole-wheat flour, and baking powder together and stir into the tofu mixture. Beat with a wooden spoon until smooth. Stir in the walnuts at this point, or save them to sprinkle on top, if preferred. Pour into the prepared pan.

5. Bake for 25 minutes, or until a knife inserted in the center comes out clean. Remove from the oven, let cool slightly, and cut into 12 brownies.

The Festivals
of Winter

Hanukkah

The Festival of Lights

In the wintry month of Kislev (mid-December) 165 B.C.E., just as the rains ceased, the crocuses blossomed like white candles all over the country. At this time too, when the olive-pressing season was almost over, an intrepid band of guerrilla warriors known as the Maccabees (their name actually an acrostic of the Hebrew, *Mi Kamocha b'Elim Adonai*—"Who among the mighty is like you, God?") fought their way to the Temple Mount in Jerusalem.

For three years, they had been battling both the Syrian-Greek king Antiochus Epiphanes—who had tried to crush the cultural diversity of the peoples under his control—as well as the Hellenized Jews, those "collaborators" among their own people who were eager to assimilate to a Greek way of life. Despite the odds, the Maccabees succeeded in liberating the Temple and ridding it of the idols Antiochus had erected. But as one tradition later claimed, when they sought to rekindle the golden seven-branched Menorah that stood in the Temple, the Maccabee victors discovered they had only one small cruse of olive oil left with the high priest's stamp, enough to last a single day.

Wonder of wonders, the oil lasted for eight days—enough time to bring newly pressed oil to the Temple in Jerusalem. With music and psalms of thanksgiving, carrying branches of trees and palm fronds, and flaming torches so brilliant they lit up Jerusalem, the Maccabees decided to celebrate the eight-day Sukkot holiday, which they had missed that year because the Temple had been defiled. From then on, they instituted a winter holiday to commemorate the rededication of the Temple, and encouraged their brethren around the country and as far away as Egypt to make it an annual celebration.

Centuries later, though, what actually happened in those days and why later generations should celebrate was no longer very clear. For the dynasty of leaders and high priests that the Maccabees established had become controversial and corrupt, and the Temple they rededicated had lasted less than three hundred years, only to be razed by the Romans after the ill-fated Bar Kochba revolt in 132 C.E. From that time on, the Jewish people had been thrust into exile.

All that was left of the old winter holiday was a vague memory of a "Festival of Lights," a phrase coined by the historian Josephus 250 years after the original event, as a result of those flaming torches.

Settled in Babylonia—the site of modern-day Iraq—the rabbis of the Talmud found themselves asking, "What's Hanukkah?" And just as it seemed that only a miracle could put an end to exile, so the crux of the rabbis' answer became the legendary "Miracle of the Oil." And to this day at Hanukkah time, it's that story we sing about as we light our Hanukkah menorahs.

No one knows the details of the first Hanukkah foods, but we can surmise that the Maccabees and their warriors depended on lentils, chickpeas, wheat, and barley, dried after the previous spring's harvest, mixed with vegetables they had preserved from the fall harvest, wild winter greens, and fresh-pressed olive oil—echoed in the hearty soups you'll find in this chapter, like Winter Vegetable Soup (page 232) and Biblical Lentil Soup with Spinach and Turnips (page 233). The concept of fried dough or bread, as in the recipe for Panfried Scallion Bread (page 236), was also familiar, for a form of it served as a grain offering in the Temple.

Over the centuries, however, the culinary heart of the Hanukkah festival came to pivot around the Miracle of the Oil. Jews who settled in the Middle East or around the Mediterranean basin, where the festival still arrives at the tail end of olive-pressing season just as it did for the Maccabees, developed a plethora of savory holiday foods heated in olive oil, like fried chicken among the Italians and Moroccans, and even fried desserts.

But in the Jewish shtetls of Eastern Europe, where no cooking oil was obtainable, the only kosher solid fat available came from chickens, ducks, and geese—and so the approach of Hanukkah was traditionally the time for fattening poultry. In fact, according to John Cooper in *Eat and Be Satisfied*, the breeding and fattening of geese was developed by Jews in the Rhineland provinces as far back as the Middle Ages. Slaughtering a duck or goose on Hanukkah was important for the festive meal, so some of the fat (schmaltz) could be used for frying latkes, while the remaining fat and skin (*gribenes*) were each rendered separately and set aside for Passover. Dairy *vareniki*, similar to kreplach, were also popular on Hanukkah, and a meat version was created stuffed with mashed potatoes, fried onions, and goose cracklings.

How did the latke come to be? Native to the New World, potatoes came to Western Europe in the sixteenth century, and by the 1840s cultivation spread throughout White Russia, Lithuania, Poland, and the Ukraine. With potatoes cheap, plentiful, and easily stockpiled in cellars for winter use, it's no wonder that they and goose fat were used to create a latke, quickly fried and just as quickly consumed.

For dessert, all Jews commemorated the holiday with their own easily accessible ingredients—a combination of flour, yeast, and water, made into puffs or rounds of dough, fried in fat (Ashkenazic) or oil (Sephardic), and served with a honey or sugar syrup, which the Sephardim scented with rose or orange-flower water. To the Greeks they were *loukomades*, to the Persians snail-shaped *zelibi*, and to North Africans the bagel-like *sfenj*. In Turkey, Jews of Spanish origin used to prepare *bumuelos* (page 254), fritters or pancakes fried in olive oil and dipped in honey or sugar syrup or a sprinkled with cinnamon and sugar, possibly deriving from the light doughnutlike *buñuelos de viento* (puffs of wind) sold in Spain on All Saints' Day (November 1), in close proximity to Hanukkah. Russian Jews also enjoyed "Flaming Tea" at the end of their Hanukkah dinner. Sitting around the table, they would each break off a spoon-size piece of sugar from the great cones in which they were sold, dip it in brandy, shut off the lights, and simultaneously ignite it, before raucously dropping it into steaming glasses of black tea.

And as for our *sufganiot*, or jelly doughnuts (pages 251 and 252), for Ashkenazim the origins lie in Christian tradition. On New Year's Eve, German Christians were accustomed to having deep-fried pastries, and in Berlin jelly doughnuts (Berliner *Pfannkuchen*) were served on the holiday. So close was New Year's to Hanukkah that German Jews eventually adopted the jelly doughnut themselves, adding apricot filling and glaze and bringing the custom with them to Eretz Yisrael in the 1930s. Some Sephardic residents of Jerusalem claim that their similar fried Hanukkah pastries date back even centuries before that.

Celebrating Hanukkah

Hanukkah has long been one of the happiest holidays, a time for more than just lighting candles and indulging in fried foods. In the old days, an old Ashkenazic tradition called "The Night of the Fifth Candle" brought long-lost and distant relatives together to feast on a pot of steaming hot mushroom-and-barley soup, roast goose or duck, winter vegetables, potato kugel or latkes, and tea. The party continued long after dinner, with everyone singing songs, and adults and even yeshiva students playing chess or card games (permitted to yeshiva students only on Hanukkah and Purim) until the late hours, and children gambling over nuts with the Hanukkah top called a dreidel. The entire family was enlisted to create and solve *katowes*, or riddles, often surrounding the number forty-four, the total number of the Hanukkah candles lit during the eight days.

The tradition of giving Hanukkah gelt—coins—to children is also an Eastern European custom, thought to date back to the seventeenth century. But in those days the children didn't keep the money; the ultimate recipients were the children's teachers at *heder* (the religious school), or the poor. Sephardic children, on the other hand, still receive their booty at Purim. Even the tradition of gift-giving, especially the "one gift each night," is a latter-day Hanukkah custom, created by parents in the Diaspora in the hope that their children wouldn't feel left out of the fun—and miss the gifts—that characterize the Christmas season.

Making a great Hanukkah party is a true pleasure, and takes only a winning blend of family and friends and the desire to have fun. One particularly memorable party our family made included, after the lighting of candles, activities such as making your own menorahs out of wood, nuts, and bolts; designing Hanukkah cookies; singing a few songs (admittedly sung most robustly by the adults), and, for the grand finale, playing a multiple-choice game designed by a 10-year-old. Everyone got a little present—even the dog. And everyone went to sleep with a smile.

In this chapter's recipes there are several suggestions for what to serve on Hanukkah's many nights, from savory and sweet latkes with different toppings, or a meal of hearty soup and bread, inspired by just the same ingredients the Maccabees might have used, to an elegant traditional Eastern European–style dinner with duck or goose. There are side dishes, salads, and accompaniments that reflect the themes of the holiday, such as Endive and Fresh Mushroom Salad in Balsamic Vinaigrette (page 244) and Ripe Olive Butter (page 248). Plus there are classic Old World seasonal dishes such as Black Radish Relish (page 246) and a selection of luscious traditional desserts, for a sweet end to the evening. Mix and match—the possibilities are many. Enjoy!

Hanukkah Recipes

Latkes

Sweet Potato Latkes with Spiced Maple Syrup **P**
Sumac or Zahtar Latkes **P**
Olive Latkes **P**
Classic Potato Latkes **P**
Bulgarian Potato Latkes **P**
Zucchini, Feta, and Basil Mini-frittatas **D**
Mini-ricotta Latkes with Cherry Sauce **D**

Appetizing Soups and Breads

Winter Vegetable Soup **P**
Biblical Lentil Soup with Spinach and Turnips **P**
Split Pea and Double-Coriander Soup **P**
No-Knead Whole-Wheat Olive and Rosemary Bread **D**
Panfried Scallion Bread **P**

Main Courses

Wild Rice–Stuffed Duck with Candied Kumquat Sauce **M**
Goose Breast with Forest Fruit Sauce **M**
Spaetzle **M**
Nostalgic Pastrami **M**

Salads, Condiments, and Toppings

Endive and Fresh Mushroom Salad in Balsamic Vinaigrette **P**
Raw Applesauce **P**
Black Radish Relish **P**
Herbed Olives **P**
Ripe Olive Butter **P**
Kumquats in Spiced Syrup **P**

Desserts

Daniel's Light-as-a-Feather Whole-Wheat *Sufganiot* **D**
Five-Minute Chocolate *Sufganiot* **D**
Sfenj **P**
Bumuelos in Red Wine Sauce **D**

Sweet Potato Latkes with Spiced Maple Syrup

**Makes 10 to 12
(serves 4 to 6)**

Although they are sweet, we've enjoyed these latkes as a main course, served with a salad alongside. As a variation, substitute Yemenite *Hawaiij* for coffee and sweets (page 300) for the ginger, nutmeg, and cloves in the sauce, or add homemade *Baharat* (page 299) to the latkes and serve with sour cream instead of sauce.

Latkes

1 pound sweet potatoes
2 eggs
¼ cup matzah meal
½ teaspoon baking powder
½ teaspoon salt
White pepper
2 to 4 tablespoons light olive oil
    for frying
Chopped fresh coriander or
    mint leaves, for garnish
Dairy sour cream or plain
    yogurt (optional)

Sauce

1 cup real maple syrup
½ teaspoon grated, peeled fresh
    gingerroot
¼ teaspoon ground nutmeg
Pinch of ground cloves
Pinch of salt
Pinch of white pepper

1. Scrub the sweet potatoes, then peel and shred them on the fine side of a grater or in a food processor. Transfer to a wire-mesh strainer and squeeze to remove moisture. Let stand in the strainer or a colander placed over a bowl for 5 minutes.

2. In a medium bowl, beat the eggs with a fork. Add the sweet potatoes, matzah meal, baking powder, salt, and pepper. Let stand an additional 5 to 10 minutes.

3. In the meantime, prepare the sauce: In a small pan, combine the sauce ingredients, heat over low heat, and keep warm.

4. Heat 2 tablespoons oil in a large skillet and add a small ladleful of the batter. Flatten gently and fry on both sides until golden brown. Add more oil to the pan as necessary, and fry the remaining latkes.

5. Place the latkes on a paper towel–lined plate to absorb excess oil. Pour some of the heated sauce on individual plates and arrange three latkes on top per serving, or use a serving platter and pass the sauce separately. Garnish with fresh coriander or mint. Serve with sour cream or plain yogurt, if desired.

Both sumac and zahtar (hyssop) were biblical spices, the former used to impart a lemony flavor to food, and the latter to season almost anything. During the time of the Maccabees' revolt in late autumn, sumac berries had just been harvested, and zahtar grew wild in the hills.

Today, the word *zahtar* refers to a spice blend of hyssop, salt, sumac, and sesame seeds, which is popular on bread, in salads, and over Yogurt Cheese (*labaneh*) (page 70). At the biblical gardens of Neot Kedumim, across from the Ben Shemen Forest near Ben Gurion Airport, Chef Nadav Granot handpicks his own sumac berries and hyssop, and pickles his own olives to create the following two recipes for unusual and flavorful latkes.

Sumac or Zahtar Latkes

Makes about 8 to 10 (serves 4 to 5)

½ cup virgin olive oil

1 cup chopped onion (1 medium-large)

2 tablespoons crushed garlic

1 cup unbleached all-purpose flour

1 teaspoon baking powder

½ teaspoon baking soda

½ teaspoon salt (slightly less if using zahtar)

1 tablespoon prepared zahtar mix or dried crushed sumac

2 eggs, beaten

2 to 2½ tablespoons hot water

Thick yogurt or dairy sour cream

1. Heat ¼ cup of the oil in a skillet. Sauté the onion and garlic until lightly golden, stirring occasionally. Set aside.

2. In a bowl, sift together flour, baking powder, baking soda, and salt. Add the sumac or zahtar.

3. Stir in the onion and garlic mixture, then mix in the beaten eggs. (The batter will be thick and sticky.) Add 2 tablespoons water (or more if necessary) so that the batter is the consistency of pancake batter.

4. Heat the remaining oil. Use a small cup or soup ladle to form 3 to 4 small latkes each time. Fry on both sides until golden. Serve with a dollop of thick yogurt or sour cream.

Olive Oil

Your wife shall be like a fruitful vine within your house,
your children like olive shoots around your table.

—Psalm 128:3

An integral part of the Hanukkah story, olive oil appears sixth in the biblical list of the Seven Species, and is the only one that captures the product of the fruit rather than the fruit itself. To the ancients, extra-virgin olive oil was more than a tasty addition to salad; it was the very source of light, both in homes and in the ancient Temple. Even olive pits were used—for fuel. If the order of the Seven Species is any indication of the life cycle, then perhaps the place of olive oil is a metaphor for enlightenment as we move into middle age.

In the home, extra-virgin olive oil was used to cook and preserve foods, and soothed the skin of babes and beauties. Today, a Druze friend of mine has become famous for her olive-oil-based soap, founded on a generations-old recipe and used in a variety of skin treatments.

The best olives were reserved for pickling in vinegar or brine, or for drying and curing in salt, and the pulp of pressed olives served as a spread or condiment akin to tapenade. Usually eaten with bread and cheese, they could also enhance the flavor and texture of cooked dishes, as they do in Chicken with Olives and Sumac (page 193) and Olive Latkes (page 227).

The olive tree grows slowly, yet attains considerable age, and the tree and its branches have come to be symbols of peace and friendship, ever since Noah's dove brought him back an olive branch as a sign that the flood waters—and God's wrath—had abated. The Bible uses the olive tree as both a metaphor and a symbol for strength, beauty, prosperity, nourishment, and purity, and tells us that olive wood embellished the Holy Temple in Jerusalem as far as the eye could see. Priests and kings were anointed with olive oil, and the word for Messiah is derived from *mashiah,* or "anointed one."

Portable, delicious, and nutritious, olives were ideal food for all seasons, for nomads, travelers, shepherds, and the average Israelite. Today we have rediscovered what the ancients knew instinctively: that olive oil, and even olive leaves, have a host of healthful benefits as well.

2 cups lightly packed pitted
  green or black olives in brine,
  drained
½ cup olive oil
1 cup chopped onion (1 medium-
  large)
2 tablespoons chopped garlic
1 cup unbleached all-purpose
  flour

1 teaspoon baking powder
½ teaspoon baking soda
1 teaspoon salt
1 teaspoon cumin
2 eggs, beaten
1 to 2 tablespoons water
  (optional)

Olive
Latkes

Makes about 8
Serves 4

1. Chop the olives finely or process in the food processor. Transfer them to a strainer and squeeze out as much moisture as possible. Set aside.

2. Heat ¼ cup of the oil a skillet. Sauté the onion and garlic until golden. Set aside.

3. In a bowl, sift flour, baking powder, baking soda, salt, and cumin. Beat in the eggs, olives, and onion mixture with a fork. Add the water if the mixture seems too thick.

4. Heat the remaining oil. Use a small cup or soup ladle to form 3 to 4 small latkes each time. Fry on both sides until golden. For a dairy meal, serve with a dollop of thick yogurt or sour cream topped with a ½ tea-spoon of *Tzoug* (page 299), if desired.

A Latke Party

The most traditional way of celebrating Hanukkah is by serving *levivot,* or latkes, which together with *sufganiot* (the Jewish version of the jelly doughnut) fit most children's idea of the perfect meal. For a party, make more than one kind of latke and different toppings. A hot soup and a green salad round out the meal.

Classic Potato Latkes

Makes 12 to 14 (serves 4 to 6)

There are many varieties of potato pancakes: some with coarsely grated potatoes, some with finely grated ones, some with flour, and others with matzah meal. Then there are those that are "dolled up" with grated carrots or other vegetables, such as Jerusalem artichokes. These are the beloved basic ones we grew up with. Serve with regular or homemade Raw Applesauce, Black Radish Relish, or Ripe Olive Butter (pages 245, 246, 248, respectively), or dairy sour cream, of course.

1 pound potatoes, peeled
1 large onion (½ pound), sliced in half crosswise
2 large eggs, beaten
1 teaspoon salt
¼ teaspoon pepper
½ cup matzah meal
¼ cup vegetable oil

1. Grate the potatoes on the medium or fine side of a grater and place in a fine wire-mesh strainer placed over a bowl. Grate the onion on the medium side of a grater and transfer to a separate strainer. Let both stand 10 minutes to drain liquids. Press down gently to extract as much moisture as possible.

2. Transfer the potatoes to a bowl. Add the grated onion, beaten eggs, and salt and pepper, and mix well. Fold in matzah meal. Let stand for 10 minutes while heating oil in a medium skillet.

3. Scoop up 1 heaping tablespoon of the mixture and place in the hot oil. Press down gently with the back of a spoon to flatten. Repeat to form 4 to 5 latkes, depending on size of pan, leaving space between them to facilitate turning.

4. Cook on medium heat until golden, turn over with a spatula (or use two—one from each side for leverage), and cook the other side. Remove and place on paper towels to absorb excess oil. Serve warm.

In Yehiel Philosof's parents' home in Dupnitza, Bulgaria, Hanukkah was always celebrated with *Prizenski-pompuchi*, little potato latkes rolled in sugar. While some pioneering Bulgarians moved to Israel in 1924, the major Bulgarian aliyah came in 1948, bringing with them this beloved Hanukkah treat.

Bulgarian Potato Latkes

Makes 12 to 13 latkes
(serves 4)

1 pound potatoes

1 egg, beaten

3 tablespoons unbleached all-purpose flour

Pinch of salt

Vegetable oil, for frying

1 cup confectioners' sugar

1. Peel the potatoes and grate on the fine side of a grater placed over a bowl. Drain and squeeze out as much moisture as possible. Mix in egg, flour, and salt, beating with a fork until a soft batter is formed.

2. Heat oil in medium skillet. Drop a small tablespoon of batter into hot oil and sauté on both sides. Remove and immediately roll in confectioners' sugar. Serve hot.

Zucchini, Feta, and Basil Mini-frittatas

Makes 8 frittatas (serves 8)

These mini-frittatas make a nice change from the traditional potato latke. Serve them with Marinated Fennel in Olive Oil and Herbs (page 38), Endive and Fresh Mushroom Salad (page 244), or a simple salad of mixed lettuces. Whole-wheat flour may be substituted for all or part of the all-purpose flour, if desired. After Hanukkah, enjoy the same combination baked in a lightly greased pan as a crustless quiche.

2 cups coarsely grated zucchini (about 4 small-medium)
2 large eggs, separated
1⅓ cups crumbled feta cheese
¼ cup chopped scallions
½ cup unbleached all-purpose flour (or slightly more if necessary)
½ teaspoon baking powder
1½ teaspoons chopped fresh basil or oregano (or a mixture)
¼ teaspoon freshly ground black pepper
Olive oil for frying

1. Wash the zucchini, grate, and place in a colander. Let drain 15 minutes and squeeze to remove excess liquid.

2. In a bowl, mix together the egg yolks, feta cheese, scallions, flour, baking powder, basil, and pepper. Add the drained zucchini, and mix well. Whip the egg whites until soft peaks form, and fold into the zucchini mixture. Heat just enough oil to cover the bottom of an 8-inch heavy or nonstick skillet. Pour in just enough batter to cover the bottom (about ¾ cup). Cook over medium heat until golden brown on one side, flip, and cook the other side. Repeat with remaining batter. Keep the finished frittatas in a warm oven until all the batter has been used.

These are the quickest latkes of all. Light and delicious for dessert, snacks, or as part of a "latke party." I also make them for Shavuot, and serve them with a berry sauce made from the ripe mulberries on the tree outside my study window.

Mini-ricotta Latkes with Sour Cherry Sauce

Makes about 34

D

Sour Cherry Sauce

1 cup canned or bottled tart cherries in syrup (measure without liquid)

1 cup liquid from can or bottle

1 tablespoon cornstarch

1 tablespoon water

1 tablespoon Cherry Heering, or other cherry liqueur

Latkes

1 pound whole- or part-skim-milk ricotta cheese

4 eggs

6 tablespoons unbleached all-purpose flour (half whole-wheat flour, if desired)

½ teaspoon baking powder (optional)

1 tablespoon walnut oil

2 tablespoons granulated sugar or turbinado sugar

½ teaspoon baking powder

½ teaspoon baking soda

1 teaspoon vanilla extract

Oil, for frying

To Make the Sauce

1. In a small saucepan, mix the cherries and syrup and heat over medium-low heat. In a small bowl, mix the cornstarch and water until smooth. Add to saucepan and continue to heat, stirring, until the mixture thickens slightly. Stir in the cherry liqueur, cover, and keep warm while preparing the latkes. (Sauce may be prepared in advance and reheated.)

To Make the Latkes

2. Put all the ingredients for the latkes in a blender and process until smooth, stopping the blender occasionally to stir the mixture with a rubber spatula and wipe down the sides.

3. Heat a small amount of oil in a skillet and drop in 1 heaping tablespoon of the mixture each time to form a mini-latke. Flatten it down with the back of the spoon into a circle. (Or make larger latkes with 2 to 3 tablespoons of the mixture.) Cook briefly on one side until lightly brown on the bottom, then flip and cook the other side for under a minute. Serve warm with the sauce.

Winter Vegetable Soup

Serves 6

To accompany your latkes, what could be more in season at this time of year than soup? It warms your insides. It provides almost instant gratification. It can last in your refrigerator for a few days of the holiday, or in your freezer for months. It can be filling and nourishing—filled with just the armor you need to fight off winter's chills and ills—provided you don't use anything instant. Our ancestors no doubt relied on many a hearty vegetable-and-bean soup to get them through this time of year. Serve in mugs or bowls along with savory latkes, or as a first course at a Hanukkah meal.

¼ cup red lentils, black-eyed peas, or mung beans, or a combination

¼ cup pearl barley

¼ cup split peas

8 cups water

1 cup chopped onion

2 medium ribs celery, sliced into ¼-inch slices

2 medium-size carrots, diced

2 tablespoons olive oil

½ to 1 cup sliced string beans

1 to 2 cups cauliflower florets

1 to 1½ cups kohlrabi (1 medium), peeled and diced or grated

4 canned tomatoes, drained, seeded, and finely chopped

1 medium sweet potato or potato, cubed, or 1 cup cubed butternut squash or pumpkin

½ cup mixed chopped fresh dill and parsley

Salt

Freshly ground black pepper to taste

1. Rinse and drain lentils, barley, and split peas. Place in a large soup pot with the water. Bring to a boil, lower heat, and cook, partially covered, for 45 minutes, skimming the top if foam develops on the surface.

2. In the meantime, in a skillet, sauté the onion, celery, and carrots together in the olive oil until tender (do not brown). Add to the pot with the green beans, cauliflower, kohlrabi, tomatoes, and sweet potato. Bring to a boil again, cover, and cook over medium-low heat an additional 30 minutes, until the vegetables are tender.

3. Remove from heat and season with salt and pepper. Add the herbs, cover, and let stand for 5 to 10 minutes before serving.

Lentils are an ancient food, mentioned throughout the Bible. Our ancestors, and certainly the Maccabees, no doubt also made use of the roots, fresh herbs, and leaf vegetables they collected during the rainy winter months. Whole coriander seeds, likened in taste to manna by one of the sages, add both visual appeal and little "capsules" of flavor. For those who prefer, ground coriander may be substituted.

2 large onions (about 1 pound)
2 medium ribs celery
¼ cup extra-virgin olive oil
2 large garlic cloves, minced or
    pressed
2 medium turnips (about 12
    ounces), peeled and finely
    diced
2 cups lentils, picked over and
    rinsed
1 bay leaf

10 cups water
1 tablespoon cumin seeds
1 tablespoon coriander seeds
10 ounces fresh spinach or frozen
    leaf spinach, thawed and
    drained
1 tablespoon salt, or to taste
Coarsely ground black pepper
    to taste
3 lemons, quartered, or sumac
    powder

1. In a food processor with a metal blade, chop the onions coarsely. Remove and chop the celery. Heat the olive oil in a skillet over medium heat, and sauté the onions for 5 minutes. Add the celery, garlic, and diced turnips, and sauté just until softened and lightly golden. Set aside.

2. In a large soup pot, mix the rinsed lentils, bay leaf, and water. Bring to a boil, cover, and cook for 30 minutes, skimming the top if foam develops on the surface.

3. Toast the whole cumin and coriander seeds in a dry skillet, stirring occasionally, until fragrant. Add to the pot together with the sautéed vegetables. Cover and simmer over low heat an additional 30 to 45 minutes.

4. If using fresh spinach, rinse, pat dry, trim stems, and tear leaves into bite-size pieces. Stir fresh or thawed and drained spinach into the soup, season with salt and pepper, and cook 15 minutes. If the soup is too thick, add boiling water until desired consistency is reached. Check and adjust seasoning. Serve with lemon quarters or sprinkled with sumac.

Biblical Lentil Soup with Spinach and Turnips

Serves 10 to 12

Split Pea and Double-Coriander Soup

Serves 6 to 8

Over the centuries, our ancestors also learned that their native spices cumin and coriander seeds, such a common pair in Middle and Near Eastern–style bean soups, are carminatives—soothing to the stomach and particularly helpful in the digestion of legumes. Turmeric, a deep yellow-gold root that arrived on camelback from India in biblical times, is often added to the above combination.

Nourishing and redolent with spices, this healthy, easy-to-digest soup is also reminiscent of the types of foods eaten during this season in biblical times. Serve with Classic Potato Latkes (page 228) and a salad.

1½ cups split peas
8 cups water
1 bay leaf
2 medium carrots, scraped and
  cut into 4 pieces each
1 large onion (½ pound),
  quartered
2 tablespoons extra-virgin
  olive oil

1 teaspoon ground cumin
1 teaspoon ground coriander
1 teaspoon ground turmeric
Salt
White pepper to taste
½ cup chopped fresh cilantro, for
  garnish

1. Put the split peas in a bowl and cover with water. Swish the water around and drain. Repeat the process until the water runs clear. Drain and place in a 3-quart pot with 8 cups water and the bay leaf. Bring to a boil and cook, partially covered, over low heat about 30 minutes, until peas are soft. Skim off any foam that develops on top. Remove the bay leaf.

2. In the meantime, finely chop carrots and onion together in a food processor. Heat the olive oil in a medium-large skillet and sauté the vegetables together until tender. Add to the split peas along with the cumin, coriander, and turmeric. Stir until blended. Season to taste with salt and pepper, and continue cooking over low heat about 10 to 15 minutes, until the vegetables are tender. Stir briskly with a wooden spoon if necessary to crush the split peas and unify the texture. Taste and adjust seasoning.

3. Divide among bowls and garnish with a sprinkling of fresh cilantro. If the soup is too thick, add boiling water and cook a few more minutes to blend flavors.

Variation

Omit the cumin, coriander, and turmeric and use *Baharat* (page 299) or Yemenite *Hawaiij* for soups (page 300) to taste instead.

H ere is a wonderfully easy, healthful, and flavorful bread that is yeast-free and takes only minutes to put together (no mixer required) and just 30 minutes to bake. Vary the olives with raisins, chopped dried fruit, or nuts, if desired.

This recipe makes one standard-size loaf, but is even more winning baked in six individual mini-loaf pans, which can be sliced for mini-sandwiches or hors d'oeuvres.

No-Knead
Whole-
Wheat
Olive and
Rosemary
Bread

2 cups whole-wheat flour
2 teaspoons baking powder
1 teaspoon baking soda
1 teaspoon salt
½ cup toasted wheat germ
2 teaspoons dried rosemary
¼ cup extra-virgin olive oil

2 tablespoons vegetable oil
1½ cups plain yogurt
1 tablespoon mild-flavored
    honey, such as clover
1 cup chopped pitted green or
    black olives (or a mixture)

**Makes 1 loaf
or 6 mini-loaves**

1. Preheat the oven to 350°F. Line the bottom and sides of an 8½-by-4½-inch loaf pan or six 4½-by-2½-inch mini-loaf pans with parchment paper affixed with a little oil if necessary.

2. In a bowl, sift the flour, baking powder, baking soda, and salt together. Stir in the wheat germ and rosemary. In a separate bowl, whisk together the oils, yogurt, and honey. Stir in the chopped olives.

3. Make a well in the center of the dry ingredients, and add the yogurt-olive mixture. Beat with a wooden spoon until smooth. Use a spoon or measuring cup to transfer the batter to the prepared pan.

4. Bake for 30 minutes (20 to 25 minutes for mini-loaves), or until a toothpick inserted in the center comes out clean.

Panfried Scallion Bread

Makes two 8-inch circular breads (serves 6 to 8)

Panfried breads are mentioned throughout the Bible, as in the famous story of incest and retribution, when Tamar prepared bread cakes for her brother Amnon, who feigned illness. The Bible tells us that she "poured them out before him" (2 Sam. 13:9), and biblical commentary suggests that "pouring out" refers to bread cakes fried in oil, and the oil "poured out" into the dish with them.

Bread could serve as a sacrificial offering in the ancient Temple, but only unleavened bread made of "fine flour"—pure wheat—was acceptable. The holy sacrifice made of "unleavened cakes mingled with oil" or "unleavened bread wafers spread with oil" was either baked in the oven or on a griddle, or made in a skillet.

This festive bread, inspired by the olive-pressing season ending just as the Maccabees' victory was assured, is a modern-day interpretation of one that might have appeared on their holiday table.

This bread can be made delicate or earthy (with the addition of whole-wheat flour), and is a fine accompaniment to the soups in this chapter. Serve with a salad for a complete and biblically inspired meal.

Another superb rendition is to substitute ⅓ cup finely chopped cilantro or 2 teaspoons fiery *Tzoug* (page 299) and 3 tablespoons toasted pine nuts for the scallions.

Note: This recipe uses the odd combination of both cold- and hot-water doughs, which together create its unique texture.

Cold-Water Dough

1 cup all-purpose flour
½ teaspoon salt
6 tablespoons cold water

Hot-Water Dough

1 cup unbleached all-purpose flour (or ½ cup all-purpose flour and ½ cup whole-wheat flour)
¼ teaspoon baking powder (½ teaspoon if using whole-wheat flour)

6 to 7 tablespoons boiling water
Extra-virgin olive oil, for brushing, plus 4 teaspoons extra-virgin olive oil
½ cup chopped scallions (white and tender part of green)
1 teaspoon coarse sea salt or kosher salt
Canola oil, for frying
Sesame seeds, zahtar, or a combination of fennel seeds, coriander seeds, and sesame seeds (optional)

To Make the Cold-Water Dough

1. Place the flour and salt in the bowl of a food processor. With the machine running, slowly pour in the water. Mix until the dough forms a ball. Remove from the mixer. Set aside.

To Make the Hot-Water Dough

2. Place the flour and baking powder in the bowl of a food processor. With the machine running, slowly add the hot water until the dough forms a ball.

3. Knead the two doughs together into a ball (on a lightly floured surface only if necessary—the dough should not be sticky). Brush or rub the ball with olive oil and let rest in an airtight container for 30 to 60 minutes or overnight in the refrigerator. Bring to room temperature before using.

4. Divide the dough in half. Roll out half the dough to a 12-by-8-inch rectangle approximately $\frac{1}{8}$ inch thick, and brush with 2 teaspoons olive oil. Spread $\frac{1}{4}$ cup chopped scallions evenly over the dough and sprinkle with $\frac{1}{2}$ teaspoon coarse sea salt.

5. Roll up from one narrow end and bend into a spiral shape. Tuck the end under the bottom and pinch to seal. Using a rolling pin, flatten the spiral into an 8-inch circle that is $\frac{1}{2}$ inch thick. Repeat the process with the second half of the dough.

6. Heat 1 inch canola oil in a skillet larger than the circle. Fry the bread on medium heat for 2 minutes, until golden (stick a spatula underneath to check), then use one or two sets of tongs to flip it over. Shake the pan slightly, and cook the other side 2 minutes. Cover and let cook another 2 minutes on medium-low heat.

7. Transfer to a plate lined with paper towels to absorb excess oil. Sprinkle with sesame seeds or zahtar while hot. To serve, cut into wedges. Serve warm.

Wild Rice–Stuffed Duck with Candied Kumquat Sauce

Serves 6 to 8

While many of our Eastern European ancestors enjoyed goose on Hanukkah, in our times duck is a far more popular choice. This is our niece Ruthie's version, made with kumquats—oval-shaped, small fruits with distinctive citrus flavor that can be eaten whole, skin and all. Although they originated in China, where their cultivation has been documented as early as 1178 C.E., Israel is one of the major producers of kumquats today. If no candied kumquats are available, you can use homemade Kumquats in Spiced Syrup (page 249).

1 4- to 5-pound Long Island duck, with neck and giblets
½ lemon
Salt
Freshly ground black pepper
Canola oil for rubbing

Stuffing

⅓ cup wild rice
½ cup short-grain brown rice
¼ cup vegetable oil
⅔ cup chopped onion (1 medium)
½ cup finely diced celery
Salt
Freshly ground black pepper

Candied Kumquat Sauce

1½ cups stock, made in advance from duck's neck and giblets
Freshly ground black pepper
⅓ cup freshly squeezed orange juice
½ cup orange marmalade with orange rinds
2 teaspoons freshly grated orange rind
½ cup brandy
Salt
6 to 8 ounces candied kumquats, sliced lengthwise
Sugar or honey (optional)

1. Trim excess fat from the duck, especially around the neck and inside the cavity. Rub the skin and inside cavity with the lemon and season the cavity with salt and pepper. Set aside.

To Make the Stuffing
2. Cook wild rice and brown rice separately according to package directions. Let cool slightly and fluff with a fork.
3. Heat oil in large skillet. Sauté onion and celery together until golden. Stir in the two kinds of cooked rice, season with salt and pepper, and let cool until easy to handle.
4. Preheat the oven to 425°F.
5. Stuff the duck with the prepared rice filling, and tie the legs together with kitchen twine. Use the tip of a sharp paring knife to prick the duck all over, inserting knife at an angle to pierce just the skin, not the

flesh. Make a 1-inch incision under each leg bone where it meets the backbone. Trim wing tips. Rub the duck with canola oil, salt and pepper to taste. Place on a rack in an aluminum-foil-lined shallow roasting pan.

6. Roast in the preheated oven for 30 minutes. Check periodically to make sure the duck is not burning.

7. While the duck is roasting, prepare the stock. Rinse the giblets and neck and place in a pot with 3 cups cold water. Bring to a boil and season lightly with salt and pepper. Cover and simmer for 20 minutes. Remove the cover and continue cooking until reduced to $1\frac{1}{2}$ cups stock. Strain.

8. Carefully remove excess duck fat from the pan, prick the duck again to release fat, and lower heat to 350°F. Continue to roast for about 1 to $1\frac{1}{2}$ hours, turning from time to time, until the duck is browned and crisp and a fork stuck into the thigh emits clear, not red, juice.

To Make the Sauce

9. Heat the prepared stock, orange juice, marmalade, grated orange rind, $\frac{1}{4}$ cup of the brandy, and salt and pepper to taste. Bring to a boil, cover, and simmer for 1 hour, while the duck roasts. Add the kumquats after 30 minutes. Taste the sauce, adding a teaspoon of sugar or honey if more sweetness is desired. Stir in the remaining $\frac{1}{4}$ cup brandy and keep warm.

10. Remove duck from the oven and brush generously with the sauce. Return to oven and roast for 5 minutes. Brush with additional sauce, and continue to roast for 5 to 10 minutes, until glazed.

11. Carve the duck and transfer stuffing to a serving platter. Spoon remaining sauce on top. Serve with the stuffing alongside.

Goose Breast with Forest Fruit Sauce

Serves 4

Inspired by his own Austro-Germanic roots and Hanukkah traditions of Eastern European Jews, chef Daniel Zach of Carmela b'Nahala, a restaurant located in a historic building just off the Carmel Market, created this classic combination that might have been served in the fine homes of yesteryear.

Look for goose breasts in specialty food shops. If you can't find them, serve Forest Fruit Sauce over crispy baked chicken or Cornish hens.

4 fresh goose breasts	½ cup pitted tart cherries
Coarsely ground black pepper	2 tablespoons blueberry jam
4 cups beef or chicken broth, reduced to 2 cups	2 tablespoons brown sugar
	6 black peppercorns
¼ cup Kirsch (or any schnapps)	4 juniper berries
4 tablespoons raspberry vinegar	1 large sprig of fresh thyme

1. Rinse the goose breasts and pat dry. Season with coarsely ground black pepper.

2. In a large, heavy (preferably cast-iron) skillet, over medium-high heat, sear the goose breasts one or two at a time, starting with the skin side, until the fat is dissolved and the breast is nicely browned. Turn and sear the other side until browned. Pour off any fat that has accumulated in the pan. Remove the goose breasts from the skillet and set aside.

3. For the sauce, mix the rest of the ingredients in the same skillet. Bring to a gentle boil over medium heat.

4. Return the goose breasts to the pan, skin side up. Cover and cook 1½ hours, until the meat is soft. Remove the goose breasts and keep warm.

5. Strain the sauce and return to the skillet. Cook over medium-high heat until thickened.

6. To serve, slice the goose breasts, pour the sauce over, and serve with Spaetzle (recipe follows). Decorate with fresh blueberries, if you wish.

Spaetzle, from the German for "little sparrow," are tiny noodles or dumplings that originated in Germany and spread in one form or another throughout Eastern Europe. Easily made with flour and eggs and very satisfying, spaetzle dough can range from batterlike consistency (this recipe) to firm enough to be rolled and cut into slivers. Briefly boiled, the small pieces are usually tossed or fried in butter (in the old days, Ashkenazic housewives used goose fat to fry them for a meat meal), and served as a side dish or added to soups. Leftover spaetzle can also be panfried with butter, finely chopped onions, and mushrooms.

Note: The best spaetzle are made with a spaetzle maker, which looks something like a grater with ¼-inch holes. If you don't own one, use a colander with ¼-inch holes and the bottom of a cup to force the mixture through the holes.

5 eggs plus 2 egg yolks	½ teaspoon salt
4 tablespoons water	⅛ teaspoon nutmeg
2 cups all-purpose flour	Goose fat or oil, for frying

1. In the bowl of a mixer or with a wooden spoon, beat together the eggs, yolks, and water. Add the flour, salt, and nutmeg. Beat on low speed until mixture is very smooth. Let the mixture rest for 20 minutes.

2. Bring a large pot of lightly salted water to a boil. Hold the spaetzle maker or colander high over the pot (the higher you make it the longer the spaetzle will be), and pour in the batter 1 cup at a time, working it through with the rectangular "rider" on top of the spaetzle maker, or the bottom of a glass or cup if using a colander.

3. Let spaetzle rise to the surface, and cook another 30 seconds. Drain the spaetzle well. If serving immediately, panfry the spaetzle lightly in oil. Serve hot with spoonfuls of Forest Fruit Sauce (page 240) on top, if desired.

4. Spaetzle may be prepared up to 4 hours ahead of time: Cook, drain, and mix with 2 teaspoons melted goose fat or oil. Cover with plastic wrap and store in the refrigerator.

The Origins of the Menorah

Shaped into nearly anything, including whimsical children's scenes, locomotives, or elaborate geometric designs, *Hanukkiyot* (eight-branch menorahs) today are fashioned in wood, metal, glass, ceramic, or the ornate silver. The eight-branched *Hanukkiya* is based on the seven-branched Golden Menorah made by the artist Bezalel for the Holy Tabernacle in the desert, described in the book of Exodus. You can still see a poignant image of it captured in stone relief on the Arch of Titus in Rome, which depicts the vanquished Judaeans holding the Temple Menorah when they were exiled as slaves to Rome, after the destruction of the Second Temple in 70 C.E. A seven-branched menorah has never been used by Jews again.

But where did the original design come from? It's to be found in the very plant life of the land of Israel: With four branches on each side, and a larger branch in the center, the Moriah sage is a dead ringer for the classic Hanukkah menorah, as the late botanists Dr. Ephraim and Hannah HaRuveni discovered (see *Nature in Our Biblical Heritage*).

It was Devora ben Yehudah (wife of Eliezer Ben Yehuda, the father of the modern Hebrew language) who coined the name *Hanukkiya,* for what was called before *Menorat Hanukkah.* Unfortunately, her husband didn't like the word, and chose not to include it in his dictionary. The ultra-Orthodox also chose not to accept *Hanukkiya,* since it came from the circles of Ben Yehudah, who had been put under *herem* (excommunicated) for developing and encouraging the use of the "Holy Language." Still, the majority of the Jewish population in Palestine lovingly adopted the word, and it remains the standard term today.

A touching letter I received in 1999 kindled memories of an old family favorite. The letter was from the late Hans Ullman, of Kibbutz Naan in northern Israel. "I am an old man," he wrote, "and I got the impression from reading your newspaper column that our present-day vitamin- and calorie-conscious women do not know or never heard how their grandmothers preserved food." And then he described how it was done nearly a century ago:

> On our farm in North Germany . . . stood a wooden shed that had double walls. The space between the walls was filled with saw-dust. Every winter the shed was filled with ice from the local mill-pond and the ice was covered with a thick layer of saw-dust. Items that had to be kept cold were buried under the sawdust.
>
> Among these items were earthenware pots in which beef was pickled in brine. When the beef was cured and was to be used it was put into fresh water, which was changed frequently in order to leach the surplus salt. Then the beef was minced (the poor servant girl who had to turn the handle of the mincer!) and the minced meat was formed into a loaf or into flattened balls without adding any condiments. The resulting dish was delicious. I think it's a pity that women do not save some room in their refrigerators and cure some meat.
>
> I had to write to you about this because we all have our memories.

Ah yes, we all have our memories. Ours is of Mom's pastrami with its crispy-sweet exterior and spicy-sweet interior. Though our mom didn't cure it herself (though she did corn her own beef on long Sunday afternoons), the memory of the rich, juicy pastrami she baked for Hanukkah has lingered with us all these years. It was then—and still is—a perfect accompaniment to Classic Potato Latkes (page 228).

4 to 5 pounds pastrami
1 large can crushed pineapple in
**   pineapple juice**

Preheat the oven to 300°F. Place the pastrami in a baking pan, and pour the crushed pineapple over. Cover loosely with aluminum foil. Bake for 2 hours. Serve with Classic Potato Latkes. To vary the recipe, substitute apricot jam for the pineapple, spreading a thin layer over the pastrami before baking.

Nostalgic Pastrami

Serves 10 to 12

Endive and Fresh Mushroom Salad in Balsamic Vinaigrette

Serves 4 to 6

Although they originate in faraway Belgium, the little heads of endive evoke the crocus flowers dotting the Israeli countryside in winter, just as they did in ancient times. You can't miss the gleaming white crocus, closed up like a candle just at Hanukkah time, among the wild mushrooms that appear suddenly after a rainfall.

This salad makes a particularly striking presentation, and is usually eaten by just scooping up the marinated mushrooms with the whole endive leaves. Or slice the leaves into bite-size pieces, mix with the mushrooms, and serve the salad on a bed of baby salad greens or fresh spinach.

4 heads endive

1½ cups mushrooms

⅓ cup extra-virgin olive oil

Salt

Coarsely ground pepper to taste

Vinaigrette
3 tablespoons balsamic vinegar

1 large garlic clove, minced or
    pressed

1. Cut the bottom end off the endives, and separate the leaves. Rinse well to remove traces of dirt, hidden particularly along the base of the leaves. Spread on a kitchen towel and let dry.

2. Wash the mushrooms quickly and dry completely. Slice thinly and place in a nonreactive bowl. Set aside.

3. In a small bowl, whisk together the balsamic vinegar and garlic. Slowly whisk in olive oil until well blended. Season with salt and pepper, pour over the mushrooms, and stir to distribute the sauce. Let stand for 30 minutes at room temperature.

4. On a large (and preferably white) serving platter, scatter the endive around and pour the marinated mushrooms over them. Stir gently and serve.

There's no need to rely on bottled processed applesauce when it's so easy and more nutritious to make your own from scratch. This method retains all the vitamins and minerals of the apples.

Raw Applesauce

Makes 2 cups

3 large Granny Smith apples
¼ cup honey
¼ teaspoon cinnamon

¼ teaspoon nutmeg
A few drops of freshly squeezed
    lemon juice

Peel and core the apples, then cut into segments. Place in a blender or food processor with the honey and the spices. Process in on/off pulses until the desired consistency is reached, adding a tablespoon of water if necessary. Stir in the lemon juice to help preserve color. Serve chilled, or cover and store in the refrigerator for up to 3 days.

Black Radish Relish

Makes about 2½ cups

Our mother's mouth waters when she sees black radishes, because they remind her of the simple delicacy her mother used to make from the cheapest vegetable in the market. With access to ingredients her mother never dreamed of, our mother has managed to create an updated delicacy that makes us salivate as well.

Serve with Classic or Bulgarian Potato Latkes (page 228 or 229), Nostalgic Pastrami (page 243), or one of the hearty soups and breads in this chapter.

Note: Always choose medium radishes; large ones tend to be woody.

2 medium black radishes
½ English (hothouse) cucumber
2 to 3 scallions, finely sliced or minced
2 tablespoons extra-virgin olive oil
2 tablespoons canola oil
1 tablespoon balsamic vinegar
1 tablespoon granulated sugar or turbinado sugar
1 teaspoon salt
¼ teaspoon freshly ground black pepper

1. Peel the radishes and shred on the large holes of a grater. Transfer to a shallow bowl. Grate the cucumber, and add to the bowl together with the scallions.

2. In a small bowl, whisk olive oil, canola oil, balsamic vinegar, and sugar until blended. Pour over the radish mixture, and blend gently just until the vegetables are coated. Season with salt and pepper. Serve at room temperature.

When our ancestors preserved their olives for winter, they learned by trial and error that the addition of certain flavoring ingredients not only enhanced the flavor of their olives, but also helped to preserve them, such as garlic and sage, which contain antibacterial properties. This updated version makes a delicious snack at a Hanukkah party. Although any olives may be used, the best are Israeli cracked green olives or Greek kalamata olives.

Herbed Olives

Makes 2 cups

2 cups cracked green (Israeli) olives or kalamata olives

1 to 2 large garlic cloves, sliced lengthwise or pressed

1 tablespoon chopped fresh thyme, or ½ teaspoon dried

1 tablespoon fresh chopped sage, or ½ teaspoon dried

½ cup extra-virgin olive oil

Mix all the ingredients together in a jar with a tight-fitting cover. Shake to blend. Cover and let stand at room temperature for several hours or overnight in the refrigerator. Let come to room temperature before serving.

. . . There are olives for eating, olives for drying, olives for oil, and the oil thereof is the finest of oils. The fashion is to enjoy fresh or dried or salted olives, or the olives that are pounded so that the pungent taste disappears.

—JT, Pesachim 2:5

Ripe Olive Butter

**Makes about
1½ cups**

*S*erve with savory latkes, such as Classic or Bulgarian Potato Latkes (page 228 or 229), Bulgarian Leek Patties (page 144), hot pita, toasted baguette slices, or crackers, garnished with additional fresh herbs, if desired.

½ pound pitted black olives,
    drained
1 to 2 tablespoons extra-virgin
    olive oil
1 large garlic clove, minced or
    pressed
1 tablespoon freshly squeezed
    lemon juice

1½ tablespoons chopped Italian
    parsley, coriander, or basil, or
    more to taste
1 teaspoon dried oregano
⅛ teaspoon dried thyme or
    marjoram
Pinch of sugar
Freshly ground black pepper

1. Grind the olives with a mortar and pestle or in a food processor (a blender is not suitable). Add 1 tablespoon of the oil and the remaining ingredients, and process to form a coarse paste. Add the second tablespoon of oil only if necessary to process.

2. Transfer to a bowl. Mix, cover, and refrigerate for several hours or overnight for flavors to blend. Bring to room temperature. Taste and adjust seasoning before serving.

Note: Finely chopped, fully drained sun-dried tomatoes in olive oil may also be added, if desired.

Kumquats in Spiced Syrup

Makes about 3½ cups

Little kumquats get a new lease on life with this recipe. Delicious used as a sauce with meats, poultry, or fish, they're also delicious on ice cream or cake. Once they're cooked, use the kumquats whole, sliced, or quartered, together with the syrup, as a dessert with vanilla ice cream or lime sorbet, or over poultry and meats. They can also be used as a substitute for candied kumquat sauce in the Wild Rice–Stuffed Duck recipe (page 238).

2 cups cold water
1 cup turbinado sugar or
    granulated sugar
½ cup flavorful honey
1 to 2 small hot, dry peppers
1½ teaspoons turmeric
1 to 2 sticks cinnamon
1½ teaspoons freshly grated,
    peeled gingerroot, or ½
    teaspoon ground ginger

¼ to ½ teaspoon nutmeg
3 whole cloves
⅓ teaspoon cumin seeds or
    caraway seeds
4 cups kumquats

1. In a pot, place the water, sugar, honey and spices and bring to a boil, stirring occasionally. Lower heat and simmer 10 minutes.

2. In the meantime, wash the kumquats well and make an **X** slit on top of each. Add to spice mixture. Simmer for 45 to 60 minutes, until the kumquats' peels are almost translucent. Cool 1 hour before transferring to a clean jar. Store in the refrigerator.

How the Dreidel Came to Be

Its name derived from the German *drehen,* which means "to spin," the dreidel is a spinning top toy that dates back to the Middle Ages. The original had a *T* on one side for "Take all," but inspired rabbis adapted it for Hanukkah use by adding a different letter, imbued with mystical meanings, to each of its four sides.

The *nun, gimel, he,* and *shin* stood for the words *New Gadol Haya Sham* ("A Great Miracle Happened *There.*"). In Kabbalistic teachings, each letter stands for one of the four empires that tried to destroy the Jewish people: Babylonia, Persia, Greece, and Rome. The world itself is like a dreidel: Though it changes and spins, with conquerors arising and conquerors falling, in the end the truth emanates from the one Stem.

In the old days, the dreidel game was played in Yiddish. A *nun* signified "*nisht,*" meaning that the spinner gave nothing to the kitty; *he,* "*halb,*" or taking half of the kitty; *shin,* "*shtel,*" or putting back in the kitty; and *gimel,* "*gantz,*" or winner-take-all. Before the Holocaust, Ashkenazic children prepared for the holiday by spending the early weeks of Kislev carving dreidels out of wood or casting them in lead. Today, children make dreidels out of many different materials, but the ones in Israel have an important difference: The letters on the sides stand for "A Great Miracle Happened *Here.*"

Daniel's
Light-as-a-
Feather
Whole-
Wheat
Sufganiot

Makes 10

Of all the *sufganiot* we've ever tasted (and we've tasted quite a few), these made by Daniel Zach, who shared his recipe for Goose Breast with Forest Fruit Sauce (page 240), are the lightest, puffiest, and most delicious. Serve in the traditional style filled with jam, and/or sprinkled with confectioners' sugar, or with some exotic jam served alongside. *Sufganiot* are best served within an hour of preparation.

2½ cups unbleached all-purpose flour	1 egg, beaten
1 cup whole-wheat flour	Pinch of salt
½ cup sugar	Oil, for frying
1 tablespoon yeast	About ⅓ cup apricot, blueberry,
¼ cup + 2 tablespoons dairy sour cream	strawberry, or other jam (optional)
1¾ cups warm milk	Confectioners' sugar

1. In the bowl of an electric mixer, mix flours, sugar, and yeast. In a small bowl, mix sour cream, warm milk, beaten egg, and salt. Make a well in the center of the flours and pour in the sour cream mixture. Mix on low speed for 5 minutes, until the dough forms a ball, then raise speed to high and beat 7 minutes, stopping occasionally to avoid overheating the mixer.

2. Transfer the dough to an oiled bowl and let rise for 1 hour, 15 minutes. Punch down and let rest 5 minutes. Divide the dough into ten 2½-ounce balls (using a kitchen scale is recommended for uniform size), and oil hands to help roll each measure of dough into an even ball. Cover and let rise 1 hour.

3. Heat 1 to 1½ inches of oil in a wide pan over medium heat. Place a wooden spoon in the oil; the oil is hot enough when it bubbles gently around the spoon. Add 4 pieces of dough (the oil should come halfway up the *sufgania*, giving it its characteristic white ring when fried on both sides) and fry about 3 to 4 minutes on each side, or until golden brown. (If they brown too quickly, lower heat slightly.) Place on paper towels and let cool until easy to handle.

4. If you wish to fill the *sufganiot*, pierce one end of each with the tip of a thin knife. Place the jam in a cookie press or pastry bag fitted with a ¼-inch hole or nozzle tip, and pipe through the slit. (If the jam is not smooth, puree in the blender.) Sift confectioners' sugar over the *sufganiot*. Serve hot, warm, or at room temperature.

Five-Minute Chocolate Sufganiot

Makes 12

These are the fastest *sufganiot* in the West, and are especially suitable for those who have no experience with yeast. They have the added benefit of whole-wheat pastry flour and turbinado sugar, and chocolate-sensitive people can substitute carob powder for the cocoa. One taste and you might never want to go back to regular doughnuts!

1 cup whole-wheat pastry flour
1 teaspoon baking powder
¼ teaspoon baking soda
3 tablespoons good-quality unsweetened cocoa powder
1 teaspoon instant coffee powder or any liqueur
¼ teaspoon cinnamon

Pinch of nutmeg
⅓ cup turbinado sugar or granulated sugar
1 cup plain yogurt
1 large egg, beaten
Oil, for frying
Confectioners' sugar, for sprinkling

1. In a bowl, sift the flour, baking powder, baking soda, cocoa, coffee, and spices together. Stir in the sugar. In a small bowl, mix yogurt and egg. Add to the flour mixture and blend thoroughly with a fork.

2. Heat 1 inch oil in a large skillet. Use a medium-size (not large) ice-cream scoop or a ¼ cup measure to drop 4 to 5 individual *sufganiot* into the pan. Fry briefly on one side, until lightly browned. Use tongs to turn them over, and lightly brown the other side.

3. Transfer to a plate lined with a paper towel and let cool slightly before sprinkling with confectioners' sugar. As with all *sufganiot,* these are best made as close as possible to serving time.

The North African answer to the *sufgania, sfenj* is a light little dough-nut that's easy to prepare once you get the technique down. Luckily, Miriyam and I received this recipe and our first lesson in *sfenj*-making from my neighbor, Miri Ben Abu.

2 cups unbleached all-purpose
   flour (or substitute ⅓ whole-
   wheat pastry flour for an
   equal amount of all-purpose
   flour)
1 tablespoon yeast
1 tablespoon sugar

2 cups warm water (or slightly
   more if using part whole-
   wheat flour)
1 teaspoon salt
Canola oil, for frying
Sugar, for dipping

1. Mix the flour, yeast, and sugar together in a large bowl. Gradually add the warm water, stirring with a wooden spoon or on the slowest speed of an electric mixer, until a thickish batter is obtained. Stir in the salt and continue stirring for 5 minutes on low speed, until the batter is thick and smooth.

2. Cover with a towel and let sit in a warm place for 1 hour to rise. The batter should be very soft and doubled in size. The traditional way to beat the batter at this point is to cup your hand and beat the batter in circular motions, easing it away from the side of the bowl. This will make it fluffy and aerated.

3. Heat about 1½ inches of oil in a large skillet. With oiled hands, take a handful of the batter from the edge of the bowl and form a large ring the size of your hand, with a hole in the center (like a bagel).

4. Gently slip it into the oil, using the handle of a wooden spoon to open the hole even wider (it usually closes somewhat when dropped in the oil). The circle will not be uniform since the dough is very soft. Fry on both sides on medium-low heat until golden. The dough will puff up and rise farther during frying. Repeat, frying 2 to 3 circles each time. Remove with a slotted spoon and dip one side in sugar. May also be served with jam. Serve warm.

Variation

Make *sfenj* even more exotic with the addition of ½ teaspoon of homemade Yemenite *Hawaiij* for coffee and sweets (page 300).

Bumuelos in Red Wine Sauce

Makes about 15

These little round balls of choux-like pastry fried in oil are the traditional Hanukkah treat among the Jews of Greece and Turkey.

Bumuelos

1 cup water

½ cup butter

2 teaspoons sugar

Pinch of salt

1½ cups sifted unbleached all-purpose flour

4 eggs

Canola oil, for frying

Confectioners' sugar, for sprinkling

Red Wine Sauce

2 cups sugar

⅔ cup dry red wine

2 cinnamon sticks

4 whole cloves

1. Prepare the sauce first: Mix the ingredients together in a small saucepan and bring to a boil. Lower heat and cook for 10 to 15 minutes, stirring occasionally until the syrup thickens to the consistency of honey. Keep warm. (Overcooking the sauce will make it harden.) Set aside.

2. In a medium saucepan, bring the water, butter, sugar, and salt to a boil. Set aside. Place the flour in the bowl of a mixer. Turn the mixer on low speed and add the boiling liquid mixture. Continue mixing on low speed until a soft dough is formed that leaves the side of the bowl. Add the eggs one at a time, mixing well after each addition.

3. Heat 1½ inches canola oil in a wide pan. Using a medium ice-cream scoop or two tablespoons, form a ball of the mixture and slip into the hot oil. If it is difficult to form the ball, beat in an additional tablespoon or two of flour. Fry 4 to 5 balls at a time on medium-high heat until golden brown. Remove with a slotted spoon and place on the paper towel-lined plate to remove excess oil. Sprinkle with confectioners' sugar.

4. Reheat the wine sauce over low heat until very warm. Pour 3 tablespoons of sauce on each serving plate. Set 2 to 3 *bumuelos* on top and serve.

*For the fruits of the Gennosar valley are
like a symphony: they tug on the heart and
fill the soul with spiritual yearning.*
    —**Nachmanides**

*If you have a sapling in your hand and
are told that the Messiah has arrived, plant
the sapling and then go out and greet him.*
    —**The Midrash**

Tu b'Shvat

The New Year of Trees and
the Seder of Fruit and Wine

When we were little girls growing up in Belle Harbor, New York, Tu b'Shvat was the day our Hebrew schools would distribute small brown paper bags of dried fruit and a mysterious, hard, twisted, and slightly sweet pod we thought was tree bark, and which the teachers called "boxer."

We'd all sing, "*Ha Shkedia porahat, Ha Shemesh ba zorahat, Tu b'Shvat higiya, hag ha ilanot! Tu b'Shvat higiya! The Jewish Arbor Day!*" ("The almond tree is flowering, the sun is shining brightly on it, Tu b'Shvat has arrived, the holiday of trees!"), but we really didn't understand why. We actually didn't even know what an "arbor" was, nor, truthfully, could we imagine almond trees.

But we *did* know that the holiday had something to do with the trees of our struggling new homeland, the State of Israel. Whatever that strange "bark" was, we knew it had come from that faraway place, and we celebrated the holiday by encouraging our parents and grandparents to buy as many Jewish National Fund "tree certificates" as possible.

Little did we realize that the custom of planting trees when a child was born—a cedar for a boy, a cypress for a girl—was an ancient one, mentioned in the Talmud (Gittin 57a). Our family bought those tree certificates not only in honor of births, bar mitzvot, weddings, anniversaries, but also to memorialize those who died. We even half-expected to someday personally greet "our" tree should we ever be fortunate enough to actually visit Israel (an expectation delightfully satirized in one of Israel's earliest movies, *Sallah Shabati*).

The New Year of Trees

Like all the major Jewish festivals, Tu b'Shvat, which means "the fifteenth day of the Hebrew month of Shvat" (January/February), has its roots in the rhythms of nature in the land of the Bible. Arriving just a few weeks after the winter solstice and exactly six months after Tu b'Av, summer's Festival of Love, the fifteenth of Shvat marks the moment in which we can actually feel the nights grow shorter and the hours of daylight increase, gently warming the earth. The dormant trees awaken from their winter hibernation, and the roots begin to absorb moisture and nutrients from the soil.

Tu b'Shvat was a tax day long before it was a holiday. Though the Bible never mentions that specific date, it does instruct the Israelites to pay a tithe (akin to an income tax) to the Temple in Jerusalem on the produce of their fruit trees and their fields, as well as on their livestock.

Gazing at the signs of nature around them centuries ago, the rabbis living in the Land of Israel tried to figure out just when the fruit trees should be tithed. They saw that the fifteenth of Shvat must be the "New Year for Trees," for until that date "the trees live off the water of the past year; from this day on, they live off the water of this year" (JT, Rosh Hashanah 1b). That's when the sap rises in the trees, and the still-hidden fruiting process begins.

To this day, around Tu b'Shvat, the change is felt even in my Tel Aviv garden; new leaves begin to unfold on the fig trees, and the earth seems to come alive again. Just as they have for millennia, the almond trees burst into glorious white bloom. The still-untamed hillsides are covered with wild leaves and roots that once helped sustain our ancestors through the winter months, and dotted throughout are the red anemones that reminded them of the beauty of the earth in this season.

Living in the hills of Safed, in the Galilee, and responding to that wintry splendor, the famed sixteenth-century mystic known as the Ari ("The Lion"), Isaac Luria, originated the custom of a special Seder for Tu b'Shvat revolving around the eating of thirty different native fruits, which he believed contained the "divine sparks" that had been scattered all over the universe when it was first created. The Seder also included a unique ritual blending red and white wines, reflecting nature's colors as winter becomes spring and the white almond blossoms slowly yield to lush carpets of red poppies, just about the time of the wheat harvest of Shavuot, in May.

With the passing centuries, the Tu b'Shvat Seder spread rapidly through many communities, especially among Jews living in Arab countries, though in the course of time it fell into obscurity. By the sixteenth century, the only tradition that remained among Ashkenazic Jews living in Germany was eating dried fruit, preferably from Israel,

But Tu b'Shvat came alive again once the State of Israel was established. Enticed by the same strange pieces of bark we chomped on as children, Jews throughout the world were encouraged to help reforest the land—vicariously—on the "New Year of Trees," the third "New Year" mentioned in the Talmud. Years later we realized that those woody fruits were carob pods, which had been chosen for shipment abroad because in those days they were the only fruit sturdy enough to make the journey from the new state to the far corners of the Diaspora.

Today, Tu b'Shvat Seders are celebrated all across the United States and Israel, thanks to the efforts of modern-day rabbis, researchers like Nogah Hareuveni and Yoel Rappel, and environmentalists who regard its rituals as a spiritual and ecological call to renew our commitment to be responsible custodians of this beautiful and fruitful world.

Setting a Tu b'Shvat Seder Table

While there are many different versions of the Seder, all involve fruit and wine. The traditional Tu b'Shvat table is set with a white tablecloth and decorated with flowers, candles to cast glowing light, fresh and dried fruit of all kinds, and both white and red wines displayed in clear glass carafes to show off their color. A particularly beautiful presentation is to make a small mound of all kinds of fresh and dried fruit down the center of the table, interwoven with flowers and candles.

At the head of the table, three bowls of fruit of varying heights are positioned, reflecting the Kabbalistic concept of the universe as "three worlds."

In the lowest bowl, the traditional combination is oranges, walnuts, and almonds. An *etrog* (citron), preserved after Sukkot with cloves, is lovely. For the mystics, these fruits, which all have a tough peel and a tasty inner flesh, represent the world of Action, the physical world around us, which they believed requires a strong outer defense. Alternative choices for this category are pecans, passion fruit, bananas, tangerines, or lemons.

In the middle bowl the traditional combination is dates, olives, and apples. The skin and flesh of these fruits are eaten, yet they contain prominent seeds to start new life. The olives remind us of the olive branch of hope that the dove returned to Noah after the destruction wrought by the Flood; the date, of the date palm, which recalls the biblical commandment against waste (*Bal Tashchit*), for every part of the date palm is used (the dates for eating, the fronds for thatching, the fibers for ropes, the trunks for building, and the branches for the lulav on Sukkot).

In mystical terms, they represent the world of Formation. Alternative fruit choices for this category could be avocados, pears, plums, cherries, loquat, apricots, peaches, melons, or papaya.

In the highest bowl are figs, carobs, and raisins. Representing the world of Creation, every part of these fruits is consumed, and so are they like those who are entirely "one" with themselves and with others. Alternative fruit choices for this category could be strawberries, blueberries, raspberries, or seedless grapes.

The Four Cups of Wine

The First Cup: Along with eating the fruit in the lowest bowl, we drink a glass of white wine, symbolic of winter and dormancy, when the rains pour down, and the long nights of winter are lit by the pale light of the moon. We withdraw into our homes, like the sweet flesh of the orange inside its inedible rind.

The Second Cup: To accompany the second bowl of fruit, we pour a second glass of white wine, this time adding a small amount of red, to signify the onset of spring, the intensifying of the sun's rays, the budding of new life, and spiritual reawakening from the slumber of winter.

The Third Cup: The third cup of wine is one-third white and two-thirds red, symbolic of summer. This is the highest level we humans can achieve, for this is the world in which, like the fruit we eat, nothing is wasted. It's a harmonious world in which we are at peace with ourselves, our neighborhoods, communities, and countries.

The Fourth Cup: The last cup of wine is entirely red, and has various interpretations: the fire of the sun, the redness of the flowers, the bounty of the harvest in the fall, and the commitment to the conservation of the earth's natural resources. We eat no fruit with the last cup.

Planning Tu b'Shvat Menus

Although the custom of eating dried fruit on Tu b'Shvat has been around since the sixteenth century, a rare number of traditional holiday dishes remain, such as Georgian Stuffed Vegetables and Pears (page 262). Instead, anything goes, from chicken to cake, as long as it contains fruit.

There *are* ways to add more meaning to your menu, however. One possibility is to do as the Kabbalists did, and include representatives of ancient Israel's Seven Species (wheat, barley, grapevines, figs, pomegranates, olive oil, and date honey) with recipes such as Whole Wheatberry Tabbouleh with Biblical Butter (page 91), Spring Barley Mini-croquettes with Tahini and Fresh Herb Sauce (page 52), and Chicken with Olives, Red Wine, Prunes, and Pomegranates (page 261). Or use the mystical number seven in a fruit-based recipe, such as Seven-Spice-Infused Meat-Stuffed Dried Fruit (page 134) or Tea with Seven Spices (page 273).

Another possibility is to create recipes around the contents of each of the three bowls, with each bowl representing a different course, such as Rich Carob Tea Cake with Fig and Raisin Confit (pages 270 and 271), the combination in the highest bowl, for dessert. And don't forget to use extra-virgin olive oil (from Israel if you can get it!) for salads and cooked dishes. That nourishing, healthful, and beautifying product of the olive tree helped sustain our ancestors during this season.

Tu b'Shvat Recipes

Appetizers

Baked Figs in Savory Tamarind Sauce (M)

Main Courses

Chicken with Olives, Red Wine, Prunes, and
  Pomegranates (M)
Georgian Stuffed Vegetables and Pears (M)

Vegetables, Grains, and Salads

Bulgur Pilaf with Mushrooms, Raisins, and Pumpkin Seeds (P)
Potatoes and Carrots with Seeds and Fragrant Spices (D)
Basmati Rice Scented with Tree Spices and Dried Fruit (D) (P)
Green Salad with Edible Flowers and Berry Vinaigrette (P)

Desserts

Warm Casserole of Seven Dried Fruits (P)
Rich Carob Tea Cake (D) (P)
Fig and Raisin Confit (P)
Natasha's Quick Russian Fruitcake (D)
Tea with Seven Spices (P)

Baked Figs in Savory Tamarind Sauce

Makes 18

This exquisite appetizer dish from the Iraqi Jewish kitchen belongs to chef Moshe Basson's childhood in Jerusalem. The figs become soft, plump, and rich—and the taste lingers in the memory for a long time to come. Use Calimyrna figs—the larger the better.

18 large dried Calimyrna figs
2 tablespoons extra-virgin olive oil
½ to ⅔ cup chopped onion
1 butterflied chicken breast, cut into small dice (less than ¼-inch cubes)
½ teaspoon salt
1 teaspoon ground cardamom
1 teaspoon ground allspice
¼ teaspoon cinnamon
Pinch of ground cloves

Sauce

3 tablespoons tamarind paste or purchased ready-made tamarind sauce
½ teaspoon ground cardamom
½ teaspoon ground allspice
1 3-inch stick cinnamon
Meat of the figs, finely chopped
2 cups water
1½ tablespoons *silan* or brown sugar
½ cup pomegranate seeds (optional)

1. Rinse the dried figs and place in a bowl. Cover with warm water and let stand 15 minutes, or until the figs are slightly softened and pliable.

2. Take one fig at a time and pull up gently from the stem end. Use a sharp knife to cut a "cap" from the top, still attached at one edge. Scoop out most of the flesh from the base section, and save for the sauce. Place the scooped-out figs on a work surface.

3. Heat the olive oil in a large pan. Sauté the onion for a few minutes until softened, stirring often. Add the chicken breast pieces, salt, and spices. Mix well and sauté quickly over high heat until the chicken turns opaque. Remove from heat and let cool slightly.

4. Carefully fill the figs with the chicken-onion mixture, replace the caps, and set aside.

5. Put the tamarind paste, cardamom, allspice, cinnamon stick, fig meat, water, and brown sugar in the same pan in which the chicken was fried. Cover and bring to a boil, stirring occasionally. Remove the cover, carefully arrange the figs in the pan, and spoon the sauce over. Reduce heat to medium-low, cover, and cook for 5 minutes, or until softened. Serve hot garnished with pomegranate seeds, if available.

Chicken with Olives, Red Wine, Prunes, and Pomegranates

Serves 6

Ⓜ

In this recipe there are fruits from the world of Action, with the pomegranate as the fruit with a protective outer skin and an edible interior; fruits from the world of Formation, with olives and prunes as the fruit whose seed represents the ability to create life; and grapes (in the form of wine) from the world of Creation—a fruit used in its entirety, with nothing wasted.

3- to 3½-pound whole chicken, in 6 pieces, or 3 whole chicken breasts, each cut in half, with bone and skin left on
1 cup extra-virgin olive oil
8 garlic cloves, peeled
1 tablespoon capers in brine, drained

1 cup pitted green olives
1 cup packed pitted prunes
½ cup red wine vinegar
½ cup pomegranate molasses
4 to 6 sprigs fresh oregano or thyme
½ cup packed dark brown sugar or honey

1. Rinse the chicken and place the pieces in a bowl. Cover with boiling water. Lift one piece of chicken out at a time, and scrape the surface gently with a knife to remove pinfeathers and excess fat. Pat dry and place the pieces in a single layer in a nonreactive (preferably glass) oven-to-table dish.

2. In a bowl, mix together the olive oil, garlic, capers, olives, pitted prunes, vinegar, and pomegranate molasses, and pour over the chicken. Tear each sprig of oregano or thyme into 2 to 3 pieces and place around the chicken. Cover and marinate in the refrigerator overnight, turning once or twice.

3. Preheat the oven to 350°F.

4. In a bowl, mix the brown sugar with the wine, and pour over the chicken, skin side up. Remove half the sprigs of fresh herbs. Bake, covered, for 45 minutes, turning once. Remove the cover and continue to bake another 15 to 20 minutes, until the chicken pieces are a rich golden brown.

Tu b'Shvat

261

Georgian Stuffed Vegetables and Pears

Serves 6 to 8

Many countries have their own version of stuffed vegetables used for every day and for holiday fare. This dish, which hails from Georgia on the Black Sea, also includes stuffed pears, and is topped with a layer of dried fruit.

The recipe for this Tu b'Shvat main course was taught to us by Marina Tofuria, a Georgian cook. Although the traditional recipe uses tomatoes and zucchini, we also like to stuff halved or whole multicolored peppers, which withstand longer cooking without losing their shape.

Note: If the quantity in the recipe seems formidable, don't hesitate to cut the recipe in half. Brown rice may also be substituted for white rice, if desired. For this recipe, you will need two large onions (1 pound)—one to stuff and one for the sauce—and a medium one for the stuffing.

2 medium potatoes (about ¾ pound)

1 medium eggplant (about 1¼ pounds)

2 large tomatoes (about 1 pound)

1 large onion (about ½ pound)

2 medium zucchini (about 1 pound)

2 large firm but ripe pears

Stuffing

12 ounces lean ground beef

8 ounces ground lamb

⅔ cup cooked white or brown rice

1 medium onion, chopped (½ cup)

Rounded ⅓ cup *each* chopped fresh cilantro, Italian parsley, and mint

2 large garlic cloves, pressed

1 teaspoon salt

1 teaspoon freshly ground black pepper

Sauce

1½ tablespoons vegetable oil

1 large onion (about ½ pound), finely chopped

1 14-ounce can crushed tomatoes

2 tablespoons tomato paste

1 bay leaf

1½ teaspoons sweet paprika

Salt to taste

Freshly ground black pepper to taste

Topping

Rounded ⅓ cup each, cut into strips, Calimyrna figs, dates, and apricots

2½ tablespoons raisins

1 small red bell pepper, seeded and diced

1 small orange or yellow bell pepper, seeded and diced

Leaves of 2 sprigs fresh mint

1. To prepare the vegetables for stuffing, wash the potatoes and use a sharp knife to hollow out a large indentation to within ⅜ inch of the rim. (Alternately, potatoes may be halved like boats.) Cut the top off the eggplant or cut in half, and hollow out the inside. Cut off a thin slice from the top of each of the tomatoes and scoop out the flesh (may be added to the cooking sauce), leaving a firm rim to hold the stuffing. Slice about ½ inch off the top of the onion, and hollow out a bowl-shaped space. Cut a slice off the bottom so the onion will stand upright. Cut off the tops and tails of the zucchini and cut into 2½- or 3-inch pieces. Hollow out each piece to within ¼ inch of the skin. Sprinkle the zucchini with salt and turn over on a rack to drain for 10 minutes. Drain, rinse, and pat dry. Set all the vegetables aside, cut side down.

2. Cut the tops off the pears and use an apple corer to scoop out the insides, leaving enough at the base so the filling will not escape (or cut in half, core, and hollow out only the base).

3. In a bowl, mix together all the ingredients for the stuffing and stuff the vegetables and pears, pressing down gently on the filling. Place in one or two of the largest, widest cooking pots you have, preferably with shallow sides.

For the Sauce

4. Heat the oil in a skillet, and sauté the onion until golden.

5. Add the crushed tomatoes, tomato paste, bay leaf, paprika, salt, and pepper, and 1½ cups water. Bring to a boil and cook, partially covered, over medium-low heat for 15 minutes.

6. Pour the hot sauce over and around the vegetables. Cover and cook over medium-low heat 30 minutes, checking occasionally to see that there is enough liquid in the pan. If not, add a little more boiling water.

For the Topping

7. Mix the dried fruit strips with the raisins, chopped bell peppers, and mint leaves. Sprinkle on top of the vegetables and pears. Cover and simmer for 8 to 10 minutes, or until the fruit is just tender but still brightly colored. Serve warm.

Bulgur Pilaf with Mushrooms, Raisins, and Pumpkin Seeds

Serves 4 to 6

Ⓟ

This recipe contains two of the Seven Species—bulgur (wheat) and raisins (grapes)—with (pumpkin) seeds, which are believed to contain the mystical energy for new life. Serve with Roasted Chicken Thighs with Honey, Olives, and Oregano (page 170) or Chicken with Dates, Olive Oil, and Twelve Garlic Cloves (page 195), if desired.

2½ cups water
1 teaspoon salt
2 cups coarse bulgur (use medium if no coarse is available)
1 tablespoon light sesame oil
1 tablespoon dark (toasted) sesame oil
2 cups thinly sliced fresh mushrooms (about 1 pound)
½ to ⅔ cup chopped onion (about 1 medium)
¼ cup raisins
⅓ cup pumpkin seeds, toasted in a dry skillet
Salt to taste
Freshly ground pepper to taste

1. In a pot, bring the water to a boil and add the salt and bulgur. Bring to a boil again and lower the heat. Turn off heat and set aside, covered, about 30 minutes, until the water is absorbed and the bulgur is tender. If any water remains, strain the bulgur.

2. In a skillet, heat the sesame oils and sauté the mushrooms and onions over medium-low heat until golden. Stir in the raisins and pumpkin seeds, and remove from heat. Add to the bulgur and fluff with a fork. Season with salt and pepper before serving.

Potatoes
and Carrots
with Seeds
and
Fragrant
Spices

Serves 6

Ⓓ

ragrant, attractive, and simply delicious, this combination of vegetables, seeds, and spices may be served as a side dish, or over Basmati Rice Scented with Tree Spices and Dried Fruit (page 266) as a vegetarian main dish. Potatoes over rice, you ask? In the Near and Middle East and parts of Asia, people eat that combination all the time.

6 medium carrots (about 1
  pound)
1 large or 3 medium potatoes
  (about 1 pound)
⅓ cup Biblical Butter (page 72), or
  safflower or canola oil
1 tablespoon freshly grated,
  peeled gingerroot, or ¼
  teaspoon ground ginger
4 to 6 garlic cloves, minced or
  pressed
4 teaspoons *each* poppy seeds,
  sesame seeds, and coriander
  seeds

2 teaspoons *each* turmeric and
  cumin
1 teaspoon chili powder or
  sweet paprika
1½ to 2 teaspoons salt
⅓ cup boiling water
1½ cups plain yogurt
Freshly chopped cilantro or
  Italian parsley, for garnish

1. To prepare the vegetables, top and scrape the carrots clean but do not peel. Halve lengthwise and chop. Scrub the potatoes well, dry (do not peel), and cut into medium dice.

2. Heat the Biblical Butter or oil in a large skillet with cover on medium heat. Add the vegetables and cook, stirring often, until lightly browned on the edges. Remove from the pan. Set aside.

3. Add the ginger, garlic, poppy, sesame, and coriander seeds to the pan and cook 1 minute, stirring constantly. Lower heat, and return the vegetables to the pan.

4. Add turmeric, cumin, chili powder or paprika, salt, and boiling water. Mix gently, cover and cook over low heat until the vegetables are tender, adding additional tablespoons of boiling water if necessary.

5. Stir in the yogurt and heat, but do not boil. Serve hot, garnished with cilantro or parsley.

Basmati Rice Scented with Tree Spices and Dried Fruit

Serves 6

Made of rice, which traditionally symbolizes fertility, and a tempting combination of dried fruits, fragrant tree bark (cinnamon), unopened tree-flower buds (cloves), seeds (cumin), roots (ginger), and greens, this dish is truly a celebration of the good earth.

1 cup white or brown basmati rice
4 tablespoons Biblical Butter (page 72), or walnut, hazelnut, or cold-pressed sesame oil
1 teaspoon cumin seeds
6 whole cloves
1 cinnamon stick
1¾ to 2 cups water
1 teaspoon salt
¼ teaspoon freshly ground black pepper
½ teaspoon ground turmeric
1 teaspoon freshly grated, peeled gingerroot
¼ cup raisins
4 dried apricots, coarsely chopped
¼ cup cashews, toasted
3 tablespoons shelled pistachio nuts, toasted (optional)
3 tablespoons chopped fresh Italian parsley or coriander, for garnish

1. Soak the rice with water to cover for 30 minutes. Drain well.

2. Melt 2 tablespoons of the butter in a medium-size pot over medium-low heat. Add the cumin seeds, cloves, and cinnamon and cook, stirring occasionally, until the spices are fragrant.

3. Add the rice and cook, stirring, for 2 minutes. Add the water (the amount of water will depend on what type of rice you use—check the package label), salt, pepper, and turmeric. Stir once and bring to a boil.

4. Cover, lower heat, and cook until the rice is tender but not soft (time depends on type of rice—brown rice will take about 10 to 15 minutes longer). Cool slightly and fluff with a fork.

5. While the rice is cooking, prepare the fruit topping: Melt the remaining 2 tablespoons butter in a small skillet and gently sauté the ginger for 30 seconds. Add the raisins and apricots and sauté 2 minutes, stirring frequently. Add the cashews and pistachios and cook an additional minute.

6. Oil a medium-size (preferably stainless steel) bowl, and pat the fruit-and-nut mixture evenly around the bottom and as far up the side as it will go.

7. Remove the cinnamon stick from the cooked rice and carefully pack the rice into the bowl until it reaches the top. Pat it down firmly but not forcefully.

8. Place a large round serving dish upside down over the bowl, and turn the bowl over onto the plate. (If the mixture doesn't reach the top of the bowl, it will lose its rounded shape when you turn it over. Rather than take it out and pack it into a smaller bowl, you can alleviate the situation by covering the rice with a dish slightly smaller than the circumference of the bowl, and turning everything over on to a serving tray or a larger plate.) Slowly remove the bowl and—voilà! Sprinkle with the parsley or coriander for garnish.

Note: If you're serving children, pick out the rest of the whole spices before serving.

Green Salad with Edible Flowers and Berry Vinaigrette

Serves 6 to 8

This elegant salad, which mixes a host of distinctive lettuces, greens, and flowers, is just perfect for a Tu b'Shvat Seder. We used nasturtium flowers, but you can choose from the wide variety of edible flowers available, including pansies and rose petals. Just make sure that the flowers are edible and have not been treated with herbicides or pesticides. Look for edible flowers at fancy greengrocers or farmers' markets. If you don't have access to edible flowers, dress up the salad with a selection of fresh herbs, such as basil and tarragon, and toasted slivered almonds.

Salad

½ pound romaine lettuce, torn in bite-size pieces

Small heads mâche or lamb's lettuce, torn into bite-size pieces

1 small red oak leaf lettuce, torn into bite-size pieces

1½ cups lightly packed sliced arugula leaves

1 cup sunflower seed sprouts (or radish or broccoli sprouts)

10 nasturtium blossoms and/or other available flowers

Vinaigrette

3 small shallots, minced (or the white part of 3 scallions)

2 garlic cloves, minced or pressed

3 tablespoons raspberry, blueberry, or strawberry preserves

2 tablespoons Dijon mustard with seeds (or without, if desired)

½ cup white wine vinegar

2 to 3 tablespoons freshly squeezed lemon or lime juice

1 cup extra-virgin olive oil

1. Rinse all the ingredients for the salad except the sprouts and flowers, and dry thoroughly. (Pay special attention to any soil that may have collected in the stem ends.) Remove stems and cores, and prepare as indicated. If not using immediately, wrap the greens in a paper or kitchen towel and place in a plastic bag in the refrigerator. (To chill more than 2 hours in advance, sprinkle a few drops of water on the towel before packing.)

2. Cut off any roots on the sprouts. Carefully wash nasturtiums or other edible flowers. Shake to dry.

3. Transfer all the ingredients except the flowers to a salad bowl and toss.

4. Put all the ingredients for the vinaigrette in a blender, except for the oil. Drizzle in the oil while the machine is running, and blend until emulsified.

5. Just before serving, toss the salad with just enough dressing to coat the leaves. Sprinkle the flowers on top, toss lightly, and serve. Pass the remaining dressing.

I n ancient times, dried fruit provided an important source of nourishment during the winter and in times of scarcity. A richly flavored and comforting dish, this casserole of dried fruits makes a superb warm breakfast, snack, or dessert throughout the holiday.

Note: Since most dried fruit is preserved with sulfur dioxide, it's best to look for organic fruit. If unavailable, immerse the fruit in boiling water for 1 minute, rinse, and pat dry to help remove sulfur dioxide and/or oil coatings.

Serves 8

2 packed cups *each* pitted
    prunes, dried pear or peach
    halves, and small Black
    Mission or other figs
1 cup golden raisins
5¾ cups bottled or canned
    white grape juice
Pinch of ground ginger, or
    1 thin slice peeled fresh
    gingerroot, or 1 cinnamon
    stick

2 bananas, peeled and sliced
1½ cups freshly squeezed
    orange juice
2 tablespoons honey

1. Rinse the fruit and snip off the tips of the figs with kitchen shears. Place in a very large bowl or nonreactive pot and cover with the grape juice. Add ginger or cinnamon. Place a heavy plate on top, and press down to immerse the fruit. Let stand overnight.

2. Preheat the oven to 350°F.

3. Transfer the fruit and juice to a casserole with a cover and arrange the sliced bananas on top. Mix the orange juice and honey and pour over the top. Bake, covered, for 1 hour.

4. Serve warm, as is, or with fresh cream, crème fraîche, yogurt, fine vanilla ice cream, or sorbet.

Rich Carob Tea Cake

Serves 6 to 8

And they gave him a fig cake, and two clusters of raisins. And when he had eaten, his spirit revived. For he had eaten no bread nor drunk any water three days and three nights.

—1 Sam. 30:12

Although it's not exactly the fig cake mentioned in the Book of Samuel, this carob cake, served with Fig and Raisin Confit (page 271), is so moist and delicious, most people would swear it's a chocolate cake. It takes only minutes to prepare and together with the confit makes a perfect dessert for a Tu b'Shvat dinner. It is an edible interpretation of the contents of the Seder's highest bowl.

1 cup unsweetened carob chips (Sunspire recommended)
½ cup (1 stick) butter or canola oil
⅔ cup turbinado sugar or packed light brown sugar
3 eggs
½ cup whole-wheat flour or unbleached all-purpose flour
1 teaspoon baking powder
Pinch of salt
2 tablespoons brandy
Confectioners' sugar, for dusting
Fig and Raisin Confit

1. Preheat the oven to 350°F. Cut out a circle of parchment paper to fit in the bottom of an 8-inch round baking pan. Cut out a strip to line the sides. Affix with a little butter or oil.

2. Place the carob chips and butter in a glass bowl. Microwave for 1 minute, until softened or melted. (If using oil, soften the carob chips in the microwave, remove, and stir in oil.) Cool slightly.

3. In the bowl of an electric mixer, beat the sugar and eggs until foamy. Using a rubber spatula, transfer the carob mixture to the mixing bowl and mix on low speed until blended. Sift in the flour, baking powder, and salt, and beat lightly. Stir in the brandy. Pour the batter into the prepared pan. Bake for 20 to 25 minutes, or until a toothpick inserted in the center comes out clean. The cake should still be moist but not wet. Do not overbake or cake will dry out.

4. Cool in the pan, run a knife around the edges, and turn out on a serving dish. Carefully remove parchment paper from the top and sides.

5. Dust the top with confectioners' sugar, passed through a wire-mesh strainer. Serve with warm Fig and Raisin Confit.

This superb confit enhances and complements the flavors of Rich Carob Tea Cake (page 270), and may also be used to stuff baked apples, spread on toast points, or served alongside any of the chopped liver renditions in this book.

½ pound Calimyrna or Black
    Mission figs
¼ cup black tea leaves
4 cups water
1 cinnamon stick
6 whole black peppercorns
4 cardamom pods, lightly
    crushed

1½-inch piece peeled fresh
    gingerroot
⅛ teaspoon ground mace
    (optional)
⅓ cup raisins

1. Rinse the figs, cut off tips with a kitchen shears, and cut each lengthwise and widthwise into 4 sections. Set aside.

2. Combine tea, water, and spices in a medium-size nonreactive saucepan and bring to a boil. Cook until reduced to 2 cups liquid. Strain, discard spices, and return to the saucepan together with the figs and raisins. Bring to a boil and cook over medium-low heat, about 8 to 10 minutes, stirring occasionally, until fruit is soft and the mixture thickens to a jam-like consistency.

3. Serve warm or store in a clean tightly closed jar in the refrigerator for up to 2 weeks. To reheat, bring the jar to room temperature, place in a half-filled saucepan of water, and heat through until warmed.

Natasha's Quick Russian Fruitcake

Serves 8 to 10

Provide our dear friend Natasha access to a variety of nuts, and she'll cook or bake you almost anything; but this concentrated little dried fruit sweet, a Tu b'Shvat family tradition taught to her by her mother, Adele, really takes the cake! Add the liqueur to the cake, or serve a choice of liqueurs alongside and let your guests dip their slices in.

½ cup (1 stick) butter
1 cup sugar
2 egg yolks
1 whole egg
1 cup unbleached all-purpose flour
1 cup walnuts, chopped

1 cup raisins
1 cup mixed thin strips of dried apricots, pitted prunes, and figs
2 to 4 tablespoons Amaretto, Kahlúa, or brandy (optional)

1. Preheat the oven to 350°F. Grease and flour a 9-inch springform or round baking pan, knocking out excess flour (or line the bottom and side with parchment paper affixed with a little butter, oil, or nonstick cooking spray).

2. In a medium saucepan, melt butter and stir in sugar, dissolving as best as possible (it does not have to dissolve completely).

3. Remove from heat, wait a moment or two, and beat in the eggs. Mix well. Work in the flour, nuts, dried fruits, and liqueur if you are using it. Beat with a wooden spoon until well blended. Pour into the prepared pan. Bake for 30 to 40 minutes, or a toothpick inserted into the cake comes out clean.

4. Run a knife along the edge of the pan, gently remove the outer ring, and peel off the parchment paper, if using. Slip a knife under the cake and slide it off the bottom of the pan onto your hand, to facilitate peeling off the parchment paper on the bottom. Transfer to a serving platter. Use a sharp knife to slice.

Black tea with seven spices is more than delicious; it contains star anise, cinnamon, and coriander to help your digestion, cloves and black peppercorns to fight germs and bacteria, ginger as a general tonic, and nutmeg to relax you. All this and the mystical "seven" in one cup! Another fragrant and delicious way to prepare tea is to add a few pinches of Yemenite *Hawaiij* for Coffee and Sweets (page 300) to already brewed strong black tea.

Serves 8 to 10

10 cups water

8 whole star anise

3 to 4 whole cloves

2 cinnamon sticks

1-inch piece peeled fresh
    gingerroot, sliced

½ whole nutmeg, broken into
    pieces

1 teaspoon coriander seeds

½ teaspoon black peppercorns

¼ cup loose black tea (like Assam
    or English Breakfast)

3 tablespoons turbinado sugar or
    honey (optional)

1. Bring the water to a boil in large saucepan, and add the spices. Lower heat, cover, and simmer for 20 minutes. Add the loose tea and steep for 3 to 5 minutes.

2. Strain through a fine wire-mesh strainer, stir in the desired sweetener, and serve in tall heatproof glasses. If the tea is too strong, add a little extra boiling water.

With the start of the month of Adar, we greatly increase joy.
   —BT Taanit 29a

Oh once there was a wicked, wicked man,
And Haman was his name, sir!
He would have murdered all the Jews,
Though they were not to blame, sir!
So today we'll merry merry be,
So today we'll merry merry be
So today we'll merry merry be,
And nosh some hamantaschen!
   —an old Purim song

Purim

The happiest, most lighthearted holiday on the Jewish calendar, Purim falls on the 14th of the Hebrew month of Adar, usually during March. Tricks are permissible, and treats essential. In Israel one year, the national television station broadcast the evening news upside down. Another year, a popular radio station announced that massive quantities of crude oil had been found under central Tel Aviv, and a major daily newspaper came out with a fake front page.

The only festival that calls not only for a *Seudah*, a grand lunch, but also for actually getting drunk, Purim commemorates the victory of Queen Esther and her Uncle Mordecai against the evil machinations of the courtier Haman, who set out to destroy the Jews of Persia somewhere between 534 and 420 B.C.E. Since then, it's been filled with a playful naughtiness expressed in its folk traditions and its amusing delicacies, like those recalling the wicked Haman's body parts and those "in disguise" as other foods.

Falling just at the vernal equinox, it's a Jewish version of Carnival, Twelfth Night, and even April Fools' Day, a topsy-turvy day whose postbiblical origins may have been in the new year celebrations of ancient Persia, which, like Purim, took place in the spring.

"Put down our story in writing for generations to come," entreat the heroes of the holiday, Mordecai and Esther, in a letter to the rabbis of their era, according to the Talmud. Centuries later, the holiday is still commemorated by the chanting of the Scroll of Esther, accompanied by foot pounding, hisses, and noisy groggers at the recitation of the very name of the wicked Haman. On this holiday, carousing is a mitzvah—there's even a Talmudic law to drink so much that you don't know the difference between "Blessed be Mordecai" and "Cursed be Haman."

Throughout the Jewish world and throughout the generations, people have translated the holiday into a variety of culinary customs, first and foremost surrounding the wicked Haman himself. In many Ashkenazic homes, Purim was the time to prepare a giant-sized braided challah called a *Keylitsh* (page 279), which represents the ropes from which Haman was eventually hanged. In Moroccan homes, a delightful Purim challah (page 280) included whole hard-boiled eggs baked right in, to represent Haman's eyes.

In Greece, Jewish bakers used their whimsy to turn the scoundrel's eyes, ears, nose, feet, and even his fleas (!) into tasty confections and pastries such as *Folorikos* ("Haman's Foot"; page 294). And on the island of Salonika, the once flourishing Jewish community destroyed by the Nazis, the Jews were known for their Purim marzipan figurines, called *Folares* (uncolored) or *Novies* (colored). To make your own homemade marzipan, see the recipe *Moshe b'Tayva* (Moses in the Basket; page 44).

And although Sephardic grandmothers might still be making *Orejas de Aman* (*Orecchi di Aman* in Italian), those crisp deep-fried twists of dough shaped like Haman's ears, dipped in sugar syrup or dusted with confectioners' sugar, the all-time quintessential delight that has succeeded in standing the test of time is no doubt the Hamantaschen, or *Ozen Haman* (page 292), developed centuries ago by Eastern European Jews. Thought to be of German origin, these triangular cookies were alternately considered Haman's pockets (taschen), ears, or three-cornered hat.

Whether baked small or oversized, using cookie dough or a yeast dough version (the latter on the verge of extinction), Hamantaschen are traditionally stuffed with poppy seeds, since tradition holds that Queen Esther chose a vegetarian diet of beans, nuts, and various seeds, including poppy seeds, rather than eat nonkosher food in the king's palace. Other common fillings are dried fruit, and in the early 1900s in Galicia, honey and nuts. Today, creative cooks might choose to fill them with halvah, exotic fruit jams, or even savory stuffings, and many children find them absolutely irresistible stuffed with nutella.

There are other amusing culinary customs as well. Since Purim is a time for masquerading—just as Queen Esther had to keep her Jewish identity hidden from King Ahasherus until it was wise to reveal it—it is customary to create "disguised" versions of traditional foods, such as the seventeenth-century

Purim kreplach dough in Poland and Prague that was kneaded with honey and spices, and filled with raisins and nuts, or jam. In this chapter you'll also find our own Apricot "Leather" Sushi (page 281), a variation on the same theme, and you can fool your guests with a dessert of Phyllis's Famous Carrot Cake (page 212) or Zucchini Tea Cake with Cinnamon and Nutmeg (page 214), and let them guess the major ingredient.

Like Yom Kippur and Sukkot, Purim is another time when it is customary to serve foods with chopped or "beaten" filling (page 181), but this time it symbolizes the way we beat our feet when Haman's name is mentioned during the scroll reading, reflected in Phyllo Envelopes Stuffed with Kasha, Mushrooms, and Onions (page 282), whose wrapping in dough is seen as a perfect Purim "disguise."

In Eastern Europe, sweet-and-sour foods such as Bubby Rose's Old World Cabbage Borscht (page 190) and Sweet-and-Sour Stuffed Cabbage (page 196) appeared as holiday fare on Purim (as well as on Sukkot), as if to echo the unfolding of the Purim story (from sour to sweet), but probably because they were festive seasonal dishes that stored well due to their acidity, counterbalanced in flavor by the addition of raisins and other sweeteners. In keeping with the sweet-and-sour theme, you might want to consider adding Sliced Avocado with Sweet-and-Sour Poppy Seed Vinaigrette (page 284) or Sweet-and-Sour Three-Bean Salad (page 286).

Though the Scroll of Esther tells us that King Ahasherus feasted for months even before meeting Esther, and later Esther herself discovered that the way to her husband's heart was through his stomach, our present-day feasting tradition is concentrated in the *Seudah*, the holiday's most festive lunchtime meal. The *Seudah* symbolizes the physical pleasure of delicious food enhanced by the simple joy that God's work has rescued us from our enemies. In keeping with Esther's spirit, we'd like to suggest a Persian-style Purim feast: Fully aware of how her royal husband Ahasherus relished a good meal, she invited him to a two-day banquet in order to expose the wicked machinations of Haman. There's no report in the Book of Esther about what they actually ate, but our friend Schelley Talalay Dardashti has helped us create a Persian banquet fit for a king!

Gifts of Food

One of the most important and beautiful customs of Purim is giving the gift of foods—*Mishloach Manot* (*Shalach Manos* in Yiddish)—capturing the essence of Judaism in both the preparation and the giving. At Purim, giving is a mitzvah, and even the poor are enjoined to give gifts to those less fortunate than themselves.

Throughout the Ashkenazic and Sephardic worlds, it was the children of the family who were employed to distribute *Mishloach Manot*, carefully arranged on a plate covered with a white cloth, among relatives and neighbors. Traditionally, the minimum requirement to fulfill the mitzvah is to send to each person a gift of at least two different kinds of ready-to-eat foods, each of which requires a different blessing. One is also required to give *tzedaka*, gifts of money or food, to at least two poor people, preferably not through a charity but directly to the people themselves.

Today, *Mishloach Manot* can be interpreted in a variety of creative ways—different cookies and sweets, savory and sweet items, gift packages that include all the ingredients for a meal, or condiments for meals to come—packed on pretty paper plates, gift plates, or in recycled baskets and tins. Working alone or together with your children, grandchildren, or a best friend, designing personal gifts of foods and their presentation is a tradition worth preserving. In this chapter you'll also find a whole slew of tempting gift ideas from which to choose.

Purim Recipes

Challot for Purim

Keylitsh Challah for Purim Ⓟ
Moroccan Purim Challah (*Boyoja Ungola Di-Purim*) Ⓟ

Appetizers and Party Food

Apricot "Leather" Sushi Ⓓ
Phyllo Envelopes Stuffed with Kasha, Mushrooms, and Onions Ⓓ Ⓟ
Sliced Avocado with Sweet-and-Sour Poppy Seed Vinaigrette Ⓟ
Shirazi Salad Ⓟ
Sweet-and-Sour Three-Bean Salad Ⓟ

Main Courses

Persian Roasted Chicken in Saffron and Lime Juice Ⓜ
Beef and Eggplant Stew (*Khoresht Mosamma Bademjan*) Ⓜ
"Drunken" Salmon in Sherry-Butter Sauce Ⓓ

Purim Pastries and Mishloach Manot—"Shalach Manos"

Makagigi (Cracow Style) Ⓟ
Almond *Makagigi* (Warsaw Style) Ⓓ
Mom's Classic Hamantaschen with Natasha's Fruit Fillings Ⓟ

Natasha's Fruit Fillings **P**
Greek *Folorikos* ("Haman's Foot") **P**
Healthy Nut and Seed Treats **P**
Yarden's Giant Chocolate-Chip Cookie **D**
Little Chocolate Snaps **D**
Black-and-White Seasoned Salt **P**
Baharat **P**
A Yemenite Flavors Gift Package of *Tzoug* and
    Two Kinds of *Hawaiij* **P**

Purim once had its own special challah. In Eastern Europe it was the *Keylitsh* (pronounced *Koilitch* by those of Russian descent), an extra-large braided challah that symbolized the ropes used to hang Haman, and little braided challot or rolls called *Brachas* (Yiddish for "blessings"), probably prepared for *Mishloach Manot*.

To make a *Keylitsh,* use the recipe for Round Challah (using raisins) in the Rosh Hashanah chapter (page 124), but instead of making two challot, divide the dough in three parts and make one giant braid. Alternately, leave a little of the dough aside, make one giant braid, and with the remaining dough make a long narrow braid to place on top (like those bakeries often make for bar mitzvot and weddings). Pinch its ends into the ends of the larger braid so it doesn't come apart during baking. Brush the top with beaten egg, as in the original recipe, and sprinkle lightly with thinly sliced blanched almonds, if desired. Bake as in the original recipe.

Keylitsh Challah for Purim

(P)

Moroccan Purim Challah

Boyoja Ungola Di-Purim

For 3 to 4 challot

These unique spiced challot, which we first encountered in the Isaac Kaplan Old Yishuv Court Museum in Jerusalem, are topped with hard-boiled eggs (sometimes one for every member of or child in the family) representing Haman's eyes.

8 cups unbleached all-purpose flour (or bread flour), plus extra for kneading

2 tablespoons yeast

1 cup sugar

1 tablespoon sesame seeds

1 tablespoon aniseed (or fennel seeds)

1 cup whole almonds, coarsely chopped (optional)

¼ teaspoon salt

3 eggs

½ cup vegetable or canola oil

2¼ cups warm water

6 to 8 hard-boiled eggs

1 egg yolk, beaten with 1 teaspoon water, for brushing

½ cup blanched whole almonds, for garnish

1. Put the flour in a wide bowl of a standing electric mixer fitted with the dough hook. Mix in the yeast, sugar, sesame seeds, aniseed, and chopped almonds, if using; add the salt.

2. In a separate bowl, whisk eggs, oil, and warm water. Make a well in the center of the dough and blend in the egg mixture. Knead with the dough hook until a soft dough is formed.

3. Remove the dough from the mixer, and transfer to a lightly floured work surface. Knead a few more minutes, adding additional flour if necessary, until dough is elastic.

4. Divide into 3 to 4 balls, cover each with a warm cloth, and let rise 2 hours. Punch down and let rest 5 minutes.

5. Preheat the oven to 400°F. Line 2 baking sheets with parchment paper or lightly grease.

6. Knead the first ball of dough briefly, and remove a small amount of dough to make strips that will hold down the hard-boiled eggs. Form the ball into a round flattened disk, and use a knife to cut crosswise shallow slits on the top in a grid. Place two hard-boiled eggs in the middle of each ball, and fasten them down individually with crosswise strips of dough. Repeat the process with the remaining balls of dough and eggs.

7. Make 1½-inch-deep slits around the edge of each disk, giving it a sunlike appearance. Brush with the egg yolk and water mixture. Stick a few blanched almonds in around the eggs. Bake in a hot oven for 30 minutes, until golden brown.

Apricot "Leather" Sushi

M any people will remember apricot "leather," an ultrathin layer of dried apricots that we literally peeled off a plastic backing. Although not as popular today as it was in *our* childhood, apricot *ledder* (as it's called in Hebrew) is still available and still a nutritious food.

Since Purim is a time for pranks, and "disguised" and topsy-turvy foods, what could be better than giving our apricot leather another incarnation—as a substitute for nori—and a funny take on sushi. This conversation piece makes a great appetizer or party food.

Look for fruit "leather" rolls in health-food stores and Middle Eastern shops, where they come in different widths and flavors. This recipe was created for a roll about 11 inches wide. If the width of your roll differs, adjust other ingredients accordingly. These rolls can be prepared a day in advance, and will last 2 to 3 days in the refrigerator.

One piece apricot or other fruit leather

4 ounces cream cheese, at room temperature

1 teaspoon honey

¼ teaspoon vanilla extract

A few drops rose water (optional)

¼ cup shelled salted pistachios, toasted

1. Cut a piece of fruit leather to approximately 11 by 4½ inches. Place the wider side closer to you.

2. In a small bowl, mix the cream cheese, honey, vanilla, and rose water, if using. With a fork, spread over the piece of fruit leather. Sprinkle the pistachios about ¼ inch from the bottom in a horizontal line. Carefully and tightly roll up the leather as you would for sushi. To seal the edge, moisten it with water.

3. Wrap the "sushi" in plastic wrap and place in the refrigerator to firm up. To serve, slice into ½-inch slices with a sharp knife and stand upright on a plate.

Phyllo Envelopes Stuffed with Kasha, Mushrooms, and Onions

Makes about 36

A variation on the kasha knish, these crispy "packages" will tempt even non-kasha lovers. They make a delicious Purim party snack, appetizer, or even vegetarian main dish, served with soup and salad.

For a spectacular buffet presentation, serve the warm packages on a bed of fresh thyme sprigs, accompanied by a bowl of thick (preferably sheep's- or goat's-milk) yogurt, and a platter of whole scallions, radishes, Tassos (salt-cured) olives, and sliced feta cheese.

9 to 10 sheets packaged phyllo dough

1 cup kasha (we prefer Wolff's)

1 egg, beaten

2 cups boiling water

3 tablespoons extra-virgin olive oil, plus ¼ cup

1 lightly beaten egg white (optional), for brushing

1 cup chopped onion (1 medium-large)

1 cup chopped fresh mushrooms, thinkly sliced

1 teaspoon salt

¼ teaspoon freshly ground black pepper

¼ cup (½ stick) butter (or an equivalent amount olive oil)

Chopped pistachios or pine nuts, toasted, for garnish (optional)

1. If using frozen phyllo dough, defrost it at least 8 hours or overnight in the refrigerator before using, and let it come to room temperature before using.

2. Grease a medium pot with a little oil or nonstick cooking spray. Stir in the kasha and toast about 2 minutes, stirring constantly. Add the beaten egg and stir quickly and constantly so that each grain is lightly covered with egg. Pour in boiling water, cover tightly, and cook on lowest possible heat for 10 to 15 minutes, or until water is absorbed. Remove from heat and let the kasha sit, covered, while you prepare the onion mixture.

3. Heat 2 tablespoons of the olive oil in a skillet. Add the onion and sauté until lightly golden, stirring often. Add the thinly sliced mushrooms with the remaining tablespoon of oil and cook, stirring, just until the mushrooms have softened.

4. Fluff the kasha with a fork and mix in the onions, mushrooms, salt, and pepper. Mix thoroughly.

5. Preheat the oven to 350°F. Lightly grease a baking sheet, or line it with parchment paper.

6. Open the phyllo out on a cutting board or dry tea towel. With a sharp knife, cut through the layers to make a stack of 4½- to 5-inch strips. Cover the stack with two slightly damp (not wet) tea towels. Work quickly. (If the dough stands for long periods of time it will dry out and tear, and if the towel is too wet the dough will stick to itself.)

7. Melt the butter in the microwave and stir in ¼ cup live oil. Keep a pastry brush handy.

8. Remove two phyllo rectangles at a time from the pile and brush with the melted butter-olive oil mixture. (Keep the remaining dough covered.) Place a tablespoon of the kasha filling about 1 inch from the bottom of the phyllo and flatten slightly. Fold the bottom over the kasha like a flap, then fold in the sides. Brush lightly with the butter-oil mixture and fold from the bottom up to form a package. Fasten the end with a dab of butter-oil or beaten egg white. Place seam side down on the prepared pan, and repeat with the remaining phyllo and filling. Brush the tops. Bake in the preheated oven for 20 minutes, or until crispy and golden brown. Transfer to a serving platter. Sprinkle with the chopped nuts, if desired.

Note: Unbaked packages may be prepared several hours in advance. Cover with plastic wrap and keep in the refrigerator. Brush with butter before baking.

Sliced Avocado with Sweet-and-Sour Poppy Seed Vinaigrette

Serves 6

This recipe proves that you can enjoy Purim's traditional poppy seeds in more ways than hamantaschen. The improvisation possibilities are plentiful, and a few suggestions are included at the end of the recipe.

Vinaigrette
¼ cup honey or sugar
½ cup sunflower or safflower oil
5½ tablespoons white wine vinegar
2 tablespoons minced scallions
½ teaspoon grainy Dijon mustard

Salt to taste
2 teaspoons whole poppy seeds

6 small avocados
6 cups baby salad or wild greens (optional)

1. Make the vinaigrette by mixing all the ingredients, except for the poppy seeds, together in a blender until emulsified. Stir in the poppy seeds. (Vinaigrette can be made in advance and stored in a covered container in the refrigerator. Shake before using.)

2. Peel, halve, pit, and thinly slice the avocados lengthwise into strips, leaving them attached at one end, so it is possible to fan out the slices. (If you don't succeed you can always overlap the detached slices.) Divide the baby greens (if using) among 6 individual plates, arrange one sliced avocado on each, and pour over the dressing.

Variations

Here's a "health salad" Queen Esther would certainly have enjoyed: A bed of thinly sliced red and green cabbage, with little mounds of freshly grated carrots, grated fresh beets, and cubed avocado, topped with sunflower seeds and the poppy seed vinaigrette.

Make alternating strips of avocado and peeled and sliced ripe pear on each plate. Top with the vinaigrette.

Use different types and textures of lettuce, add chopped scallions and fresh tarragon leaves, and top with the avocado and vinaigrette.

Create an interesting fruit cocktail, adding sliced bananas, seedless red grapes, and sliced carambola (Chinese star fruit) to the avocado, and top with the vinaigrette. For a festive touch, serve in chilled cocktail glasses with rims moistened and dipped in sugar.

Although this is one of the typical appetizers you'd find at any Persian feast, the Shirazi salad of plenteous fresh herbs and vegetables can be served as a healthy and delicious start to any meal.

Note: If you were to visit a Persian home, Jewish or not, you'll also find a Sabzi fresh herb platter on the table at the beginning of the meal, its contents chomped on throughout the many courses. Such a platter should consist of equal amounts of mint, Italian parsley, tarragon, and basil sprigs, along with baby radishes and scallions. The radishes are often sliced into fans, and dipped in ice water to open them up, and the scallions are quartered halfway up, and placed in ice water to open and curl. Very pretty!

1 cup fresh parsley
1 cup fresh mint
½ cup fresh tarragon
1 cup fresh dill
½ cup fresh basil
3 English (hothouse) cucumbers
4 beefsteak tomatoes, or 12 to 16
    small Roma tomatoes
1 medium onion

Dressing
½ cup freshly squeezed lime
    juice or lemon juice
¼ to ⅓ cup extra-virgin olive oil
1½ teaspoons freshly ground
    black pepper
2 teaspoons salt, or to taste
½ teaspoon sugar
2 garlic cloves, minced (optional)

1. Wash the five herbs well, remove the stems, and chop. Place in a bowl, cover with plastic wrap, and refrigerate.

2. Wash, peel, and seed the cucumbers. Cut in very small dice (the smaller the dice, the tastier the salad will be). Wash and seed tomatoes, and cut in very small dice. Dice the onion very small. Place cucumbers, tomatoes, and onions in a separate bowl, cover, and refrigerate for at least 2 hours.

3. An hour before serving, make the dressing: Combine lime juice, olive oil, pepper, salt, and sugar.

4. Remove the bowl of cucumbers, tomatoes, and onions from the refrigerator, and drain off all the liquid that has accumulated. Add the chopped herbs and the dressing, and mix well. Return to refrigerator until just before serving, to allow time to marinate. Check seasoning. Add minced garlic, if desired.

Sweet-and-Sour Three-Bean Salad

Serves 6 to 8

Ⓟ

Whenever we make this easy and nutritious salad, everyone always asks for the recipe, which our mother has been making for decades, and our friends all hoped it would appear in this book. Two things make it eminently suitable to be a part of the Purim chapter, however: its sweet-and-sour flavor, and the fact that according to legend, chickpeas were one of vegetarian Queen Esther's favorite foods.

Serve a bowl of this three-bean salad along with Phyllo Envelopes Stuffed with Kasha, Mushrooms, and Onions (page 282) at a party, or as a side dish with "Drunken" Salmon in Sherry-Butter Sauce (page 289).

1 14-ounce can cut green beans drained

1 16-ounce can red beans, drained

1 15-ounce can chickpeas, drained

¾ cup thinly sliced small red onion

1 cup thinly sliced small carrot

½ cup celery cut into ¼-inch slices

⅔ cup olive oil

⅓ cup apple cider vinegar

1 teaspoon salt

¼ teaspoon freshly ground black pepper

⅓ to ½ cup honey

1. Drain beans thoroughly and put in a deep bowl. Add onion, carrot, and celery.

2. Whisk together oil, vinegar, salt, pepper, and honey, or place in a jar with a tight-fitting lid and shake well. Pour over vegetables and beans and mix together gently, trying not to mash any of the beans. Let stand for 1 hour at room temperature before serving.

3. To store, let stand 1 hour, then cover and store in the refrigerator. Best used within 4 days—if it lasts that long.

I n this Persian dish, the whole roasted chicken is served on a separate dish, with Herbed Rice with Seasoned Currants (page 169) alongside. Ladle the pan juices from the chicken over the rice.

Note: A turkey breast may be substituted for the roasted whole chicken.

(page 169)

Persian Roasted Chicken in Saffron and Lime Juice

Serves 6 to 8

M

1 teaspoon saffron threads

A few grains of sugar

1 tablespoon very hot water

1 3- to 3½-pound chicken

½ cup freshly squeezed lime juice (about 4 medium limes)

2 tablespoons olive or canola oil

Salt

Freshly ground black pepper

1 cup sliced onion

1. Preheat the oven to 350°F.

2. Grind the saffron using a small mortar and pestle, adding a few grains of sugar to help to break up the threads. When reduced to a powder, put in a small cup and add 1 tablespoon hot water. Mix, and set aside to steep.

3. Wash and dry the chicken well. Mix the steeped saffron, lime juice, oil, salt, and pepper in a small bowl.

4. Lay the onion slices in a roasting pan, add the chicken, and pour the saffron mixture over it. Roast for 1 hour, or until the thigh juices run clear, basting frequently with the pan juices.

Beef and Eggplant Stew

Khoresht Mosamma Bademjan

Serves 6 to 8

A lovely dish, perfect to warm the insides on a cold or chilly evening.

2 to 2½ pounds very lean stew beef, cut into 2-inch cubes
1 to 2 teaspoons salt
2 teaspoons freshly ground black pepper
2 pounds red onions (about 4 large)
2½ pounds large purple eggplants (about 2), or 1 small Japanese eggplant per person
Coarse salt
Oil, for frying

1 teaspoon ground turmeric
1 28-ounce can crushed Italian tomatoes
1 28-ounce can whole Italian tomatoes
1 6-ounce can tomato paste
⅓ to ½ cup freshly squeezed lime juice
1 to 2 tablespoons brown sugar
2 teaspoons cinnamon
3 cups water or beef bouillon

1. Season the beef cubes, pressing salt and pepper into the meat. Set aside while preparing eggplants and onions.

2. Peel and thinly slice the onions in half, then crosswise, and set aside.

3. Peel eggplants and slice horizontally into ½-inch-thick slices. Place in a colander and sprinkle with coarse salt. Let bitter juices drain for about 30 minutes. If using small Japanese eggplants, peel but leave whole, and immerse in a bowl of salted water for 30 minutes. Drain and dry eggplants with a paper towel.

4. Heat oil in large nonstick skillet. Add the eggplants and sauté, in batches if necessary, until golden brown. Remove to a platter as they are brown. Sauté beef cubes in the same pan a few at a time (you may need to add more oil). Remove to a bowl as they brown.

5. Scrape all the oil from the skillet into a heavy nonstick pot, heat, and add all the onion slices (you may need to add more oil). Sauté slowly, until browned but not burned. After 10 minutes, add the ground turmeric, and mix in well. Continue sautéing until almost caramelized.

6. Add the browned beef cubes, crushed tomatoes, the liquid from the canned whole tomatoes, tomato paste, lime juice, brown sugar, cinnamon, water or bouillon, and 1 slice of sautéed eggplant or 1 small fried eggplant.

7. Bring to a boil, lower heat, and simmer, covered, about 45 minutes, until beef cubes are tender and sauce is thick, not watery. Add the canned whole tomatoes and simmer for another 5 to 10 minutes. Taste and adjust seasoning, adding more salt, pepper, cinnamon, or lime juice, if necessary.

8. Serve beef stew in a wide, shallow bowl or rectangular Pyrex dish. Place small eggplants or slices on top, or serve eggplant separately in another bowl.

The consumption of alcohol is a tradition on Purim, so why shouldn't the fish enjoy the same treatment? This recipe is a delicious contribution from our niece Ruthie Levi-Schuster. Serve with Back-to-the-Roots Casserole (page 205) and Sweet-and-Sour Three-Bean Salad (page 286), if desired.

¾ cup (1½ sticks) butter
4 cups dry sherry
2 tablespoons brown sugar
1 2-pound salmon filet

Salt
Freshly ground white pepper
    to taste

1. Preheat the oven to 400°F. Line a baking pan with parchment paper.
2. In a small saucepan, over low heat, melt the butter, sherry, and brown sugar together. Do not boil.
3. Rinse the salmon and pat dry. Dust with salt and white pepper, and place in the prepared pan. Pour half the sauce over the salmon and place in the oven.
4. Bake about 35 to 40 minutes, basting every 10 minutes, until the salmon is done. The fish should be moist inside with a delicious crispy glaze.
5. Pour any remaining sauce or pan juices into a small saucepan, and heat over medium heat until thickened. Pass the sauce at the table.

Mishloach Manot (Shalach Manos)

When planning gifts of food for Purim, make a list of the recipients and start collecting plastic or wood produce baskets, boxes, decorative bottles, ribbons, and bows in the months before the holiday. Here are some wrapping ideas:

If you're crafty or looking for a crafts project to do with children, create your own memorable gift baskets and recycle at the same time. Upgrade pint- or quart-size wooden berry (cherry tomato, mushroom) boxes by painting with a brush or spray paint. Line with a cloth or paper napkin, or paste fabric into place with craft glue. Plastic produce baskets can be upgraded by weaving them with colorful ribbons. Recycle tins or cans or boxes with reclosable covers as cookie or sweet containers by gluing on decorative wrapping paper or a page from a Hebrew newspaper and adding a coat of shellac, or by simply covering with Con-Tact paper. Use the top to add your blessing.

Discovering a Lost Recipe

When it comes to music, art, theater, culture, and even food, so many Eastern European and Mediterranean Jewish traditions were lost during the Holocaust, there seems no way back—unless somehow, some way, we can rediscover threads of it through someone's however faint memory. This is the story of *makagigi,* a long-lost Polish Purim recipe of beloved memory.

Several years ago, I received this letter, sent to my regular "Feedback" column:

> *Always around Purim, I recall my grandmother's Purim concoction called* makagigi. *If you ask someone from Cracow, Poland, they will start beaming and say that they had it too. But the people I know were children when World War II started and did not know how to prepare it themselves. It was made of honey and nuts and who-knows-what. Of course, homes and grandmothers were lost forever, so I have no one to ask and would like to pass this on to my grandchildren. Would one of your readers know how to prepare it?*
>
> —Eva Toren, Tel Aviv

Another reader's response:

> *My parents and my parents-in-law are also from Cracow. Makagigi was a part of my childhood, made always by my grandmother. While my grandmother was alive, however, I was too young to be interested in preserving this or any other recipes; later on, she was no longer alive for me to ask. My father always loved* makagigi, *and I wanted very much to surprise him with some. I searched and searched for recipes until I came across the one he said is exactly like the one his mother used to make. I also include a recipe I found for Warsaw-style* makagigi.
>
> —Ruth Galai, Tel Aviv

Eva's reply:

> *I feel overjoyed, not just because of being finally able to taste it again, and to pass family tradition on to the next generation, but also because something that was snatched away by the Holocaust has been brought back to us. Thank you from the depths of my heart. Always grateful,*
>
> —Eva Toren

Makagigi (Cracow Style)

Makes 3 dozen

½ pound honey
½ cup sugar
Juice of ½ lemon
1 pound mixed nuts, chopped finely

1. In a pot, mix together honey, sugar, and lemon juice. Bring to a boil over low heat and cook until mixture starts to brown. Add the nuts and cook, stirring, over very low heat about 5 to 7 minutes, until the mixture has thickened.

2. Pour onto a moistened baking sheet or pan (for easy cleaning line with moistened parchment paper). Flatten with the back of a wooden spoon dipped in cold water, until evenly spread into a 9-by-5½-inch rectangle. Let cool until just set. Use a sharp knife to cut widthwise into 9 pieces, then slice down the center to form rectangular shapes. Store in a closed container in the refrigerator. To give as *Mishloach Manot*, place in paper muffin cups or wrap individually in plastic wrap.

Almond Makagigi (Warsaw Style)

Makes about 2½ dozen

M ade with the addition of butter, this is a richer version of *makagigi* (our personal favorite!).

¼ cup sugar
½ cup honey
⅔ cup butter
1 pound almonds, coarsely chopped

1. Heat the sugar in saucepan over low heat until caramelized, stirring frequently with a wooden spoon to avoid burning. Add honey and butter and cook for 20 minutes over very low heat. Add nuts and cook over very low heat for 10 minutes.

2. Spread waxed paper or parchment paper on a board. Moisten with water. Use a wooden spoon dipped in water to drop small cookie-sized lumps of the mixture on the sheet. Flatten with the back of a spoon.

3. Allow to harden in the refrigerator, then pack in an airtight jar. Because they tend to get sticky, we also store these in the refrigerator. Serve in gold or silver petit four cups.

Mom's Classic Hamantaschen with Natasha's Fruit Fillings

Makes about 5 dozen

Our friend Natasha, who can munch on dried fruit and nuts day in and day out, was happy to oblige our mother when she asked for some new ideas for hamantaschen fillings. Together they came up with tempting new ways to pick Haman's pockets.

4 eggs
1¼ cups sugar
1 cup canola or corn oil
3 tablespoons cognac, or 2
    teaspoons vanilla extract

5 cups unbleached all-purpose
    flour
4 teaspoons baking powder
Natasha's Fruit Fillings (recipe
    follows)

1. In the bowl of a standing mixer, beat eggs until lemon-colored. Beat in sugar, oil, and cognac. Gradually stir in 4 to 4½ cups of flour, mixing until a soft dough is formed. Oil hands and make a ball out of the dough, cover it in plastic wrap, and chill for at least 2 to 3 hours. (Can be chilled overnight.)

2. Preheat the oven to 350°F. Line a baking sheet with parchment paper.

3. Divide the dough into 3 sections. Knead one section until it is smooth enough to roll out. Use the remaining flour to flour a rolling pin and a work surface, and roll the dough out to ¼-inch thickness.

4. Use a tea glass or round cookie cutter to cut rounds, and put a rounded teaspoon of filling (see page 293) in the center of each. Close the top of the cookie with a pinch, and pinch both sides and bottom to form a triangular shape, leaving the filling exposed in the center. Pick up scraps and form another ball. Repeat until all dough is used. Transfer to the prepared baking sheet. Bake for 25 to 30 minutes, until just lightly browned.

Each of these fillings can also be rolled into little balls.

Makes about 4 cups

1½ cups chopped dried apples

¼ cup raisins

½ cup chopped dried mango

¼ cup chopped dried apricots

½ cup chopped walnuts

3 tablespoons apricot jam

1 teaspoon cinnamon

1 to 2 teaspoons brandy
  (optional)

Makes about 1¾ cups

¼ cup chopped dried pineapple
  pieces

½ cup toasted blanched almonds,
  chopped

¼ cup chopped dried apricots

¼ cup chopped dried apple

½ to 1 teaspoon freshly grated,
  peeled gingerroot

½ cup pitted dates

2 to 3 tablespoons honey

1 to 2 teaspoons Calvados
  (optional)

Makes about 2½ cups

1 teaspoon grated orange rind

1 cup chopped pitted prunes

½ cup raisins

1 cup chopped dried apples

2 to 3 tablespoons orange
  marmalade

2 teaspoons port wine

To make any of the fillings, coarsely chop the fruit and nuts, measure, and transfer to the bowl of a food processor. Add 1 to 2 tablespoons of jam, honey, or marmalade at a time, and process in on/off pulses until the filling looks sticky but not mashed. Mix in the liqueur if using and fill the hamantaschen.

Greek *Folorikos* ("Haman's Foot")

℗

Wherever they were throughout the Jewish world, our great-grandmothers probably made many holiday foods that have long since been forgotten. In Salonika, and in other Jewish communities around Greece devastated by the Holocaust, one of these foods was *Folorikos*, which were alternately considered Haman's foot or his shoe, and made especially for children on the holiday.

At the center of all *Folorikos* is a hard-boiled egg, a tradition that may have arisen from the holiday's close proximity to Easter (Turkish Jews made Purim *Folorikos* in the shape of a basket). But the egg has Jewish associations as well, such as fertility and wholeness.

Whatever its derivation, the original *Folorikos* was egg surrounded by a simple flour, salt, and water dough. Instead, we use half or all the "Birds of Prayer" Challah Rolls dough (page 156), which is both easy to use and eminently edible.

Prepare hard-boiled eggs in advance, and bring to room temperature before using.

1. There are many designs for *Folorikos*, but almost all involve an **X** of dough on top (which serves as both the laces and a strap to hold the eggs in place). The egg can be set in a dough "nest" or, if you're creative, in a realistic-looking foot or shoe, decorated with smaller pieces of the dough that have been brushed with oil and "glued" with a little beaten egg white. Brush the *Folorikos* with a beaten yolk mixed with a teaspoon of water, or a little warmed honey. Bake until golden brown, 15 to 20 minutes. Serve warm.

2. To serve, let everyone tear the dough away from the egg, peel the egg, and enjoy the two together. The yolk will have a creamier consistency after baking.

Healthy Nut and Seed Treats

Makes 1 dozen

P

Packed with vitamins, minerals, and fiber, these are among the healthiest *Mishloach Manot* you can make. For a Middle Eastern touch, add a few drops of rose water to the oil mixture.

1½ cups quick-cooking oats
¼ cup untoasted sunflower seeds
¼ cup coarsely chopped regular
   or toasted cashews
¼ cup coarsely chopped regular
   or toasted almonds
2 tablespoons wheat germ
⅛ teaspoon salt
⅛ teaspoon cinnamon
¼ cup corn, safflower, or
   peanut oil
¼ teaspoon real vanilla extract
¼ cup mild-flavored honey
3 tablespoons molasses

1. Preheat the oven to 350°F. Grease an 8-inch square pan or line the bottom with parchment paper.

2. Mix the dry ingredients together in a medium-size bowl.

3. In a smaller bowl, mix oil, vanilla, honey, and molasses until smooth. Pour the oil mixture into the dry ingredients and stir with a wooden spoon until coated. Knead the mixture with oiled hands until uniform. Press into the prepared pan. Bake for 15 to 20 minutes, or until golden on top. Remove the pan from the oven and cut into square or diamond shapes. Let cool in the pan and remove carefully.

4. Divide the pieces among colorful and/or contrasting large petit four or decorative paper muffin cups. Place on a paper or gift plate.

Yarden's Giant Chocolate-Chip Cookie

Makes 1

My older daughter, Yarden, invented this giant cookie for a class Purim party in seventh grade, and it met with such great success that she was asked to repeat it for other class parties as well. It's another example of how Purim fun doesn't have to restrict itself to games. Purim foods can be fun as well!

1 cup (2 sticks) butter or margarine, at room temperature

¾ cup granulated sugar or turbinado sugar

¾ cup packed brown sugar or turbinado sugar

2 large eggs

2 teaspoons real vanilla extract

1¾ cups unbleached all-purpose flour

½ cup whole-wheat or whole-wheat pastry flour

1 teaspoon baking soda

½ teaspoon salt

2 cups chocolate chips

1. Preheat the oven to 375°F. Line a 14-inch-wide baking sheet with parchment paper, and set aside.

2. In the bowl of a standing mixer, beat butter and sugars together until light and fluffy. Add the eggs and vanilla, beating until incorporated. Sift the flours, baking soda, and salt, and beat into the butter mixture. Stir in the chocolate chips.

3. Turn the dough out on the prepared baking sheet and flatten it down with wet hands to form a single round 11½-inch-diameter cookie, leaving 1½ inches between the cookie and the sides of the sheet. Bake for 25 to 30 minutes, until the top is dry to the touch and a toothpick inserted in the center comes out clean. Do not overbake.

4. Serve warm, cut into wedges, or let cool completely (the cookie will harden) and break off pieces.

Note: If you are carrying the cookie to another location, place it on a piece of cardboard or carton covered with aluminum foil, and wrap the package with paper or foil to avoid breakage.

*S*uper easy, these little snaps are low in fat, high in taste. Crisp and firm, their portability makes them perfect for *Mishloach Manot.*

1½ cups unbleached all-purpose flour

⅓ cup whole-wheat pastry flour

½ teaspoon baking soda

½ cup (1 stick) butter, at room temperature

2 cups granulated or turbinado sugar

⅔ cup good-quality unsweetened cocoa powder

2 large eggs

2 teaspoons vanilla extract

1. Preheat the oven to 350°F. Line a baking sheet with parchment paper.

2. Sift flours and baking soda into a bowl. In another bowl, beat butter and sugar together until fluffy. Blend in cocoa, eggs, and vanilla until smooth. Mix in the dry ingredients until blended.

3. Form the mixture into 48 small balls and place 1½ inches apart on the prepared baking sheet. Flatten with a fork or the bottom of a glass.

4. Bake for 12 minutes. Remove from the oven and cool for a few minutes before transferring to a wire rack to cool completely.

Variations

For mocha snaps, substitute 1½ teaspoons of strongly brewed coffee for 1 teaspoon of the vanilla.

For chocolate mint snaps, substitute a few drops of mint extract for 1 teaspoon of the vanilla.

The Gift of Homemade Spice Mixtures

Although they are not a traditional gift for *Mishloach Manot,* Miriyam and I love to make homemade spice mixtures for friends and family. Not only do they add flavor and interest to various dishes, they also take us on a culinary journey to their countries of origin every time we use them. What's more, they're a welcome gift. You'll find that they also appear in several of the recipes in this book, such as Middle Eastern *Baharat* (page 299) in Spiced Butternut Squash Soup (page 189), as well as beans, meat and poultry, and *Tzoug* (page 299).

Pack spice mixtures in small Mason jars, recycled spice jars, or even test tubes with cork tops. Label each (label designs are sold in handicraft, stationery, and office-supply stores). Tie several together with a ribbon or twine. Or use the suggestions included with each recipe.

Black-and-White Seasoned Salt

Makes about ½ cup

This delicious seasoning, inspired by Claudia Roden's Egyptian combination, is helpful as a salt substitute for those who wish to reduce their sodium intake. But everyone loves it sprinkled on salads, with bread and olive oil or cream cheese, and in Pistachio-Coriander Cheese Balls (page 73).

½ cup sesame seeds
1 tablespoon whole coriander seeds
¼ to ½ teaspoon sea salt or kosher salt
½ tablespoon cumin seeds
1 teaspoon nigella or black sesame seeds

Toast the ingredients together in a dry skillet for 3 to 4 minutes, until fragrant, stirring often with a wooden spoon. Grind in a mortar and pestle or a coffee grinder briefly, so that the sesame seeds do not release too much oil.

To Gift-wrap

Pour into a piece of plastic wrap, draw up the edges, and twist to form a bundle (or use a plastic sandwich bag, twist and fasten the top with a rubber band, and cut off the excess plastic at the top). Place in the center of a square of fabric and tie with a piece of yarn, ribbon, or twine. Attach a little note with suggestions for how to use the salt.

Baharat

The word *baharat* comes from the Arabic word *bahar*, or allspice, which only reached the Old World because Columbus mistook it for black pepper. A native of Jamaica, allspice has the same essential oils found in cloves and nutmeg, which are grown on the other side of the world in Indonesia.

Because it has encompassed such a complex flavor, the word was applied to both the spice itself and a blend of pungent spices. Today, Sephardim from Syrian, Lebanese, Egyptian, Armenian, and Iraqi households still tend to add a good pinch of homemade *Baharat* blend to soups, stuffed vegetables, and meat dishes.

For Syrian-style *Baharat*

Combine the following ground spices: 1 tablespoon cinnamon, 4 tablespoons black pepper, 4 tablespoons paprika (hot or sweet), and 6 tablespoons cumin. If possible, grind the same proportions of whole spices yourself in a coffee or spice grinder.

For Lebanese *Baharat*

Combine 1 tablespoon of each of the following ground spices: allspice, cinnamon, cloves, and black pepper.

A Yemenite Flavorings Gift Package

Another much-appreciated gift for the holiday is a package of assorted Yemenite flavorings—including the fiery *Tzoug* condiment, and two kinds of *hawaiij* spice mixtures—one for cooking and the other for coffee and sweets. They'll add a delicious and exotic taste to all kinds of foods in the months to come.

Tzoug

Some like it hot, among them the Yemenites, who invented a mixture called *Tzoug* that packs both a nutritional and a sensational wallop. *Tzoug* can be red, like the recipe below, perfect for those who love the taste of fire (and there are many of you out there), or green, with coriander and fresh hot green or red peppers instead.

This *Tzoug* recipe comes from the Gamlieli family in Tel Aviv, who make vast quantities of it at a time and store it in the refrigerator for up to six months. This is only half the recipe!

Serve *Tzoug* alongside Biblical Cream Cheese or Biblical Yogurt Cheese (page 71 or 70) and as an addition to Fresh Corn Casserole (page 203); rub on chicken before baking; add to pasta sauce; or mix a little into extra-virgin olive oil and use as a dressing for salads or cooked potatoes, green beans, and other vegetables.

½ pound garlic cloves
2 ½ tablespoons small dried hot red peppers
¾ cup black peppercorns
Rounded ⅓ cup cumin seeds
¼ cup cardamom seeds

Peel the garlic and grind in a food processor (or as the Gamlielis do, in a meat grinder). Use a spice or coffee grinder to grind the peppercorns, cumin seeds, and cardamom seeds separately, and mix with the ground garlic. Pack into jars, label, and store in the refrigerator.

Hawaiij

*H*awaiij is the Yemenite version of Chinese five-spice powder, Middle Eastern *Baharat*, and Indian *garam masala*. This blend is used to flavor soups, meats, and vegetable dishes. The recipe comes from Ba-li, a Yemenite lunch place on Ibn Gvirol Street in Tel Aviv.

5 teaspoons ground black pepper
5 tablespoons ground cumin
2 tablespoons ground cardamom
3 teaspoons ground turmeric
2 teaspoons ground coriander seeds

Mix together and store in a tightly covered jar, away from light.

Hawaiij for Coffee and Sweets

Mix 3½ ounces ground ginger, 8 cardamom pods, 1 whole nutmeg, 7 whole cloves, and 3 cinnamon sticks. Grind all the spices together in batches, and use a funnel to transfer the mixture to individual bottles. Add a note to the package to suggest adding a pinch of this blend to coffee, tea, and cake and cookie batters.

Menu Suggestions

Though the recipes in each chapter have been organized to make it easy for you to design festive meals yourself, these menu suggestions may help inspire you. They include traditional, ethnic, biblical, and vegetarian meals and snacks, as well as ideas for entertaining, and, on Purim, gift-giving.

Most of the menu suggestions appear in that holiday's chapter; those marked with an (*) appear elsewhere in the book. Consult the index.

Passover

A Traditional Ashkenazic Seder

Ida's Classic Chopped Liver*
Mom's Russian-Style Gefilte Fish
The Ultimate Chicken Soup* with the Perfect Knaidlach
Stuffed Shoulder of Veal
Adi's Tzimmes*
Melon with Crystallized Ginger—*Eingemacht*
Pecan Meringue Cookies

A Vegetarian/Dairy Seder

Vegetarian "Chopped Liver"*
Cream of Root Vegetable Soup
Roasted Salmon with Marinated Fennel and Thyme
    and/or Spring Vegetable Kugel
Braised "Bitter Herbs" with Pistachios or
Lemony Nut Cake with Lemon Topping and Berries

A Passover Flavors Seder

Nanuchka's Fabulous Walnut-and-Herb-Stuffed
    Eggplant Rolls
Golden Thyme-Scented Vegetable Broth with The
    Perfect Knaidlach
Roasted Chicken with Two Potatoes, Garlic, and Rosemary
Marinated Fennel in Olive Oil and Herbs
Fresh Fruit
Moshe b'Tayva (Moses in the Basket)

Passover Week Breakfasts

Glazer Family Matzah Brei
Fresh Mushroom and Vidalia Onion Frittata

Passover Week Lunches

Tarragon-Scented Savory Goat Cheese Cheesecake
Baby Spinach Salad with Arugula, Basil, and Pine Nuts

or

Moroccan Egg-Stuffed Potato *Pastelim*
    or Iraqi Chicken-Stuffed Patties
Roasted Vegetables in Olive Oil and Spring Herbs

or

Fresh Beet Salad in Honey Dressing
Assorted Cheeses
Passover Thumbprint Seeded Rolls
Fudgy Passover Brownies

Lag b'Omer

A Lag b'Omer Bonfire and Picnic

Cheese in the Fire
Pita or Baguettes
Feta Cheese in Seven-Ingredient Olive Oil Marinade
Cherry Tomatoes, Basil, and Tassos Olives in Olive Oil
Baked Potato and Sprout Salad with Fresh Parsley Dressing
Barley Salad with Lemon and Cilantro
Carob Walnut Brownies

A Lag b'Omer Barbecue

Spring Barley Mini-croquettes
    with Tahini and Fresh Herb Sauce
Grilled Cornish Hens in Lemon and Hot Pepper Sauce
Yehiel's Famous Kabob
Wilted Cabbage with Mustard Seed
Aromatic Chickpeas
Rich Carob Tea Cake
Tea with Fresh Mint / Coffee with *Hawaiij**

Shavuot

A Shavuot Breakfast

Fresh Mushroom and Vidalia Onion Frittata*
Quick Garlic-and-Chive Rolls
Biblical Yogurt Cheese
Biblical Butter
Anise-Scented Milk

A Shavuot Lunch

Schav and Spinach Borscht with Nutmeg
Tarragon-Scented Savory Goat Cheese Cheesecake*
Zucchini *Fattoush* Salad
Fresh Fruit

A Biblically Inspired Lunch

Taratour with Walnuts
Spring Barley Mini-croquettes
    with Tahini and Fresh Herb Sauce*
Whole-Wheatberry Tabbouleh
Feta Cheese with Seven-Ingredient Olive Oil Marinade
Quick Garlic-and-Chive Rolls (or Pita)
Lishansky's Halvah Cheesecake

A Shavuot Dinner

Stuffed Mushrooms with Wheat Germ, Sunflower Seeds,
    and Fresh Herbs*
Hot and Bubbling Semolina and Sage Gnocchi

or

Ricotta-Stuffed Ravioli with White Wine Sauce*
Spring Green Salad with Tangerine and Fennel Seed Vinaigrette
Mom's Famous Buttermilk Pie
Fresh Fruit

Shavuot Munchies

Pistachio-Coriander Cheese Balls
Feta Cheese in Seven-Ingredient Olive Oil Marinade
Bourekas b' Milui Badinjan (Short-Crust Pastries Stuffed with
  Eggplant and Feta)
Cheese and Olive S'Mores
Anise-Scented Milk

A Shavuot Dessert Party

Ida's Classic Cheese Blintzes
Cabbage Salad with Grapes and Almonds
Double-Ginger Granola Cheesecake
Fresh Fruit

Tu b'Av

A Romantic Dinner

Champagne and Melon Soup with Feta Cheese
Yellowtail Ceviche in Lemon-Coriander Marinade
Ricotta-Stuffed Ravioli with White Wine Sauce
Hearts of Palm Salad
Mango Brûlée
Chocolate Frangelico and Hazelnut Truffles

A Romantic Brunch

Peach Champagne Cocktail
Brioche French Toast with Fruit and Honey-Yogurt Sauce

or

Salad of Goat Cheese, Arugula, and Figs
Melt-in-Your-Mouth Breakfast Scones
Cherna's Favorite Lemon Curd*

Rosh Hashanah

An Ashkenazic-Style Menu

Apples and Honey

Round Challah with Seven Seeds

Ida's Classic Chopped Liver

The Ultimate Chicken Soup with Any-Way Kreplach

Roasted Chicken with Two Potatoes, Garlic, and Rosemary*

Mixed Greens Salad

The Best Honey Cake Yet

A Sephardic Menu

"Birds of Prayer" Challah Rolls*

Seven Blessings Tray, Including

Bulgarian Leek Patties, *Lubia* Salad, Moroccan Carrot Salad

Bowl of Pomegranate Seeds, Cooked Beets, Fish Head, Dates,
   Apples, and Honey

Sweet-and-Sour Bass in the Style of Iraq and Salonika

Chicken with Dates, Olive Oil, and Twelve Garlic Cloves*

Rice

Quince in Spiced Muscat Wine

A Biblically Inspired Menu

Sesame-and-Herb-Stuffed Grape Leaves*

Cornish Hens Stuffed with Bulgur, Raisins, and Caraway

Roasted Eggplant and Pomegranate Seed Salad

Figs Stuffed with Halvah, Nuts, and Honey

A Vegetarian Menu

Golden Thyme-Scented Vegetable Broth (with
   vegetables added)*

Vegetarian "Chopped Liver"

Bulgarian Leek Patties (vegetarian version)

with

Avas Frescas (Green Beans in Tomato Sauce)

Roasted Eggplant and Pomegranate Seed Salad

Moroccan Carrot Salad

Chocolate Honey Brownies

New Moon Butter Cookies

Yom Kippur

A Pre-Fast Meat Yom Kippur Meal

"Hands in Blessing" Spiral Challah
Two-Mushroom Lentil Barley Soup with Thyme
Roasted Chicken Thighs with Honey, Olives, and Oregano
Green Salad
Honey-Sautéed Pineapple
Little Almond Cookies

A Pre-Fast Dairy Yom Kippur Meal

Spiced Butternut Squash Soup*
"Birds of Prayer" Challah Rolls
Rainbow Trout Stuffed with Tomatoes and Honey-Basil Pesto
Herbed Rice or Plain Rice
The Best Honey Cake Yet*
Sorbet or Ice Cream

A Vegetarian Yom Kippur Meal

"New Age" "Chopped Liver"
"Birds of Prayer" Challah Rolls or "Hands in Blessing" Spiral
    Challah
Seven-Spice Vegetable Soup
Raisin and Pine Nut Couscous
Bulgarian Leek Patties (vegetarian version)*
Festive Mandelbrot

Foods to Break the Fast

Choice of
Festive Mandelbrot
Ka'a'him (Sephardic Sesame and Seed Rings)
Sutlage (Jerusalem Star-of-David Rice Pudding)

A Bagel Buffet After the Fast

"Birds of Prayer" Challah Rolls or Bagels

Choice of
Avocado Spread
Mozzarella and Sun-dried Tomato Topping
Daniel's Schmaltz Herring Salad with Sour Cream and Apples
Poached Halibut Salad*
Warm Casserole of Seven Dried Fruits*

Sukkot

A Biblically Inspired Meal

Sesame-and-Herb-Stuffed Grape Leaves
Chicken with Dates, Olive Oil, and Twelve Garlic Cloves
Bulgur and Pomegranate Seed Salad
Figs Stuffed with Halvah, Nuts, and Honey*

Sukkot Meat Menus

I. The Ladder Challah
   Albondigas Soup with Jerusalem Artichokes
   Chicken with Olives and Sumac
   Multicolored Roasted Pepper Salad
   Bulgur and Pomegranate Seed Salad
   Zucchini Tea Cake with Cinnamon and Nutmeg

II. Sesame-and-Herb-Stuffed Grape Leaves
   Lamb Stew with Chickpeas, Pomegranates, Squash,
      and Cilantro
   Jerusalem Artichoke Salad with Crispy Garlic
      and Rosemary
   Mixed Greens Salad
   Pears in Red Wine and Spices

Sukkot Vegetarian Menus

I. Stuffed Mushrooms with Wheat Germ, Sunflower Seeds,
      and Fresh Herbs
   Spiced Butternut Squash Soup
   Fresh Corn Casserole
   Multicolored Roasted Pepper Salad
   Sweet-and-Sour Cabbage and Carrot Slaw
   Tofu Brownies

II. Bubby Rose's Old World Cabbage Borscht (vegetarian
      option)
   The Balaban Family's *Vareniki*
   Mixed Greens Salad
   Green Lentils and Barley with Tomatoes and Rosemary
   Phyllis's Famous Carrot Cake

Hanukkah

A Latke Party

Winter Vegetable Soup

Choice of
  Classic Potato Latkes
  Olive Latkes
  Sumac or Zahtar Latkes
  Zucchini, Feta, and Basil Mini-frittatas
  Bulgarian Potato Latkes
  Sweet Potato Latkes with Spiced Maple Syrup
  Mini-Ricotta Latkes with Sour Cherry Sauce

Choice of
  Raw Applesauce
  Black Radish Relish
  Ripe Olive Butter
  Herbed Olives

Kumquats in Spiced Syrup
Vanilla Ice Cream

or

Bumuelos in Red Wine Sauce

Hanukkah Inspired by Biblical Foods

I. Split Pea and Double-Coriander Soup
  Olive, Sumac, or Zahtar Latkes
  Roasted Beets
  Black Radish Relish
  Sfenj

II. Biblical Lentil Soup with Spinach and Turnips
  Feta Cheese in Seven-Ingredient Olive Oil Marinade*
  Panfried Scallion Bread
  Herbed Olives
  Warm Casserole of Seven Dried Fruits*

An Elegant Eastern European Dinner

The Ultimate Chicken Soup
Goose Breast with Forest Fruit Sauce and Spaetzle
Endive and Fresh Mushroom Salad in Balsamic Vinaigrette
Daniel's Light-as-a-Feather Whole-Wheat *Sufganiot*

Tu b'Shvat

A Meat Menu

Baked Figs in Savory Tamarind Sauce
Chicken with Olives, Red Wine, Prunes, and Pomegranates
Rice
Green Salad with Edible Flowers and Berry Vinaigrette
Warm Casserole of Seven Dried Fruits
Tea with Seven Spices

A Vegetarian Menu

Winter Vegetable Soup*
Potatoes and Carrots with Seeds and Fragrant Spices
Basmati Rice Scented with Tree Spices and Dried Fruit
Mixed Greens Salad
Rich Carob Tea Cake with Fig and Raisin Confit
Tea with Seven Spices

Purim

Keylitsh Challah or Moroccan Purim Challah

Openers and Purim Party Food

Phyllo Envelopes Stuffed with Kasha, Mushrooms, and Onions
Apricot "Leather" Sushi
Folorikos

A Dairy Purim Dinner

Sliced Avocado with Sweet-and-Sour Poppy Seed Vinaigrette
"Drunken" Salmon in Sherry-Butter Sauce
Green Salad
Phyllis's Famous Carrot Cake* or Zucchini Tea Cake with
    Cinnamon and Nutmeg*
Hamantaschen

A Persian-Style Purim Feast

Shirazi Salad
Persian Roasted Chicken in Saffron and Lime Juice
Herbed Rice with Seasoned Currants*

Beef and Eggplant Stew (*Khoresht Mosamma Bademjan*)
Melon Bowl and Fresh Fruit
Moshe b'Tayva (Moses in the Basket)*

Mishloach Manot (Shalach Manos)
A Basket of Edible Gifts

Choose from
    Classic Hamantaschen
    Greek *Folorikos* ("Haman's Foot")
    Healthy Nut and Seed Sweets
    Kumquats in Spiced Syrup*
    Moshe b'Tayva (Moses in the Basket)*
    Yarden's Giant Chocolate-Chip Cookie
    Little Chocolate Snaps
    Makagigi (Cracow or Warsaw Style)
    Black-and-White Seasoned Salt
    Baharat
    Tzoug
    A Yemenite Flavorings Gift Package

New Holidays During the Omer Period

Since the establishment of the State of Israel in 1948, the Israeli Knesset (Parliament) added four new holidays to the Jewish calendar during the Omer period between Passover and Shavuot. Two of them are somber. *Yom Hashoah,* Holocaust Martyrs' and Heroes' Day, on the twenty-seventh of Nisan (April/May), in memory of the victims of the Nazis, and the fourth of Iyar (May) is *Yom Hazikaron,* Israel's Remembrance Day, which commemorates the soldiers and victims of terror who have died in defense of the Jewish state.

Two holidays have a joyful ring: *Yom Ha'atzmaut,* Israel's Independence Day, which, on the fifth of Iyar, follows on the heels of the somber Remembrance Day, and *Yom Yerushalayim,* Jerusalem Day, the twenty-eighth of Iyar (May/June), commemorating the reunification of the city during the Six Day War of 1967.

Israel's Independence Day

While there are parades in New York and Los Angeles, anyone traveling around Israel on Independence Day might be led to think that the Jews were again making collective animal sacrifices to their Maker. Indeed, thousands of sheep, lambs, fowl, and cows are offered up on that day, but not to God. To guests.

Whether or not it reflects a kind of sudden mass throwback to our ancient Temple ritual, Independence Day in Israel is devoted to the barbecue—*man-gal,* as the locals call it—which consists of one or more standard rectangular low-to-the-ground tin grills, charcoal, and a lot of meat.

Along with the animal sacrifice, most people consume one or more kinds of hummus, tahini, eggplant and cabbage salads, along with roasted peppers, tabbouleh, olives, pickles, and homemade cake, ending with the obligatory first-watermelon-of-the-season dessert!

Whether or not you parade down the streets of American cities for the holiday, you may want to plan an Israel Independence Day menu. We recommend indulging in the foods and beverages that Israelis love best, starting with *café hafuh* (café au lait) in the morning, and a barbecue with Israeli wines, beers, and Turkish coffee or mint tea in the evening. And don't forget a snack of falafel in pita somewhere in between!

Jerusalem Day: "Getting Used to the Taste"

Many stones are scattered and strewn on the sides of the road leading to Jerusalem. Where did they come from? Who put them there? Legend says that when Jews in exile remember the destruction of the city, they feel as if a heavy stone presses their heart. If the day comes when they are granted the privilege of going up to the city, just seeing it in the distance relieves them of their burden. It is as if the stone on their heart were lifted. And so they take a stone, and place it on the roadside, to testify that the very sight of the Holy City a source of comfort. (Based on *"Where Are the Stones From?"* by Zev Vilnay, *Legends of Jerusalem* [Jewish Publication Society, 1973], p. 306.)

Ever since the biblical King David came dancing with the Ark of the Covenant up and down the hills from the city of Hebron to the southern slopes of Mount Moriah, Jerusalem has been the beloved capital of the Jewish people, whether they were longing for it during centuries of exile or enjoying its culture and cafés in modern times.

In the 1948 War of Independence, cut off from the rest of the country, Jerusalem barely survived a long and desperate siege that led to food and even water being minutely rationed. The war left the city fragmented. East Jerusalem and the Old City fell to the troops of King Abdullah of Jordan, and West Jerusalem, to the new state of Israel. Separating them was the ramshackle Mandelbaum Gate.

And then, at the beginning of June 1967, less than forty-eight hours after Jordan's King Hussein made the fateful decision to join Syria and Egypt in a war against Israel, Israeli forces swept through the Mandelbaum Gate. By June 7, 1967, the city was in their hands. The exhaustion and awe of the young Israeli soldiers were photographed for history as they gazed upon the newly recaptured Western Wall in the Old City, the only section of the Second Temple that had survived the endless wars suffered over the centuries by the city whose very name paradoxically evokes a still elusive dream. For "Jerusalem" means the "City of Peace."

Yom Yerushalayim, Jerusalem Day, commemorates the physical unification of the city. We asked Jerusalem-born chef Gil Hovav to describe how his family's special Jerusalem Day menu came to be. Here's what he told us:

My grandmother was always braver than I. In 1948, long before I was born, Jerusalem suffered from a long siege. My grandmother would hang laundry out on her porch—a simple enough thing to do, one would think, but during a war, when the distance between her porch and the enemy snipers was only 200 meters, it was dangerous. In fact, doing the laundry at all wasn't easy—in Jerusalem in 1948, water was even more expensive than food. But my grandmother refused to give up: every week she confiscated a little of the family's expensive water ration, laundered the bedding and the clothes, and then, with the same water, washed the floors in room after room, hoarding it in the pail till every room was washed. When she'd finished, she'd wring out her mop three times, till she extracted every last drop, and then she would water the few plants that had managed to survive in the garden. Finally she'd hang out the laundry to dry on the porch, right opposite the enemy snipers.

"But Mom," my shocked mother used to say, "you'll be killed! They'll shoot you! Isn't it enough that they shot the neighbor's daughter on her way to work, and killed her? Didn't you hear that yesterday someone was killed lining up for their water ration in Yemin Moshe? Why do you do it?"

My grandmother refused to pay attention. "How will we live?" she'd respond, "without clean bedding? I'm only hanging out laundry. Why would they kill an old woman hanging out laundry? I don't understand. No, if this war has come down to not being able to do laundry, and young men shoot old woman—nu, from my point of view it's better to die."

And so, enveloped in an armor of laundry, detergent, and solid principles, my grandmother became a commander on the first front of the Independence War, hanging laundry.

I, as I said, was much less heroic. Twenty years later the first alarm of the Six-Day War found me in a kindergarten without a bomb shelter. Right after the all-clear siren sounded, forty five-year-old children were herded out in one long row from the teacher's house, which was five terrifying minutes from the kindergarten, but had a bomb shelter. But I wanted to go home, so even though we heard the sirens rising and falling, I fled outside and ran up the hill to our house. I remember the shells in the air. I remember porches collapsing from the houses around me. And I remember myself so frightened that I couldn't even cry.

Only when I got to our shelter and my mother hugged me with all her strength and wept, did I burst out in tears, too. And then, I recall, my grandmother took me, caressed my head, and said, "Don't cry . . . it will pass. Senor Dilmondo, the Master of the World, will protect you. And tomorrow you'll help me cook."

The next day, as the shells and explosions roared around us, and my mother protested just as loudly, my grandmother and I went out to our courtyard to gather mallow leaves to prepare meatballs. The leaves were what had been eaten in the Jerusalem of 1948, and my grandmother, who like all of us had no idea when the new war would end and how long our supplies would last, decided that the time had come to go back to the practices of the siege and to eat the wild grasses in the garden. "And I give them until tomorrow to end this war," she said angrily, "because if it doesn't end, you and I are going to hang up laundry." And she kissed me.

The war ended in six days. In Jerusalem it took just four. Ever since, on Yom Yerushalayim, my grandmother celebrated in two ways: first of all, she laundered everything she could find in the closets—even if it was already clean—with lavender and rosemary, and she hung it all out to dry in the sun on special steel laundry cords strung on the porch and in the garden. That's how she celebrated freedom.

Afterwards, she would cook us especially rich dishes, like albondigas soup from Jerusalem artichokes, bourekas b'milui badinjan, sutlage, on which she drew a Star of David with cinnamon, and, for safety's sake, she also prepared mallow leaves "because you never know when the next war is, so I want us to get used to the taste."

Note: Gil's grandmother's recipes for *Albondigas* Soup, *Bourekas*, and *Sutlage* appear in this book. See the index.

A Sabbath for the Land

In Jewish tradition and Kabbalah, the number seven has both a mystical and a special status. The Promised Land was a "good land," says the Bible, where Seven Species flourished:

> *a land of streams*
> *of springs and underground waters flowing*
> *out in valley and hills,*
> *a land of wheat and barley, of vine*
> *and fig trees and pomegranates,*
> *a land of olive trees and honey.*

—**Deut. 8:7–8**

Every seventh day is Shabbat, the Sabbath on which, says the book of Genesis, God rested after completing the creation of the world and on which the Jewish people are also commanded to rest.

And every seventh year, says the Bible, is a Sabbath for the land itself, called the *shmitah* (sabbatical year): "Your field you are not to sow, your vineyard you are not to prune, the aftergrowth of your harvest you are not to harvest. You may eat whatever the land during its Sabbath will freely produce—you, your male and female servants, your hired hand, your settlers who sojourn with you, your cattle and wild animals in your land may eat all its yield" (Lev. 25:4b–7).

And then, just as the harvest celebration of Shavuot comes on the fiftieth day after Passover, so the Jubilee comes on the fiftieth year after "seven sabbaticals." In the Jubilee, says Leviticus, the people of Israel should return to their "ancestral holding: every one of you, to your family. . . . You shall not sow, nor reap what grows, nor gather the grapes of the unpruned vines"

(25:10b–11). All debts are forgiven, and any land that was sold is returned, for, says the Bible, the land of Israel ultimately belongs not to human beings but to God.

What About Today?

The commitment to a sabbatical for the land is alive and flourishing even in modern industrialized Israel. In 1973, the late rabbi Benyamin Mendelsohn established a nationwide center for "Shmitah Observing Farmers" in Israel, of whom there are about 4,000 today, whose farms cover about 62,000 acres. Because Jews are forbidden to work the land in the seventh year, many food manufacturers purchase agricultural produce in advance, putting it in cold storage. Journalist Idele Ross describes a particularly creative method of growing produce during *shmitah:* Instead of in the earth, it is grown on a raised platform above the soil!

When a newly established kibbutz asked rabbinical experts how to observe the *shmitah* year, Rabbi David Golinkin of the *Masorti* (Conservative) Movement's Law Committee cited earlier precedents to explain that today *shmitah* should be considered not a commandment, but an act of piety. *Shmitah* is about more than letting the land rest, says Rabbi Golinkin. "One of the ultimate goals of the *shmitah* year is 'that the poor of thy people may eat' (Exod. 23:11)."

Thus, just as Boaz, in the Book of Ruth, left a corner of his field for gleaners, so today when a *shmitah* year comes around on the Hebrew calendar, Jews who grow food may discover that the most meaningful way to honor the law is to donate a part of their year's profits to help their community's poor.

A Sabbath for the Land

Appendix IV

Keeping Kosher

One of the most persistent misconceptions about the laws of kashrut (keeping kosher) is that they were designed for reasons of health, as if somehow the Torah knew pork could cause trichinosis, and a pepperoni pizza with "extra cheese" could give you a stomachache. It's a misconception we owe foremost to the rabbinic sage (and physician!) Maimonides, who thought that the Torah proscribed certain foods because they were "unwholesome."

But as Isaac Arbabanel (1437–1508) pointed out centuries ago, the Torah was not a "minor medical book." Plenty of people did just fine eating pork ("and insects" too!), he saw. The laws of kashrut, he insisted, did not come "to heal bodies" but to "seek the health of the soul."

Living in the paradise of Eden, Adam and Eve were vegetarians: "Behold, I have given you every herb-yielding seed which is upon the face of the earth, and every tree in which is the fruit of tree yielding seed—to you it shall be for food" (Gen. 1:29). Only after the Flood, when human beings are recognized as imperfect, does God permit the eating of meat (Gen. 9:3). But there are caveats. According to the Bible, Moses instructed the people of Israel at Mount Sinai not to kill animals for food any which way, and not to eat just *any* meat or fish. And if they do eat the *meat* of an animal, they are not to eat it together with the same or another animal's *milk*.

In general, the rules developed by the rabbis of the Talmud are that all fruits and vegetables are permitted, all seafood that has fins and scales, and all animals that part the hoof, are cloven-footed, and chew the cud, such as cattle, sheep, goats, buffalo, and deer. In addition, chickens, turkeys, ducks, geese, pigeons, and, according to some authorities, pheasants can be as well.

But all animals must be slaughtered according to the laws of kashrut, which are designed to prevent excessive cruelty to the animal. The process, called *shechitah*, involves a highly trained person, equipped with a special kind of knife, cutting both the windpipe (trachea) and the food pipe (esophagus). Activists today have sought additional processes (such as ending the hoisting and shackling of the animal, and ending to "factory farming" of veal calves) to realize that goal more effectively. Others have urged Jews today to "update" the laws of kashrut by becoming vegetarians.

Since the eating of blood is forbidden to Jews, poultry and meat must first be salted by the butcher (or at home) to remove any trace of blood, unless first broiled.

Meat and milk products may not be eaten together in the same meal. After eating dairy foods, meat may be eaten without waiting. After eating meat, however, the custom is to wait until the next meal before eating dairy. How *long* one waits depends upon custom—Eastern European Jews traditionally waited six hours, West European, three, and some Dutch and Scandinavian Jews, 72 minutes.

Meat and dairy should also be cooked in separate pots, and served on separate dishes with separate utensils.

If the laws of kashrut are new to you or if you'd like to adopt a kosher way of life, there are many sources to consult. One of the finest is Samuel H. Dresner's *The Jewish Dietary Laws: Their Meaning for Our Time*, along with Seymour Siegel and David M. Pollock's *Guide to Their Observance* (Revised and expanded edition. New York: The Rabbinical Assembly, 1982).

Bibliography

Contemporary Sources

Cooper, John. *Eat and Be Satisfied: A Social History of Jewish Food.* Jerusalem: Jason Aronson, 1993.

Crowfoot, Grace M., and Louise Baldensperger. *From Cedar to Hyssop: A Study in the Folklore of Plants in Palestine.* London: The Sheldon Press, 1932.

De Vaux, Roland. *Ancient Israel: Its Life and Institutions.* London: Darton, Longman, and Todd, 1976.

Elon, Ari, Naomi Hyman, and Arthur Waskow, eds. *Trees, Earth, and Torah: A Tu b'Shvat Anthology.* Philadelphia: Jewish Publication Society, 1999.

Gaster, Theodor. *Festivals of the Jewish Year.* New York: Morrow Quill Paperbacks, 1978.

Glazer, Miriyam. *Dancing on the Edge of the World: Jewish Stories of Faith, Inspiration, and Love.* Los Angeles: Roxbury Press, 2000.

Glazer, Phyllis. *Foods of the Bible.* Published as *Milch und Honig*, Neuhausen-Stuttgart: Hanssler Press, 1988, and *Mense et Cibi ai Tempi della Bibbia*, Casale Monferrato: Edizioni Piemme, 1994.

———. *From Phyllis's Kitchen.* Published as *HaMitbach shel Phyllis.* Jerusalem: Keter-Books, 2002.

Goodman, Philip. *The Passover Anthology.* Philadelphia and Jerusalem: Jewish Publication Society, 1993. Other volumes in the series: *The Purim Anthology*, 1992; *The Rosh Hashanah Anthology*, 1992; *The Shavuot Anthology*, 1992; *The Sukkot/Simhat Torah Anthology*, 1988.

Hareuveni, Nogah. *Nature in Our Biblical Heritage.* Translated and adapted by Helen Frenkley. Israel: Neot Kedumim, 1996.

Kremezii, Aglaia. *The Mediterranean Pantry.* New York: Artisan, 1994.

Roden, Claudia. *Book of Jewish Food.* New York: Alfred A. Knopf, 1996.

Schwartz, Oded. *In Search of Plenty: A History of Jewish Food.* London: Kyle Cathie Ltd., 1992.

Stavroulakis, Nicholas. *Cookbook of the Jews of Greece.* Port Jefferson, N.Y.: Cadmus Press, 1986.

Waskow, Arthur. *Seasons of Our Joy: A Modern Guide to the Jewish Holidays.* Boston: Beacon Press, 1982.

Waskow, Arthur, ed. *Torah of the Earth: Exploring 4,000 Years of Ecology in Jewish Thought.* Vol. I. Woodstock, Vt.: Jewish Lights Publishing, 2000.

Yaffe, Martin. *Judaism and Environmental Ethics: A Reader.* Lanham, Md.: Rowman & Littlefield, 2001.

Rabbinic Sources

Pesikta Rabbati is a collection of medieval Midrash, arranged according to the cycle of the Jewish festivals. It draws material from the other collections of Midrashim, the *Pesikta d'Rav Kahana* and the *Tanhuma.*

Genesis (Braishit) Rabbah, Leviticus Rabbah, and *Song of Songs Rabbah* are collections of Midrash based on the respective books of the Bible.

Mahzor Vitri is an eleventh-century halakic work focusing on Jewish liturgy written by Rav Simcha of Vitri (France). It includes material that related to the daily lives of Jews (such as the laws of Shabbat).

Maimonides (1135–1204) was Moses ben Maimon, known in Hebrew as the Rambam. A brilliant rabbi, physician, and philosopher, he was born in Spain but, because of religious persecution by the fanatical Muslim regime there, had to flee, first to Morocco, then to Israel, and finally to Cairo, where he served as the private physician to the sultan of Egypt. Maimonides not only wrote many medical books and served as a leader of Cairo's Jewish community, but he also produced some of the most important books in Jewish legal, religious, and philosophical history, including his *Guide to the Perplexed* and the *Mishneh Torah,* the very first attempt to codify the religious laws (halakah) of Judaism.

Nahmanides (1194–1270) was Rabbi Moshe ben Nahman, known as the Ramban, a physician, Torah scholar, and the foremost authority on Jewish law of his age. However, unlike the rationalist Maimonides, Nahmanides had strong mystical leanings. His commentaries on the Bible are the first ones to include the mystical teachings of kabbalah. Expelled from Spain, he moved to *Eretz Yisrael.* Although the land was devastated when he arrived, "even in its destruction," he wrote, "it is a blessed land."

Originally transmitted orally from generation to generation, the Talmud is the collected and edited conversations of the rabbis of Palestine and Babylonia on the intricacies of Jewish law, which they learned from the Mishna. It also includes much aggadic material—legends and stories. The Palestinian Talmud—also called the Jerusalem Talmud—was compiled in the early fifth century C.E., and the longer Babylonian Talmud, in the sixth century C.E. In our book, we refer to the Babylonian Talmud as "BT" and the Palestinian Talmud as "JT," followed by the name of the tractate and the page number.

Index